NOTES ON THE

THEORY OF CHOICE

UNDERGROUND CLASSICS IN ECONOMICS

Consulting Editors
Kenneth Arrow, James Heckman, Joseph Pechman,
Thomas Sargent, and Robert Solow

Progress in economics takes place in many different forums. Many of these forums are not "above ground," in the sense of published work freely available. They are in the form of unpublished notes, dissertations, government reports, and lectures. This series is dedicated to making the best of this underground literature more widely available to libraries, scholars, and their students. In so doing it will serve to fill a large gap in the contemporary economic literature.

Entries in this series can be on any topic of interest to economists, and they may occasionally be in rough and sometime unfinished form. The only criteria are that the works have been influential, widely cited, of exceptional excellence, and for whatever reason, never before published.

Other Titles in This Series

Functional Form and Utility: A Review of Consumer Demand Theory, Arthur S. Goldberger

Game Theory, Robert A. Aumann

Behind the Diffusion Curve: Theoretical and Applied Contributions to the Microeconomics of Technology Adoption, Paul A. David

The Allocation of Scarce Resources: Experimental Economics and the Problem of Allocating Airport Slots, David M. Grether, R. Mark Issac, and Charles R. Plott

Notes on the

Theory of Choice

David M. Kreps

WESTVIEW PRESS / BOULDER AND LONDON

Underground Classics in Economics

This Westview softcover edition is printed on acid-free paper and bound in softcovers that carry the highest rating of the National Association of State Textbook Administrators, in consultation with the Association of American Publishers and the Book Manufacturers' Institute.

Published in 1988 in the United States of America by Westview Press, Inc.; Frederick A. Praeger, Publisher; 5500 Central Avenue, Boulder, Colorado 80301

Library of Congress Cataloging-in-Publication Data
Kreps, David M.
    Notes on the theory of choice/by David Kreps.
        p.   cm. – (Underground classics in economics)
    ISBN 0–8133–7553–3
    1. Demand (Economic theory).   2. Utility theory.   3. Uncertainty.
4. Game theory.   5. Microeconomics.   6. Consumers' preferences.
I. Title   II. Series.
HB801.K73 1988
338.5′212–dc19   88-4975
                                                                                    CIP

Printed and bound in the United States of America

∞ The paper used in this publication meets the requirements of the American National Standard for Permanence of Paper for Printed Library Materials Z39.48-1984.

7   8   9   10

For my parents

Contents

Preface

This book compiles some teaching notes on axiomatic choice theory which were developed from 1976 to 1981 at the Graduate School of Business, Stanford University. The notes have been updated a bit, and they have been cleaned up a bit, but they are otherwise much as they were in 1981. They were used in conjunction with a one term course for first year Ph.D. students, and they provide about enough material for just such a course, when supplemented with one or two advanced topics. The course was originally required of all the first year Ph.D. students in the Business School, and so the level of mathematical complexity that could be permitted for most of the development was low. Nonetheless, the purpose of the course was to give students some basic training in the theorem proving parts of economic theory, and the notes are written in the style of theorem-proof. Hence the reader will find the book to be somewhat schizophrenic. The style is such that it seems to want to be taken seriously as a reference book on choice theory, but then whenever the mathematical going gets tough, arms start to wave and the reader is sent to a real book on the subject. Appearances notwithstanding, this is not intended to be a reference book on choice theory. It is meant instead to be a first course on the subject for graduate (Ph.D.) students, although I imagine it could be used by really good undergraduates. Serious students of the subject can use this book as a chatty introduction to some of the basic ideas and logic, but it must be supplemented by a serious reference book. When I taught the course, I would send students to Fishburn's *Utility Theory for Decision Makers*, to Krantz et al. *Foundations of Measurement*, and, of course, to Savage's *Foundations of Statistics* for the "real stuff"; those recommendations are still quite good and valid. The reader will notice as well that the general lines adopted are those of Fishburn. It is hard to improve on that classic, although in places I do move some stuff around. In any case, much of what is reported here I learned by reading Fishburn, and an enormous intellectual debt is owed to him.

The reader will note that the style of writing is both informal and uneven. I have not made a great effort to clean up the original notes, which were not intended for this sort of dissemination, and excursions into the first person or phrases masquerading as sentences will have to be excused. Students have said that they found this style more accessible than the standard texts; and I hope (a) this is correct and (b) you will find it so.

At the end of most chapters are some homework problems. They were an integral part of the course, and I would urge any serious reader to try them out. This being a series in "Underground" writings, perhaps the publisher will allow me to suggest here that there are copies of suggested solutions floating around in the deep underground.

The book comes roughly in three parts. After an introduction (Chapter 1), we have a very brief excursion into the theory of choice and preference without any uncertainty (Chapters 2 and 3). This goes by very quickly, since the interesting questions in this development become too mathematical in short order.

The second part of the book, and the bulk of it, is devoted to the standard models of choice under uncertainty. Chapter 4 provides an introduction to what will be sought, and then Chapter 5 takes on von Neumann-Morgenstern expected utility, first for finite outcome lotteries and then more generally, via the mixture space approach of Herstein and Milnor. Chapter 6 discusses the special case of utility functions defined on dollar prizes, which is to say, a brief development of the Arrow and Pratt measures of risk aversion. Chapter 7 presents the development of subjective expected utility with extraneous objective randomizing devices, as given by Anscombe and Aumann. Chapters 8 and 9 then introduce (but far from cover) the classic development of Savage – subjective probability is discussed in Chapter 8, with expected utility in Chapter 9. Finally, Chapter 10 gives a very short discussion of conditional preference and conditional probability within the Savage framework, and it introduces ideas about the use of static theories of choice in the context of dynamic choice.

The third part of the book discusses a number of special topics, the selection of which was entirely idiosyncratic and formed in part by my then current research. Chapter 11 introduces the concept of exchangeability and gives a simple version of de Finetti's theorem. In Chapter 12 we discuss why the classical models don't work when they are applied to pieces of a larger problem. Chapter 13 gives the reader a quick taste of what I think dynamic choice theory ought to look like (which is not what was discussed in Chapter 10). And in Chapter 14 the reader, by now exhausted, is given a very quick introduction to the bad news about the experimental evidence.

The course on which these notes are based was taught first by J. Michael Harrison, and so much of the credit for the basic organization of the course, left over after the large allocation of credit to Fishburn, goes to him. He is also to be credited with any artistry in the drama of Chapter 11, and I am grateful for his permission to include my bastardized version of his classic. The teaching of the course subsequently was shared by Joel Demski, who made many contributions. Comments and suggestions on the notes also came from the students who suffered through them; without trying to recall everyone who made suggestions, Rick Antle, Elchanan Ben-Porath, and Paul Milgrom come to mind as individuals who deserve special thanks. Renee Gibb turned a badly typed typescript into serviceable TeX files, from which this book eventually emerged, and Hideo Suehiro and the students of Faruk Gul's 1988 edition of the course read pieces of the final manuscript and pointed out numerous typos.

The hero of this book is a character named Totrep, Mike Harrison's acronym for a Trade-Off Talking Rational Economic Person. With apologies, Totrep will use male pronouns throughout.

David M. Kreps

1

Introduction

The subject matter of this book is the axiomatic development of single-person choice theory, also known as decision theory and preference theory. This includes bits of the philosophy of probability. The easiest way to describe what we'll be doing is to give an example. If you've read a book on decision analysis or the economics of uncertainty, you probably will be familiar with this example, although not in quite so formal a manner.

Let P denote the set of all *simple probability distributions* on the interval $[0, 100]$, where a simple probability distribution is one with a finite number of outcomes. Such things can be represented graphically by chance nodes, as in figure 1.1a below.

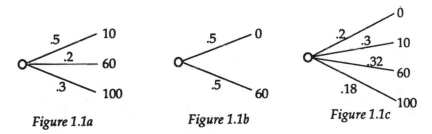

Figure 1.1a   *Figure 1.1b*   *Figure 1.1c*

This represents a .5 chance at the prize 10, a .2 chance at 60, and a .3 chance at 100. If p and p' are two such probability distributions and a is a number between 0 and 1, we can define a new probability distribution $ap + (1 - a)p'$ which is the "$a, 1 - a$ mixture of p and p'." For example, suppose that p is as above and p' is the distribution given by the chance node in figure 1.1b. Then $.6p + .4p'$ is the distribution given by the chance node in figure 1.1c.

Interpret these probability distributions as gambles or lotteries with dollar prizes between $\$0$ and $\$100$, based on devices such as fair coins, dice, roulette wheels, etc.

An individual – you, your friend, the man in the street – whom we will call *Totrep*, for Trade-Off Talking Rational Economic Person, has preferences among these lotteries. These preferences are described by a *binary relation* $\succ$ which stands for "strict preference" – we write $p \succ p'$ if and only if Totrep strictly prefers p to p'. (If you aren't sure what a binary relation is exactly, just go with the spirit of the thing for the moment.)

Consider the following properties of such a binary relation:

Axiom (1.1). If $p \succ p'$, then not $p' \succ p$.

Axiom (1.2). If not $p \succ p'$ and not $p' \succ p''$, then not $p \succ p''$.

Axiom (1.3). If we let δ_r denote the lottery which gives the prize r with certainty, then $r > r'$ implies $\delta_r \succ \delta_{r'}$.

Axiom (1.4). If $p \succ p' \succ p''$, then there exist a and b in $(0,1)$ such that $ap + (1-a)p'' \succ p' \succ bp + (1-b)p''$.

Axiom (1.5). If $p \succ p'$, then for all $a \in (0,1)$ and $p'' \in P$ it follows that $ap + (1-a)p'' \succ ap' + (1-a)p''$.

These five axioms may not be in a form familiar to you, but the following results are probably familiar. Some notation: If u is a function from $[0, 100]$ to R (the real line), and if p is a simple probability distribution, then $E_p[u]$ means the expectation of u taken with respect to the probability distribution p. That is,

$$E_p[u] = \sum_{r \in [0,100]} u(r)p(r).$$

Theorem (1.6). A binary relation $\succ$ on P satisfies Axioms (1.1) through (1.5) if and only if there exists a strictly increasing function $u : [0, 100] \to R$ such that

(1.7) $p \succ p'$ if and only if $E_p[u] > E_{p'}[u]$.

Theorem (1.8). Suppose $\succ$ on P satisfies Axioms (1.1) through (1.5) and that u and u' are two functions : $[0, 100] \to R$ such that (1.7) holds. Then there exist real numbers $c > 0$ and d such that $cu + d = u'$.

This book will be spent developing results like Theorems (1.6) and (1.8). Note carefully the steps:

(a) Some set of objects, the *choice set* X, is identified. Typically the objects in X will have some structure; for example, in this example, X is the set P of probability distributions on the set $[0, 100]$.

(b) *Axioms* concerning Totrep's preferences among members of X are proposed. These are qualitative statements about the relation $\succ$, typically involving the structure in X.

(c) A *representation theorem* is stated and proved. Most of the time we seek a function from the choice set to the real numbers (called a *utility function*) such that higher utility corresponds to more preferred items. The representation will typically exploit the structure; e.g., in the example we have an *expected utility* representation.

When we look at a set of axioms and a representation, we will sometimes wonder whether the axioms are *sufficient* for a representation, which means that if the axioms hold, then a representation is possible, and whether the axioms are *necessary* for the representation, which means that if the representation holds, then the axioms must hold. Note that in our example, Theorem (1.6) establishes that the five axioms are both necessary and sufficient for the representation (1.7).

(d) A *uniqueness* result is given – this characterizes the extent to which two similarly structured representations of a given preference relation can vary. Theorem (1.8) is an example of this. These sorts of results are called uniqueness theorems because of the stock phrase: "The representation is *unique* up to ..." (in the case of Theorem (1.8), "... a positive affine transformation.")

What constitutes a "good" set of axioms? This largely depends on the application that you have in mind – cf. the next section. In general, axioms should be basic, primitive, intuitive, qualitative, etc., whatever these things mean. But there are two technical properties of sets of axioms that should be watched out for:

A *consistent* set of axioms is a set of axioms which can be satisfied simultaneously. That is, there is some identifiable collection of objects which satisfies the axioms. For example, suppose I added to Axioms (1.1) through (1.5) the following:

Axiom (1.9). If p assigns probability .5 or more to prizes below the value r, and p' assigns zero probability to this range, then $p' \succ p$.

Then I'd have an inconsistent set of axioms. (Can you prove this?)

An *independent* set of axioms is a set of axioms where no subset of them implies the others. For example, consider adjoining to Axioms (1.1) through (1.5) the following:

Axiom (1.10). If $p \succ p'$ and $a, b \in (0,1)$ are such that $a > b$, then $ap + (1 - a)p' \succ bp + (1 - b)p'$.

This larger set of axioms is not independent, because Axioms (1.1) through (1.5) imply (1.10). (Can you give a proof?) Good sets of axioms should be both consistent – for obvious reasons – and independent – for reasons of parsimony.

That, more or less, is what constitutes choice theory. "So," you ask, "Why would anyone be interested?" There are two basic reasons for this, with a lot of fuzzy middle ground between. Everything, we shall see, depends on who is to play the role of Totrep.

NORMATIVE APPLICATIONS

Suppose that you, or a friend, had to choose one of the following three lotteries:

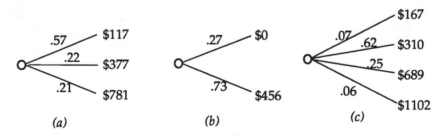

(a)   (b)   (c)

The choice is not an easy one, because there are lots of prizes and "strange" probabilities such as .62. But *if* you examine the five axioms, you *might* be able to conclude that in this particular choice situation you want your choice behavior to conform to the axioms. (Alternatively, you might be able to convince your friend that the five axioms are reasonable guides to how a choice should be made in this circumstance.) If you do come to this conclusion then the theorems guarantee that you *want* your choice behavior to conform to expected utility maximization. And you can then assess your utility function u by making judgments about simpler lotteries and use the assessed u to choose among the three complicated lotteries above. That is, you solve the problem by analysis: (a) Decide that you want to obey the axioms because they seem reasonable guides to behavior. (b) Assess your utility function using simpler lotteries. (c) Combine the logical conclusion of (a), the representation theorem, with the numbers derived in (b) to make your choice. (Similarly, for your friend.)

In this sort of normative application, there is obviously going to be great emphasis on finding axioms that are reasonable guides to behavior; intuitive axioms will be much prized. Also, you'll be content with a sufficient set of axioms.

One normative application deserves special mention. Social scientists, and often physical scientists, go around making pronouncements about their theories being based on empirical evidence. This involves statements of *likelihood* or degree of belief – if any sense is to be made of such things, then "probability" had better be defined in terms that social scientists can agree on. We'll touch on the very basics of this problem, but we won't get too far with it. Since axiomatizations of probability and empirical proof should be of paramount concern to any social scientist who is reading this book, you can supplement the little we do here with the book of readings by Kyburg and Smokler listed in the references.

DESCRIPTIVE APPLICATIONS

Insofar as individuals' preference (as revealed by their choices – more about this in the next chapter) conform to the five axioms, their behavior can be modeled *as if* they are expected utility maximizers.

Much of modern micro-economic theory, and its applications in Accounting, Finance, Marketing, and so on, is done in this fashion: Models of organizations/economies are studied wherein all the agents or actors are copies of Totrep in one or more of his various guises.

The obvious question in such applications is empirical: To what extent *do* individuals' choices conform to a given set of axioms and/or a given representation? In looking at this question, the emphasis will be on testable axioms, on necessary sets of axioms, and on testable *implications* of a given set of axioms/representation.

Descriptive applications, at least in the realm of economics that I know best, raise all sorts of tough philosophical questions. No one that I know of would seriously maintain that individuals do conform exactly to the sorts of axiomatic systems that will be studied here. Indeed, in the last chapter we'll see some empirical evidence which casts great doubt on the standard models of choice that economists use. At best then, individual behavior *approximates* the axiomatic based behavior that we shall study. Why then does it make sense to study the behavior of systems (economies, organizations) where the actors are presumed to satisfy exactly the axiom systems? The answer must be: Because if their behavior is approximately what is modeled, then the model will tell us something about how their behaviors interact or intertwine in the system. This, the reader will surely note, takes a somewhat large leap of faith; a leap for which this book will not provide assistance.

PROBLEMS

(1) Assume the truth of Theorem (1.6). Show that the set of axioms (1.1) through (1.5) and (1.9) are inconsistent. Show, on the other hand, that Axioms (1.1) through (1.5) are consistent.

(2) Assume the truth of Theorem (1.6). Show that the set of axioms (1.1) through (1.5) imply axiom (1.10).

(3) Show that Axiom (1.1) is independent of Axioms (1.2) through (1.5). This is not a trivial exercise. You are being asked to prove that there is no possible proof that (1.2) through (1.5) imply (1.1). Even if you can't do this for the particular axioms here, discuss how such a thing could conceivably be proved. If you are really up for a challenge, show that each of the first five axioms is independent of the other four. You will be in better shape to tackle this assignment after you finish Chapter 5, including the problems given there.

2

Preference Relations and Revealed Preference

BINARY RELATIONS

For a given set X, let $X \times X$ denote the usual Cartesian product of all ordered pairs (x, y), where both x and y are from X.

A *binary relation* B on the set X is formally defined as a subset of $X \times X$ – write $B \subseteq X \times X$, and $(x, y) \in B$ if the ordered pair (x, y) is in the relation B. Another, quicker way to write $(x, y) \in B$ is xBy, which can be read as "x Bees y" or "x stands in the relation B to y." If $(x, y) \notin B$, I'll write "not xBy" or $x\tilde{B}y$.

Examples:

(a) Let $X = \{1, 2, 3\}$ and $B = \{(1, 1), (1, 2), (1, 3), (2, 3), (3, 1)\}$.
(b) Let $X =$ all people in the world and let B be the relation "shares at least one given name with."
(c) Let $X = R$ (the real line, remember) and let B be the relation "greater or equal to"; that is, $B = \geq$.
(d) Let $X = R$ and let B be the relation: xBy if $|x - y| > 1$.
(e) Let $X = R$ and let B be the relation xBy if $x - y$ is an integer multiple of 2.

There is a long list of properties that a given binary relation might or might not have. The properties that will be important in this book are the following. A binary relation B on a set X is:

reflexive if xBx for all $x \in X$;
irreflexive if $x\tilde{B}x$ for all $x \in X$;
symmetric if xBy implies yBx;
asymmetric if xBy implies $y\tilde{B}x$;
antisymmetric if xBy and yBx imply $x = y$;
transitive if xBy and yBz imply xBz;

negatively transitive if $x\tilde{B}y$ and $y\tilde{B}z$ imply $x\tilde{B}z$;

complete or connected if for all $x, y \in X$, xBy or yBx (or both; "or"s are never exclusive in this book unless specifically mentioned);

weakly connected if for all $x, y \in X$, $x = y$ or xBy or yBx;

acyclic if $x_1Bx_2, x_2Bx_3, \ldots x_{n-1}Bx_n$ imply $x_1 \neq x_n$.

Example (a) (above) is weakly connected, but nothing else. Example (b) is reflexive and symmetric. Example (c) is reflexive, antisymmetric, transitive, negatively transitive, complete, and weakly connected. Example (d) is irreflexive, symmetric. Example (e) is reflexive, symmetric, transitive.

PREFERENCE RELATIONS

In this section, we take up the following simple story. There is a set of items X, and Totrep is willing to express his preferences among these items by making paired comparisons of the form: "I strictly prefer x to y" which is written $x \succ y$. "Strict preference" is a binary relation on X. Consider the following properties that this binary relation might possess:

(a) *Asymmetry* – if x is strictly preferred to y, then y is not strictly preferred to x. (What do you think of this? Reasonable normatively? How about descriptively? Think of these questions for each of the following.)

(b) *Transitivity* – if x is strictly preferred to y and y is strictly preferred to z, then x is strictly preferred to z.

(c) *Irreflexivity* – no x is strictly preferred to itself.

(d) *Negative transitivity* – if x is not strictly preferred to y and y is not strictly preferred to z, then x is not strictly preferred to z.

Negative transitivity is a hard property to deal with intuitively in the form given, so let me develop an alternative statement that is completely equivalent.

Lemma (2.1). A binary relation B is negatively transitive iff (if and only if) xBz implies that, for all $y \in X$, xBy or yBz.

Proof. (Very pedantic.) The statement [M implies N] is the same as the statement [N or not M], thus [M implies N] is the same as [not N implies not M]. (The second equivalence is called contraposition.) Thus [{xBz} implies {xBy or yBz for all $y \in X$}] is the same as [{not(xBy or yBz for all $y \in X$)} implies {not xBz}] which is [{there exists $y \in Z$ with $x\tilde{B}y$ and $y\tilde{B}z$} implies {$x\tilde{B}z$}], which is negative transitivity.

Now back to $\succ$. Is negative transitivity reasonable? Is it reasonable to say that if x is strictly preferred to z, then for all y either x is strictly preferred to y or y is strictly preferred to z? As a normative property, I think it is (barely) reasonable. But as a descriptive property, I don't think it is reasonable. Suppose $X = (0, \infty) \times (0, \infty)$, where $x = (x_1, x_2) \in X$ is interpreted as the commodity bundle x_1 bottles of beer and x_2 bottles of wine. Totrep (if his tastes are like my own) would certainly say that $(10, 10) \succ (9, 9)$. But consider $(15, 6)$. Totrep might *not* be willing to say either that $(10, 10) \succ (15, 6)$ or $(15, 6) \succ (9, 9)$ – he might plead that comparisons called for are too difficult for him to make.

Despite these difficulties with negative transitivity, it is standard to proceed assuming that $\succ$ is asymmetric and negatively transitive.

Definition (2.2). A binary relation $\succ$ on a set X is called a *preference relation* if it is asymmetric and negatively transitive.

Proposition (2.3). If $\succ$ is a preference relation, then $\succ$ is irreflexive, transitive, and acyclic.

Proof. (a) Asymmetry directly implies irreflexivity.
(b) Suppose $x \succ y$ and $y \succ z$. By negative transitivity (and Lemma (2.1)), $x \succ y$ implies that either $z \succ y$ or $x \succ z$. But $z \succ y$ is impossible because $y \succ z$ is assumed and $\succ$ is asymmetric. Thus $x \succ z$, which is transitivity.
(c) If $x_1 \succ x_2, x_2 \succ x_3, \ldots, x_{n-1} \succ x_n$, then by transitivity $x_1 \succ x_n$. Since $\succ$ is irreflexive, this implies $x_1 \neq x_n$. Thus $\succ$ is acyclic.

When we are given a binary relation $\succ$ that expresses strict preference, we use it to define two other binary relations:

$$x \succeq y \text{ if } y \not\succ x, \text{ and } x \sim y \text{ if } x \not\succ y \text{ and } y \not\succ x,$$

where we are using $\not\succ$ as shorthand for $\tilde{\succ}$ or for "not $\succ$." The relation $\succeq$ is called *weak preference*, although it really expresses the absence of strict preference. The relation $\sim$ is called *indifference* – it expresses the absence of strict preference in either direction, which is perhaps not quite the same thing as active indifference.

Proposition (2.4). If $\succ$ is a preference relation, then:
(a) For all x and y, exactly one of $x \succ y, y \succ x$ or $x \sim y$ holds.
(b) $\succeq$ is complete and transitive.
(c) $\sim$ is reflexive, symmetric, and transitive.
(d) $w \succ x, x \sim y, y \succ z$ imply $w \succ y$ and $x \succ z$.
(e) $x \succeq y$ iff $x \succ y$ or $x \sim y$.
(f) $x \succeq y$ and $y \succeq x$ imply $x \sim y$.

Proof. (a) follows from the definition of $\sim$ and the fact that $\succ$ is asymmetric.
(b) By the asymmetry of $\succ$, either $x \not\succ y$ or $y \not\succ x$ (or both) for all x and y, thus $\succeq$ is complete. For transitivity of $\succeq$, note that this follows immediately from the negative transitivity of $\succ$.
(c) $\sim$ is reflexive because $\succ$ is irreflexive. $\sim$ is symmetric because the definition of $\sim$ is symmetric. For transitivity, suppose $x \sim y \sim z$. Then $x \not\succ y \not\succ z$ and $z \not\succ y \not\succ x$. By negative transitivity of $\succ$, $x \not\succ z \not\succ x$, or $x \sim z$.
(d) If $w \succ x \sim y$, then by part (a) one of $w \succ y$ or $y \sim w$ or $y \succ w$. But $y \succ w$ is impossible, since then transitivity of $\succ$ would imply $y \succ x$. And $y \sim w$ is impossible, since then transitivity of $\sim$ would imply $x \sim w$, contradicting $w \succ x$. Thus $w \succ y$ must hold. The other part is similarly done.
(e) $x \succeq y$ iff $y \not\succ x$ iff $x \succ y$ or $x \sim y$ (by part (a)).
(f) This is immediate from the definitions of $\succeq$ and $\sim$.

Note well the plot: Totrep expresses strict preferences, from which *we* define weak preferences and indifference. It is strict preference that is basic – Totrep is not being called upon to express any judgments concerning weak preference or indifference, and he might disagree with our use of those terms to describe the negation of strict preference.

Another possible plot would be to ask Totrep to express weak preferences or preference or indifference. That is, the basic relation is

$\succeq$. This is a plot that is followed in many developments of choice theory, and in the standard treatment it leads to the same mathematical results:

Proposition (2.5). Given a binary relation $\succeq'$ on a set X, define two new binary relations $\succ'$ and $\sim'$ from $\succeq'$ by

$$x \succ' y \text{ if } y \not\succeq' x, \text{ and } x \sim' y \text{ if } x \succeq' y \text{ and } y \succeq' x.$$

Then *if* $\succeq'$ is complete and transitive, $\succ'$ will be a preference relation. Moreover, if we start with a binary relation $\succ'$, define $\succ'$ and $\sim'$ as above from $\succeq'$, and then define $\succeq$ and $\sim$ from $\succ'$ by

$$x \succeq y \text{ if } y \not\succ' x, \text{ and } x \sim y \text{ if } y \not\succ' x \text{ and } x \not\succ' y,$$

then $\succeq'$ and $\succeq$ will agree, as will $\sim'$ and $\sim$.

The proof is left as an exercise. So it doesn't matter whether we start with a strict preference relation that is asymmetric and negatively transitive or with a weak preference relation that is complete and transitive – we end up in the same place. For reasons of interpretation I prefer to take strict preference as being basic. But it is a matter of personal taste, and most authors do it the other way.

REVEALED PREFERENCE THEORY

In the previous section, the story was that Totrep was making paired comparisons between items in X. But especially from a descriptive point of view, we would like to start with an even more basic concept – that of choices made rather than preferences expressed. That is, from a descriptive point of view what we see is an individual's choice behavior – we have to connect that behavior as best we can with his preferences which are never directly expressed. The individual's choice behavior *reveals* his preferences, hence the name of this subject: revealed preference theory. This subject also has some normative justifications – taking preferences as given, how should choices be made? But this subject is of greatest interest from the descriptive viewpoint.

To keep matters simple, throughout this section I'll assume that
the choice set X is finite. Especially if the application you are thinking of is demand for consumption bundles or for any item that is infinitely divisible, this is not a very nice simplification. For nonempty
subsets of X, I'll use notation such as A, B, etc. The set of all
nonempty subsets of X will be denoted $P(X)$.

Definition (2.6). A *choice function* for a (finite) set X is a function
$c : P(X) \to P(X)$ such that for all $A \subseteq X$, $c(A) \subseteq A$.

The interpretation is: If Totrep is offered his choice of anything
in the set A, he says that any member of $c(A)$ will do just fine.

If Totrep's preferences are given by the binary relation $\succ$ (and by
the corresponding $\succeq$ and $\sim$), it is natural to suppose that he chooses
according to the rule that from a set A, anything that is *undominated*
will be okay. In symbols, define a function $c(\cdot, \succ) : P(X)$ by

$$c(A, \succ) = \{x \in A : \text{ for all } y \in A, y \not\succ x\}.$$

It is clear that for any $\succ$, $c(A, \succ) \subseteq A$, but it isn't clear whether
$c(A, \succ) \neq \emptyset$. Thus it isn't clear that $c(\cdot, \succ)$ is a choice function.
That will be something to be investigated.

The other questions to be looked at are:
(a) From the normative point of view: Given a relation $\succ$ (not necessarily a preference relation), when is $c(\cdot, \succ)$ a choice function? If $\succ$
is a preference relation, what properties does $c(\cdot, \succ)$ have?
(b) From the descriptive point of view: Given a choice function c,
when is there a binary relation $\succ$ such that $c(\cdot) = c(\cdot, \succ)$? When is
this binary relation a preference relation? (N.B., this last question is
the critical one, as we're going to be building models where individuals
are assumed to be maximizing their preferences according to some
preference relation.)

Proposition (2.7). If a binary relation $\succ$ is acyclic, then $c(\cdot, \succ)$ is a
choice function.

Proof. We need to show that for $A \in P(X)$, the set

$$c(A, \succ) = \{x \in A : \text{ for all } y \in A, y \not\succ x\},$$

is nonempty. Suppose it was empty – then for each $x \in A$ there exists a $y \in A$ such that $y \succ x$. Pick $x_1 \in A$ (A is nonempty), and let x_2 be x_1's "y". Let x_3 be x_2's "y", and so on. In other words, $x_1, x_2, x_3, \ldots$ is a sequence of elements of A where

$$\ldots x_n \succ x_{n-1} \succ \ldots \succ x_2 \succ x_1.$$

Because A is a finite set, there must exist some m and n such that $x_m = x_n$ and $m > n$. But this would be a cycle, and $\succ$ is assumed to be acyclic. The necessary contradiction is established.

Note the following instant corollary: If $\succ$ is a preference relation, then $c(\cdot, \succ)$ is a choice function. Also, we can strengthen (2.7) as follows.

Proposition (2.8). For a binary relation $\succ$, $c(\cdot, \succ)$ is a choice function iff $\succ$ is acyclic.

Proving this is left as an exercise.

Next we survey some properties of choice functions. The classic axiomatic property of choice is Houthakker's axiom of revealed preference.

Houthakker's axiom (2.9). If x and y are both in A and B and if $x \in c(A)$ and $y \in c(B)$, then $x \in c(B)$.

In words, if x is sometimes chosen (from A) when y is available, then whenever y is chosen and x is available, x is also chosen.

Houthakker's axiom is broken into two pieces by Sen:

Sen's property α *(2.10).* If $x \in B \subseteq A$ and $x \in c(A)$, then $x \in c(B)$.

Sen's paraphrase of this is: If the world champion in some game is a Pakistani, then he must also be the champion of Pakistan.

Sen's property β *(2.11).* If $x, y \in c(A)$, $A \subseteq B$ and $y \in c(B)$, then $x \in c(B)$.

Sen's paraphrase: If the world champion in some game is a Pakistani, then all champions (in this game) of Pakistan are also world champions.

Note that Houthakker's axiom concerns A and B such that $x, y \in A \cap B$. Property α specializes to the case $B \subseteq A$, and property β specializes to the case $A \subseteq B$. Property α is sometimes referred to as Independence of Irrelevant Alternatives, the idea being that the choice out of a larger set of options doesn't change when some of the (unchosen, hence) irrelevant alternatives in the set are removed.

Proposition (2.12). For an arbitrary binary relation $\succ$, $c(\cdot, \succ)$ satisfies Sen's property α.

The proof is left as an exercise. It is interesting that even if $\succ$ is acyclic, $c(\cdot, \succ)$ may fail to satisfy property β. Providing an example makes a good homework exercise.

Proposition (2.13). If $\succ$ is a preference relation, then $c(\cdot, \succ)$ satisfies Houthakker's axiom, hence both Sen's α and Sen's β.

Proof. Suppose x and y are in A and B, $x \in c(A, \succ)$ and $y \in c(B, \succ)$. Since $x \in c(A, \succ)$ and $y \in A$, we have that $y \not\succ x$. Since $y \in c(B, \succ)$, we have that for all $z \in B$, $z \not\succ y$. Thus by negative transitivity of $\succ$, for all $z \in B$ it follows that $z \not\succ x$. This implies $x \in c(B, \succ)$.

Question: In this proof we seemingly only used the negative transitivity of $\succ$. Does this mean that $c(\cdot, \succ)$ satisfies Houthakker's axiom whenever $\succ$ satisfies negative transitivity?

Proposition (2.14). If a choice function c satisfies both properties α and β, then there exists a preference relation $\succ$ such that c is $c(\cdot, \succ)$.

Before proving this, note that it combines with (2.13) to imply that if a choice function c satisfies Sen's α and β, then it also satisfies Houthakker's axiom. Also, since we didn't use the asymmetry of $\succ$ in the proof of (2.13), it seems to imply that negative transitivity of $\succ$ implies that $\succ$ satisfies asymmetry. Or does it?

Proof. Define $\succ$ as follows:

$$x \succ y \text{ if } x \neq y \text{ and } c(\{x, y\}) = \{x\}.$$

The relation $\succ$ so defined is obviously asymmetric. We need to check that this relation is negatively transitive, and that $c(A, \succ) = c(A)$ for all sets A. We will do the latter first.

Fix a set A.

(a) If $x \in c(A)$, then for all $z \in A, z \not\succ x$. For if $z \succ x$, then $c(\{x, z\}) = \{z\}$, contradicting property α. Thus $x \in c(A, \succ)$.

(b) If $x \notin c(A)$, then let z be chosen arbitrarily from $c(A)$. We claim that $c(\{z, x\}) = \{z\}$ – otherwise property β would be violated. Thus $z \succ x$ and $x \notin c(A, \succ)$.

Combining (a) and (b), $c(A, \succ) = c(A)$ for all A.

Finally, to prove negative transitivity, suppose that $x \not\succ y$ and $y \not\succ z$, but $x \succ z$. $x \succ z$ implies that $\{x\} = c(\{x, z\})$, thus $z \notin c(\{x, y, z\})$ by property α. Since $z \in c(\{y, z\})$, this implies $y \notin c(\{x, y, z\})$. (Why?) Which, since $y \in c(\{x, y\})$, implies $x \notin c(\{x, y, z\})$. Which isn't possible, as c is a choice function. Contradiction – proving that $\succ$ is negatively transitive.

Propositions (2.13) and (2.14) are exact converses. It is interesting to speculate on a possible converse to (2.12). Is it true that if a choice function c satisfies property α, then there exists some acyclic relation $\succ$ such that $c = c(\cdot, \succ)$? The answer to this is no. which makes another good exercise for homework. So what fills in the following blank?

c obeys property α and satisfies ..... iff
there exists some acyclic $\succ$ such that $c = c(\cdot, \succ)$.

It is possible to fill in the blank, and you can find some blank fillers in the literature, but none that you will find are, in my opinion, particularly intuitive. Any suggestions?

CONCLUDING REMARKS

A summary of these results follows:

There exists a preference relation $\succ$ such that $c(\cdot) = c(\cdot, \succ)$
if and only if
$c(\cdot)$ satisfies Houthakker's axiom
if and only if
$c(\cdot)$ satisfies Sen's α and β.

> *A binary relation* $\succ$ *is acyclic*
> if and only if
> *there exists a choice function* $c = c(\cdot, \succ)$ *for* $\succ$
> which implies that, but is not implied by
> *c satisfies Sen's* α,
> and none of the previous three imply or are implied by
> *c satisfies Sen's* β.

This is just an introduction to revealed preference theory – there is a very large literature on the subject. Two important questions, both related to the applications of these ideas to classical demand theory in microeconomics, that we haven't discussed are:

What if X is an infinite set? (Where did we use the finiteness of X in the development above?) For one approach to an answer to this question, see problem 8 of the next chapter.

Suppose we can't observe Totrep's choices from *all* subsets of X. That is, suppose c is defined only for a subset of $P(X)$. You can see how this would provide problems, especially if sets of the form $\{x, y\}$ are not in the domain of c. And you can see why this is a natural question – especially if we have in mind a descriptive theory of choice. What can be said in such cases?

PROBLEMS

(1) For each of the five examples on page 7, show that the binary relation has precisely the list of properties that are ascribed to it on page 8 (from the list of properties on pages 7 and 8).

(2) A binary relation E that is reflexive, symmetric and transitive is called an equivalence relation. (For example, if $\succ$ is a preference relation, then $\sim$ is an equivalence relation; cf. Proposition (2.4)(c).) Here is an easy proof that if E is symmetric and transitive, then it is automatically reflexive (thus reflexive could be deleted from the list of properties): Fix $x \in X$ and take some y such that xEy. Then yEx by symmetry, and hence xEx by transitivity. Unfortunately, this easy proof is spurious. Why?

(3) Prove Proposition (2.5).

(4) Show that the properties (for a binary relation) of asymmetry and negative transitivity are independent.

(5) Prove Proposition (2.8): For a binary relation $\succ$ (on a finite set X), $c(\cdot, \succ)$ is a choice function if and only if $\succ$ is acyclic. In what sense is it important here that X is finite?

(6) Prove that for any binary relation $\succ$, $c(\cdot, \succ)$ defined as in the display on page 12 satisfies Sen's α. (Is it important here that X is finite? In what sense is it important that $\succ$ is acyclic, even though you weren't told to assume acyclicity?)

(7) Give an example of a finite set X and an acyclic binary relation where $c(\cdot, \succ)$ does not satisfy Sen's property β.

(8) In and around Propositions (2.13) and (2.14), I seem to get very confused about whether negative transitivity is all I need to prove Houthakker's axiom, and thus asymmetry. Unconfuse me. Have I implicitly used asymmetry in the proof of (2.13), and if so, where? Deal with the proof. I *know* (and so do you, if you did problem (4)) that negative transitivity doesn't imply asymmetry, and I don't want an example of that – I want to know what is going on in the proof.

(9) Give an example of a finite set X and a choice function c on $P(X)$ that satisfies Sen's α but such that there is no binary relation $\succ$ such that $c(\cdot, \succ) = c$.

3

Ordinal Utility

The storyline for this chapter is that there is a set of objects X, and Totrep makes pairwise comparisons expressing strict preference for some objects over others, formalized by the binary relation $\succ$. From $\succ$ are defined $\succeq$ and $\sim$ as in Chapter 2. We are looking for a numerical representation of $\succ$; i.e., a function $u : X \to R$ such that

(3.1) $$x \succ y \quad \text{iff} \quad u(x) > u(y).$$

FINITE X

We begin with the case of finite X.

Proposition (3.2). If X is a finite set, a binary relation $\succ$ is a preference relation if and only if there exists a function $u : X \to R$ such that (3.1) holds.

Proof. We first prove that if such a function exists, then $\succ$ is a preference relation. Assume the existence of such a function u.
(a) $x \succ y$ iff $u(x) > u(y)$ iff $u(y) \not\geq u(x)$ which implies $y \not\succ x$, thus $\succ$ is asymmetric.
(b) If $x \not\succ y$ and $y \not\succ z$, then $u(x) \not> u(y) \not> u(z)$, which is the same as $u(x) \leq u(y) \leq u(z)$ which implies $u(x) \leq u(z)$ or $u(x) \not> u(z)$ which implies $x \not\succ z$. Thus $\succ$ is negatively transitive.
   That was easy. Now to go the other way. (The method of proof that I'm about to use is the most straightforward way to proceed, and it has the advantage of introducing the uninitiated to the principle of mathematical induction. But it is far from the most elegant proof that can be given. To see an elegant method of proof, which could be used here quite handily, see the proof of Theorem (3.5).) I'm going to use mathematical induction on the size (or cardinality) of the set X.

(Brief aside: The principle of mathematical induction says: Suppose that I want to prove that a statement is true for all strictly positive integers $n = 1, 2, 3, \ldots$. Then a valid method of proof is to show that the statement is true for $n = 1$, and that for every $n = 2, 3, \ldots$, if the statement is true for $n - 1$, then it is also true for n.)

I'm going to prove inductively: If X has n elements ($n = 1, 2, 3, \ldots$) and $\succ$ is a preference relation on X, then there exists a function $u : X \to R$ such that (3.1) holds. In fact, in the proof I'm going to show that this can be done with the range of u being the interval $(0, 1)$.

First I must prove that this result is true for $n = 1$. In this case X is a singleton, say $\{x\}$, and if I define $u(x) = 1/2$, then neither $x \succ y$ nor $u(x) > u(y)$ is possible for $x, y \in X$ (the former because $\succ$ is asymmetric), so (3.1) holds trivially.

Now I fix an integer $n = 2, 3, \ldots$ and hypothesize that the result is true for sets of size $n - 1$. (This working hypothesis is called the *induction hypothesis*). Fix a set X with n elements, and let $\succ$ be a preference relation on X. Let x° be any arbitrary element picked from X, and let X' denote $X \setminus \{x^\circ\}$. X' has $n - 1$ elements, so by the induction hypothesis there exists a function $u' : X' \to (0, 1)$ such that (3.1) holds for all $x, y \varepsilon X'$. (Oops, I forgot something! In order to apply the induction hypothesis, I must show that $\succ$ restricted to X' is a preference relation. It is, and I'll spare you the details. But be sure that you understand (a) what this means, (b) why it is necessary, and, if you can't "see" the proof immediately, (c) how it would be proved formally.)

I have to consider four cases.

Case 1: There exists some $x'' \in X'$ such that $x^\circ \sim x''$. In this case define $u : X \to (0, 1)$ by

$$u(x) = \begin{cases} u'(x) & \text{if } x \in X', \\ u'(x'') & \text{if } x = x^\circ. \end{cases}$$

I claim that the range of this function u is indeed $(0, 1)$ (obvious) and that it satisfies (3.1) for all $x, y \in X$:

If both x and y are from X', then $x \succ y$ iff $u'(x) > u'(y)$ (by the induction hypothesis) iff $u(x) > u(y)$ (since $u \equiv u'$ on X').

If $x \in X'$ and $y = x^\circ$, then $x \succ y$ iff $x \succ x''$ (since $x'' \sim y = x^\circ$) iff $u'(x) > u'(x'')$ iff $u(x) > u(x^\circ)$ (since $u(x) = u'(x)$ and $u(x^\circ) = u'(x'')$).

If $x = x^\circ$ and $y \in X'$, then $x \succ y$ iff $x'' \succ y$ iff $u'(x'') > u'(y)$ iff $u(x^\circ) > u(y)$.

If $x = y = x^\circ$, then both $x \succ y$ and $u(x) > u(y)$ are impossible, and (3.1) is satisfied trivially.

Case 2: If $x^\circ \succ x$ for all $x \in X'$. In this case define

$$u(x) = \begin{cases} u'(x) & \text{if } x \in X' \\ [\max_{x \in X'} u'(x) + 1]/2 & \text{if } x = x^\circ \end{cases}$$

Again the range of u is $(0,1)$ and it satisfies (3.1):

If both x and y are from X', then just as in case 1.

If $x \in X'$ and $y = x^\circ$, then $x \succ y$ is impossible by the hypothesis of this case, and $u(x) > u(y)$ is impossible by the construction of u.

If $x = x^\circ$ and $y \in X'$, then $x \succ y$ by the hypothesis of this case, and $u(x) > u(y)$ by construction.

If $x = y = x^\circ$, then just as in case 1.

Case 3: If $x \succ x^\circ$ for all $x \in X'$. In this case define

$$u(x) = \begin{cases} u'(x) & \text{if } x \in X', \\ [\min_{x \in X'} u'(x)]/2 & \text{if } x = x^\circ. \end{cases}$$

and proceed as in case 2. (These details can be awfully tedious.)

Case 4: If $x \not\sim x^\circ$ for any $x \in X'$ and there exist at least one $x \in X'$ such that $x \succ x^\circ$ and at least one $x \in X'$ such that $x^\circ \succ x$. In this case, let $\overline{x}$ be such that $u'(\overline{x}) = \min_{\{y \in X' : y \succ x^\circ\}} u'(y)$ and let $\underline{x}$ be such that $u'(\underline{x}) = \max_{\{y \in X' : x^\circ \succ y\}} u'(y)$. In words, $\overline{x}$ is the "worst" thing in X' that is better than x°, and $\underline{x}$ is the "best" thing in X' that is worse than x°. (How do I know that such $\overline{x}$ and $\underline{x}$ exist? You should be sure that you know how to provide this missing step.) Then define u by

$$u(x) = \begin{cases} u'(x) & \text{if } x \in X', \\ [u'(\overline{x}) + u'(\underline{x})]/2 & \text{if } x = x^\circ. \end{cases}$$

Note that if $x \in X'$ is such that $x \succ x^\circ$, then $u'(x) \geq u'(\overline{x})$ so that $x \succeq \overline{x}$. Similarly, $x^\circ \succ x$ implies that $\underline{x} \succeq x$. And since $\overline{x} \succ x^\circ \succ \underline{x}$, we know by transivity that $\overline{x} \succ \underline{x}$, and thus $u(\overline{x}) > u(\underline{x})$, so that $u(\overline{x}) > [u(\overline{x}) + u(\underline{x})]/2 = u(x^\circ) > u(\underline{x})$. Clearly, the function u has the range $(0,1)$. And (3.1) holds:

If x and y are from X', proceed as in case 1.

If $x = x°$ and $y \in X'$, then $x \succ y$ iff $x° = x \succ \underline{x} \succeq y$ iff $u(x°) = u(x) > u(\underline{x}) \geq u(y)$.

If $x \in X'$ and $y = x°$, proceed as immediately above.

If $x = y = x°$, proceed as in case 1.

Cases 1 through 4 exhaust all possibilities (if pressed, could you show this formally?), so that the induction step (extending the result from a set of size $n - 1$ to a set of size n) is complete, and the proposition is proven.

There is so much detail above that it is easy to lose track of what is going on. Basically, it can be paraphrased as follows: Assume (inductively) that the representation is possible for sets of size $n - 1$. Then take a set of size n and a subset of size $n - 1$, X'. Produce a representation for X', called u'. Let $x°$ denote the point left out.

Now look for where $u(x°)$ should fall. It will either be (case 1) on top of some $u'(x')$, (case 2) to the right of all $u'(x')$, (case 3) to the left of all $u'(x')$, or (case 4) between two $u'(x')$'s. Put it where it belongs. All the detail in the proof is to show that if you do this, then what results does indeed satisfy (3.1).

Now for the acid test of your comprehension. *Nowhere* in the proof of the second half of the proposition (that a representation was possible for a preference relation) did I use the words "negatively transitive." But the first half of the proof shows that somewhere I *must* have assumed that $\succ$ possesses this property. Where? Until you can answer that question, you don't comprehend the proof.

COUNTABLY INFINITE X

Now we can work on extending this result to infinite sets X. We begin with the case of a *countable* set X.

(Aside: A set X is *countable* (or *denumerable*) if it is possible to "count" the elements of X by listing them $X = \{x_1, x_2, \ldots\}$. More formally, a set is countable if there is a function f with domain $\{1, 2, 3 \ldots\}$ and range X which is *onto* X. (That is, f hits everything in X at least once.) Finite sets are always countable, so the expression *countably infinite* is sometimes used to distinguish sets that are countable and infinite from finite sets. A set is countably infinite iff there is a one-to-one and onto function from $\{1, 2, 3, \ldots\}$ to the set. Examples of countable sets are the integers and the rational numbers. The set of real numbers R is *uncountable*, as is the unit interval $[0, 1]$ (and if you've never seen this last statement proved, get someone to do it for you).)

Proposition (3.3). For X countable, a binary relation $\succ$ is a preference relation if and only if there exists a function $u : X \to R$ such that (3.1) holds.

Proof. The proof of: "If there exists a function u satisfying (3.1), then $\succ$ is a preference relation" is exactly as in Proposition (3.2) – nowhere in that part of the proof of (3.2) did we use the fact that X is finite.

To prove that if the relation $\succ$ is a preference relation, then such a u exists, it suffices to look at the case where X is countably infinite – if X is finite then (3.2) applies. So let $X = \{x_1, x_2, \ldots\}$ (that is, *enumerate* X) and for each $n = 1, 2, \ldots$, let $X_n = \{x_1, \ldots, x_n\}$. Note that $\succ$ restricted to X_n (for each n) is a preference relation. ('This needs a proof, if you didn't do it before.) I claim that for $n = 1, 2, \ldots$, there exist functions $u_n : X_n \to R$ such that

(a) for all $x, y \in X_n$, $x \succ y$ iff $u_n(x) > u_n(y)$, and

(b) for all $x \in X_{n-1}, u_{n-1}(x) = u_n(x)$.

The last bit is the key. It says that once $u_n(x_n)$ is defined, the values $u_{n+1}(x_n), u_{n+2}(x_n), \ldots$ are all fixed and equal to $u_n(x_n)$. The proof of my claim is by induction in n – in fact the proof is identical to the proof of (3.2): Define $u_1(x_1) = 1/2$, and if you have u_{n-1} produce u_n by the procedure given with u_{n-1} in place of u', u_n in place of u, and x_n in place of x°. (For rigor freaks in the audience, I'm being a bit sloppy here. Can you come up with an exact statement which, when proved by induction, yields the result desired?)

Now define $u : X \to (0, 1)$ by $u(x_n) = u_n(x_n)$. (3.1) holds for this because if $x, y \in X$, then $x = x_n$ and $y = x_m$ for some integers n and m. Let $k = \max\{m, n\}$. Then $u_k(x_n) = u(x_n), u_k(x_m) = u(x_m)$, and $x_n, x_m \in X_k$, thus $x \succ y$ iff $x_n \succ x_m$ iff $u_k(x_n) > u_k(x_m)$ iff $u(x) > u(y)$. (For the rigor freaks who know something about mathematical set theory: Is what I just did legit? In particular, do I need the power of the axiom of choice to make this construction work?) (If you don't know what the axiom of choice is, please ignore the previous remark at peril of your sanity!)

UNCOUNTABLE X

Can we go any further? For example, is the following true?

Pseudo-proposition (3.4). For arbitrary X, a binary relation $\succ$ is a preference relation if and only if there exists a function $u : X \to R$ such that (3.1) holds.

It should be clear that *if* such a function u exists, then $\succ$ is a preference relation. This is just the first half of the proof of (3.2), where we made no assumptions at all about the size of the set X. But if $\succ$ is a preference relation, and X is "large", then there needn't exist such a u.

To develop an example, let $X = [0,1] \times [0,1]$ and define

$$(x_1, x_2) \succ (y_1, y_2) \text{ if } x_1 > y_1 \text{ or } [x_1 = y_1 \text{ and } x_2 > y_2].$$

This is a preference relation (can you verify this?), and it even has a name – it's called the *lexicographic* preference relation. It is so called because it resembles the rule by which things are ordered in the dictionary: First alphabetize all the words you have by the first letter, and only then (if there is a tie) go on to the second letter. This preference relation cannot be represented by a numerical function u.

To see why this is, suppose such a representation is possible. Let u do the job. Then for every $r \in [0,1]$, it is the case that $(r,1) \succ (r,0)$, thus $u((r,1)) > u((r,0))$. Define $d(r) = u((r,1)) - u((r,0))$. We know that $d(r) > 0$ for each r. Thus we have that

$$[0,1] = \bigcup_{n=1}^{\infty} \{r : d(r) > 1/n\}$$

Now on the left hand side I have an uncountably infinite set (see the end of the previous aside), while on the right hand side I have a countable union of sets, so some of the sets on the right hand side must be uncountable.

(Mathematical aside: A countable union of countable sets is countable. So if all of the sets on the right hand side were countable, then the union would be countable. But the union, we know, or at least we were told, is uncountable.)

So suppose that $\{r : d(r) > 1/n°\}$ is uncountable.

Let $u((1,1)) - u((0,0)) = K$, and let N be an integer larger than $Kn° + 1$. Pick a subset of N elements out of $\{r : d(r) > 1/n°\}$ and index the subset $\{r_1, r_2, \ldots, r_N\}$ so that $r_1 < r_2 < \ldots < r_N$. Since

$$(r_n, 0) \succ (r_{n-1}, 1),$$

we know that $u((r_n, 0)) > u((r_{n-1}, 1))$. Hence

$$u((r_n, 0)) - u((r_{n-1}, 0)) > u((r_{n-1}, 1)) - u((r_{n-1}, 0)) > 1/n°.$$

Thus finally
$$K = u((1,1)) - u((0,0)) =$$
$$[u((1,1)) - u((r_N, 0))] + [u((r_N, 0)) - u((r_{N-1}, 0))] + \ldots$$
$$+ [u((r_2, 0)) - u((r_1, 0))] + [u((r_1, 0)) - u((0,0))]$$
$$> 0 + 1/n° + 1/n° + \ldots + 1/n° + 0 > (N-1)/n° > K.$$

This establishes the necessary contradiction.

So what can be done for uncountable sets X? The "answer" is somewhat technical and not always useful, but here it is, for the record.

Definition. Suppose $\succ$ is a binary relation on a set X. A subset Z of X is called $\succ$-*order dense* if for all $x, y \in X$ such that $x \succ y$, there exists some $z \in Z$ with $x \succeq z \succeq y$.

Theorem (3.5). For an arbitrary set X and binary relation $\succ$, there exists a function $u : X \to R$ such that (3.1) holds if and only if $\succ$ is a preference relation and there is a countable $\succ$-order dense subset Z of X.

Proof. It is left to you to show that if a representation is possible, then there is a countable $\succ$-order dense subset of X.

Suppose there is a countable $\succ$-order dense subset $Z = \{z_1, z_2, \ldots\}$ of X. For each $z_n \in Z$, let $r(z_n) = 1/2^n$.

For each $x \in X$, let $\overline{Z}(x) = \{z \in Z : z \succ x\}$ and let $\underline{Z}(x) = \{z \in Z : x \succ z\}$. We claim that is $x \succeq x'$, then $\overline{Z}(x) \subseteq \overline{Z}(x')$ and $\underline{Z}(x) \supseteq \underline{Z}(x')$. (Details are left to you.) Moreover, if $x \succ x'$, then one of the two set inclusions just given is strict. This follows because if $x \succ x'$, there is some $z \in Z$ with $x \succeq z \succeq x'$, and either $x \succ z \succeq x'$ or $x \succeq z \succ x'$ or both. Now define

$$ u(x) = \sum_{z \in \underline{Z}(x)} r(z) - \sum_{z \in \overline{Z}(x)} r(z). $$

Since the sequence $\{r(z_n)\}$ is summable, $u(x)$ is clearly well defined. In fact, $u(x) \in [-1, 1]$. And by the remarks above, if $x \succeq x'$, then $u(x) \geq u(x')$, while if $x \succ x'$, then $u(x) > u(x')$. Thus $x \succ x'$ if and only if $u(x) > u(x')$. That does it.

UNIQUENESS

The uniqueness result for the ordinal representation of preference is easy.

Theorem (3.6). Given a set X, a preference relation $\succ$ and functions u and u' that represent $\succ$ in the sense of (3.1), there exists an increasing function $f : R \to R$ such that
(a) f is strictly increasing on $\{r : r = u(x) \text{ for some } x\}$ and
(b) $u' = f \circ u$ (that is, $u'(x) = f(u(x))$).
Moreover, for any strictly increasing function $g : R \to R, g \circ u$ represents $\succ$.

This is loosely paraphrased: u is unique up to a strictly increasing transformation. I'll omit the proof.

BELLS AND WHISTLES

(The material in this section requires some knowledge of real analysis).

Now we move on to bells and whistles on the basic story. One seemingly natural variation on the results above, for the case of uncountable X, is to imagine that X and $\succ$ together are "nice." Specifically, we consider cases in which X is a subset of a separable metric space, and $\succ$ is continuous.

(If you don't know what it means for X to be a subset of a separable metric space, then perhaps you can follow this if we say that X is a subset of R^k for some integer k. That is, X is a subset of k-dimensional Euclidean space. This is natural in many applications to economics, where X is a commodity space. And in this case X will qualify as a subset of a separable metric space.)

What does it mean for $\succ$ to be continuous? Simply this:

Definition. A binary relation $\succ$ defined on a separable metric space X is *continuous* if for all sequences $\{x_n\}$ from X with limit x, (a) if $x \succ y$ for some $y \in X$, then for all large n, $x_n \succ y$, and (b) if $y \succ x$ for some $y \in X$, then for all large n, $y \succ x_n$.

So what do we do with a preference relation that is continuous on a separable metric space? One can show in this case that there is a countable $\succ$-order dense subset of X and hence that $\succ$ admits a numerical representation. But we might want more. We might want that $\succ$ is represented by a numerical function u that is continuous on X. We state without proof:

Theorem (3.7). If X is a subset of a separable metric space, then $\succ$ is a continous preference relation if and only if there exists some continuous function $u : X \to R$ such that (3.1) holds.

For a proof, consult a standard reference book in choice theory. For the real math jocks in the audience, we can go further than this: We can suppose that X is a topological space, and define continuity of preferences by insisting that, for all x, the sets $\{y \in X : x \succ y\}$ and $\{y \in X : y \succ x\}$ are both open. Then, if the topological space is well-behaved – something akin to separability, we get an analogous result to (3.7).

Another natural extension, at least for economists, is to consider choice sets X that are convex subsets of linear spaces, and to define that a binary relation is *convex* if $\{y \in X : y \succ x\}$ is convex for all $x \in X$. Any u that represents such a $\succ$ will be quasi-concave. (If you don't know what that means, don't worry.) But in general, representation of a convex preference relation with a concave utility function will not be possible. Necessary and sufficient conditions for representation by a concave utility function – if the choice space is a subset of finite dimensional Euclidean space – are known and are quite messy.

PROBLEMS

(1) In many of the proofs in this chapter, I made implicit use of the result that if $\succ$ is a preference relation on a finite set X and if X' is a subset of X, then $\succ$ restricted to X' is a preference relation. Provide a proof. (What if $\succ$ restricted to X'? If we think formally of $\succ$ as a subset of $X \times X$, then it is $\succ \cap X' \times X'$.)

(2) Recall that right after the proof of Proposition (3.2), I remarked that I didn't seem to have used negative transitivity of $\succ$ in order to show that a representation exists. Of course, I must have used this somewhere, even if implicitly. (Why "of course"?) Where?

(3) Recall that in the middle of the proof of Proposition (3.3), I said that I was being sloppy in my use of mathematical induction. Unslop me. What statement, when proved by induction, gives the desired result? And, if you know about such things: A little later on I remark that my proof may require the axiom of choice. Does it? If so, why? If not, why not?

(4) Complete the proof of Theorem (3.5). Show that if $u : X \to R$ represents $\succ$ in the sense of (3.1), then there is a countable $\succ$-order dense subset of X.

(5) Concerning Theorem (3.6), suppose I modify it to read "... there exists a strictly increasing function $f : R \to R$ such that $u' = f \circ u$." Show by example that this modification renders the theorem false.

(6) In Chapter 2, we questioned the assumption that strict preference "ought" to be negatively transitive. So suppose we tried to get by with a strict preference relation that was only asymmetric and transitive:

(a) If $\succ$ is asymmetric and transitive, is it acyclic? Either give a proof or a counterexample.

(b) Define $\sim$ by $x \sim y$ if $x \not\succ y$ and $y \not\succ x$. If $\succ$ is asymmetric and transitive, then $\sim$ is reflexive and symmetric. Provide a proof. But $\sim$ needn't be transitive – provide a counterexample.

(c) Prove that if $\succ$ is asymmetric and transitive, then there exists a function $u : X \to R$ such that $x \succ y$ implies $u(x) > u(y)$. Assume X is finite.

(d) Suppose $\succ$ is a binary relation and $u : X \to R$ satisfies $x \succ y$ implies $u(x) > u(y)$. Is $\succ$ necessarily irreflexive?, asymmetric?, transitive?, negatively transitive?, acyclic? For each, either provide a proof or a counterexample. Again assume X is finite.

(e) One rationale for $\succ$ that are not negatively transitive is that there needs to be a "perceptible difference" between two items x and y before Totrep will express strict preference. This suggests the following representation (for finite X):

$$x \succ y \text{ iff } u(x) > u(y) + 1.$$

If $\succ$ has this sort of representation, is $\succ$ asymmetric and transitive? If $\succ$ is asymmetric and transitive, can it necessarily be represented in this fashion? Provide either proof or counterexample in answering these questions.

(7) Prove as much of Theorem (3.7) as you can. Take this in four parts. You should be able to show that if $u : X \to R$ represents $\succ$ and u is continuous, then $\succ$ is continuous. (If you can't do this, give up on the rest.) You will have a bit harder time with: If $\succ$ is continuous and X is a subset of a complete and separable metric space, then X has a $\succ$-order dense subset. Even if you can't do this, assume it and comment on whether the function u constructed in the proof of Theorem (3.5) will be continuous. And, if it isn't, try to prove that there is a continuous u that represents $\succ$.

(8) Recall from Chapter 2 that we didn't try to think about revealed preference theory for infinite sets X. Now it is time to think about it. Suppose that X is, say, a subset of finite dimensional Euclidean space. (If you have the math skills, you can generalize this setting substantially.) We will not require that a choice function c is defined for all subsets A of X, but only for all compact subsets. (If you think in terms of the application to demand theory, thinking that c is defined for all compact subsets of X is not natural. But to

weaken this really complicates matters.) And we will restrict attention to preference relations that are continuous. With this as a starting point, how much of the development of the previous chapter can you replicate?

(9) In the last mentioned bell-or-whistle, I said that $\succ$ was said to be convex if $\{y \in X : y \succ x\}$ was convex for all x. And I said that any representation u of a convex preference relation was necessarily quasi-concave. In case you didn't know, a real-valued function f on a convex set X is said to be quasi-concave if for all $x, y \in X$ and $\alpha \in [0, 1]$, $f(\alpha x + (1 - \alpha)y) \geq \min\{f(x), f(y)\}$. Prove that if $\succ$ is a convex preference relation as defined above and u represents $\succ$ in the sense of (3.1), then u is quasi-concave. If $\succ$ is represented by u in the sense of (3.1) and u is quasi-concave, is $\succ$ a convex preference relation? Give a proof or supply a counterexample. What would happen in this problem if I defined convexity of preference differently, saying that preferences (now specified by weak preference $\succeq$) are convex if, for all x, $\{y \in X : y \succeq x\}$ is convex? Finally, provide a counterexample to the statement that if $\succ$ is convex, then there must exist some concave function u that represents $\succ$ in the sense of (3.1). Note well, this doesn't say that all functions u that represent $\succ$ must be concave – but only that there is some one concave function. You have to produce a convex $\succ$ such that *every* u that represents it is not concave. And remember, the rules are that X must be a convex set. If you want a real challenge, give a counterexample where X is a subset of R^2 *and* all the indifference sets (sets of the form $\{y \in X : y \sim x\}$ for some x) are "thin." I won't try to give a definition of the term thin here – if you see the point of this addition to the problem, you'll know what I mean. This last challenge, by the way, ought to point you towards a counterexample to the proposition without the added condition on indifference sets.

4

Choice Under Uncertainty: Formulations and Representations

The topic for the next few chapters is choice under uncertainty. Basically, we seek to expand upon the story of the last section, where we had a binary (preference) relation $\succ$ on a set X and we sought a function $u : X \to R$ representing in the sense of

$$x \succ y \text{ if and only if } u(x) > u(y).$$

Now we'll make assumptions about the mathematical structure of the objects in the set X – we'll want $x \in X$ somehow to represent *uncertain prospects*. And by imposing further conditions on $\succ$ having to do with the mathematical structure of X, we'll try to specialize the form of the function u.

This leaves us with two immediate questions: How *mathematically* do you model an uncertain prospect? Given the structure of the mathematical model, what corresponding forms of functions u will we seek?

The literature contains (basically) three sets of answers to these questions, differing in whether they treat uncertainty as objective or subjective. The two polar cases are associated with the names of *von Neumann-Morgenstern* (hereafter abbreviated NM), for objective uncertainty, and *Savage*, for subjective uncertainty. I'll use those names as designators. A third, middle course is taken by *Anscombe and Aumann* – I'll refer to this either as the A-A or the horse lottery-roulette wheel theory.

What I want to do in this chapter is to lay out these three formulations – the point is for you to understand how they differ as representations of uncertain prospects and, especially, to think of why one might give a more appropriate model than another.

31

NM MODELS

The NM model views uncertainty as objective, in the sense that there is given a quantification of how likely the various outcomes are, given in the form of a probability distribution. Formally, there is given some arbitrary set Z of *prizes* or *consequences*, together with a second set P of *probability measures* or *probability distributions* on Z. P is the choice set – Totrep is choosing/expressing preference among probability distributions.

Which set of probability distributions? There is some leeway here: If Z is finite, we always take P to be all the probability distributions on Z, where by a probability distribution p we mean a function $p : Z \to [0,1]$ such that $\sum_{z \in Z} p(z) = 1$.

If Z is countably infinite, we may still define P exactly as above – *all* the probability distributions on Z. (If you are well trained in mathematics, you should have just smelled a rat. See problem 4 of Chapter 8.) But when Z is infinite, countable or not, we sometimes take P to be the set of all *simple* probability measures on Z. A simple probability measure (or distribution – I use the terms interchangeably) is represented mathematically by a function $p : Z \to [0,1]$ such that $p(z) \neq 0$ for at most finitely many z and $\sum_{z \in Z} p(z) = 1$, where in this sum we mean to sum over the Z such that $p(z)$ is nonzero. The idea is simple (ouch): simple probability measures are measures that charge/put mass on/give positive probability to a finite subset of the prize set.

For infinite Z, we might also take P to be the set of all *discrete* probability measures on Z, where a discrete probability measure is just like a simple measure, but the set of nonzero probability prizes can be either finite or countably infinite.

And for infinite Z, we can take P to be more complicated sets of probability measures. For example (not expected to be quite comprehensible for many readers), if Z is a topological space, we might take P to be the set of all Borel probability measures on Z. If Z is some interval on the real line, we might take P to be the set of all probability measures on that interval that have continuous density functions. We might take P to be the set of *all* probability measures on Z. (The technically minded and extremely well-educated reader will note: I haven't said that these probabilities must be σ-additive – finite additivity may be all I desire). Now for each of these more complicated sets P I have to be more exact than I am being – I have to be mathematically precise concerning what I mean by a probability distribution. But whenever I can do that I am potentially in business according to the terms of NM style theory.

Note well: In this theory, the externally imposed objects are (a) a set Z of prizes, and (b) a set P of some sort of probability measures on Z – an $x \in X$ represents an uncertain prospect where as part of the objective description of the prospect we have what probabilities it assigns to various prizes and/or sets of prizes.

Inside such a setting, we seek conditions on binary relations $\succ$ defined on P that give an expected utility representation: There is a function $u : Z \to R$ such that

(4.1) $\qquad p \succ p'$ if and only if $\displaystyle\sum_{z \in Z} p(z)u(z) > \sum_{z \in Z} p'(z)u(z).$

Note that the summation in (4.1) definitely makes sense if either Z is finite or if P is the set of simple probability measures on some (arbitrary) Z – it may make sense if P is the set of discrete probability measures on some Z. (Math jocks: it certainly makes sense if u is a bounded function, since then the sums converge absolutely for all $x \in X$). And it definitely doesn't make sense in the more general types of P that are referred to above. For those more general types, we will have to generalize (4.1) so that integrals, appropriately defined, can replace the summations, and again we'll want to assume that any such integrals are well defined for all $x \in X$.

But however we finesse the definition, the idea of the representation should be clear: u gives some index of how good each prize z is. And then a probability distribution over prizes is indexed by the expected value of that index.

SAVAGE STYLE MODELS

In the Savage style models, uncertainty is viewed as being subjective in the sense that there are no objective (externally) imposed probabilities. Probabilities will enter the story, being part of the eventual representation, but they will be supplied by Totrep on the basis of his subjective preferences.

The basics of the Savage formulation are

(a) a set of prizes or consequences, denoted Z; and

(b) a set of *states of the world* or *of nature* denoted by S with typical element denoted by s. Each $s \in S$ is a compilation of all character-istics/factors about which Totrep is uncertain and which are relevant to the consequences that will ensue from his choice. The set S is to be an exhaustive list of mutually exclusive states – some *one* s is/will be the state.

From Z and S we construct the choice space, which is denoted by F, as the set of *all* functions from S to Z. Formally we would write $X = Z^S$. Elements of X are called *acts*. The idea is that Totrep cannot fully specify the consequences that will ensue from the action chosen. Instead, Totrep's choice of action sets up a function f from states of nature to the consequences for Totrep – Totrep *chooses* one such action from some set of available actions, and Totrep's pref-erences over actions are given by a binary relation $\succ$ defined on F.

The representation that we look for in this setting goes as follows: There exist a function $p : S \to [0,1]$ such that $\sum_{s \in S} p(s) = 1$ and a function $u : Z \to R$ such that

(4.2) $f \succ f'$ if and only if $\displaystyle\sum_{s \in S} p(s)u(f(s)) > \sum_{s \in S} p(s)u(f'(s)).$

Actually, Savage is looking for something a bit more complicated – the above makes sense if S is finite, but for reasons we'll discuss in due course, Savage will need to assume that S is infinite (and, loosely, uncountable, although this isn't really quite accurate). So in the eventual Savage representation, the probability measure p will need to be fancier, and the summations in (4.2) will need to be replaced by integrals.

Still, the form above communicates the basic nature of the Savage formulation and representation – I'd like to discuss it a bit here making the assumption that S and Z are both finite so that no mathematical difficulties get in the way of the conceptual content.

There are three things to note about this representation:

(a) Both *tastes*, given by the utility function u, and *beliefs*, given by the probability measure p, are subjective. That is, both arise from the relation $\succ$. Compare with the representation in NM theory, where the probabilities are given objectively or exogenously.

(b) Tastes and beliefs are independent. That is, the utility of a conse-quence does not depend on the state in which it is received, nor does the prize received in a state affect the probability of that state.

(c) The probability measure p is independent of the action taken, and the utility of a particular consequence is independent of the action taken.

Point (a) is obvious. In order to understand points (b) and (c), let's look at a couple of standard examples that are hard to fit into the Savage setup if we're going to get the representation (4.2).

Suppose, to begin, that you are going on a picnic, you're unsure about the weather, and you're trying to decide what equipment to bring. A naive formulation would have:

The state space gives the various possible states of the weather: $S =$ {rain, cloudy, sunny}.

Prizes in Z are of bundles of equipment. For example, suppose that you can take on this picnic any/all of: fried chicken; fruit; coffee; iced tea; umbrella; frisbee; suntan lotion. Then a typical prize z would be some subset of these items, such as {fruit, iced tea, frisbee}, and Z would be the set of all subsets of the items above.

An act $f \in F$ then is a function from states to bundles of equipment; say the act f which is {fruit, iced tea, frisbee} if it rains, {fruit, iced tea, umbrella} if it is cloudy, and {fried chicken, suntan lotion, umbrella} if it is sunny. The nature of this problem is such that it seems natural to look only at *constant acts* – acts where the prize doesn't change with state – because those presumably are what are truly feasible acts. That is, you can't take some act which will make the bundle of equipment that you have available depend on the weather. (You might be able to do this if you could arrange to have some picnic equipment service agree to deliver to your picnic site a bundle which is contingent on the weather.) But as part of the Savage setup we have to think about *all* the functions from S to Z as acts. From a normative point of view, we do this so that the axioms eventually stated will give us the strongest possible results, being applicable to the largest possible set of objects – that is, for "for all" types of axioms. Of course, the problem with this is that Totrep will need to be able to conceptualize any incredible acts and to sign off on the axioms as regards incredible acts as well as the credible acts. This is a point we've seen once already (where?) and that we'll keep coming back to.

With this setup, is it reasonable to suppose that we can find p and u so that (4.2) is satisfied? Not if we're talking about my pref-

Chapter 4

erences. Note that the utility of a bundle of equipment is supposed to be given by a function u in the representation which is independent of the state s, while the desirability to me of, say, the bundle {umbrella, fried chicken} depends on the weather. That is, the utility of a prize may depend on the state that occurs.

How do we deal with this? There are two standard cures: First, reformulate prizes so that the problem goes away – instead of making the prizes bundles of "capital equipment," make prizes the *flow of services* derived from the capital. That is, a typical prize would be a vector $z = (z_1, z_2, ..., z_6)$ where z_1 gives the level of food satiety, z_2 the level of thirst, z_3 the level of body comfort in terms of temperature, z_4 the level of body comfort in terms of wetness/dryness, z_5 whether or not sunburned, and z_6 the level of entertainment. Then the act of taking along {fried chicken, iced tea, frisbee} results in the act f that is given by:

$f(\text{rain}) = (\text{satiated, not thirsty, cold, wet, no sunburn, not amused});$

$f(\text{cloudy}) = (\text{satiated, not thirsty, cool, dry, no sunburn, amused});$

$f(\text{sunny}) = (\text{satiated, not thirsty, warm, dry, sunburned, amused}).$

The problem with this cure is that in some cases the prize space you'll need to formulate is so far removed from what is objectively describable that the representation becomes tautological.

A second cure is to give up on trying to have a state independent representation – look instead for a representation of the form: There exist functions $p : S \to [0,1]$ with $\sum_s p(s) = 1$ and $u : Z \times S \to R$ such that

(4.3) $\qquad f \succ f'$ iff $\sum_s p(s) u(f(s), s) > \sum_s p(s) u(f'(s), s).$

In the literature this is called a "state-dependent expected utility" representation. With regard to which, note that the function p plays no real role here – if you can find functions p and u satisfying (4.3), then for "almost any" other p' there is a u' that together with p' also satisfies (4.3). (Question which, if you can answer it, means that you understand what I just said: What is the needed restriction on p'?) So it is "more honest" to write this as follows: There exists a function $v : Z \times S \to R$ such that

(4.4) $\qquad f \succ f'$ iff $\sum_s v(f(s), s) > \sum_s v(f'(s), s),$

and call this an "additively-separable-across-states" representation, which is (in my opinion) a much more appropriate description than "state dependent expected utility." In any case, having additive separability is *something*, but clearly it is less than a Savage representation.

Question: Why didn't we encounter this sort of problem when we discussed the NM setup? Does that setup somehow avoid this problem?

The second example to illustrate (b) and (c) concerns Totrep as a marketing manager: Consider the decision to advertise a new product, which will either sell like hotcakes or bomb. Consequences in terms of dollar profits are: if Totrep doesn't advertise and it sells, profits are $1M; if Totrep does advertise and it sells, profits are $.9M; if Totrep doesn't advertise and it bombs, profits are $0; or if Totrep does advertise and it bombs, profits are $-.1M

The naive formulation of this would run:

the state space S is the set {sells, bombs};

the set of prizes Z = {$1M, $.9M, $0, $-.1M};

and then the two feasible acts out of the sixteen in total that Totrep will have to think about are

$$f_1(\text{sells}) = \$1M, \quad f_1(\text{bombs}) = \$0,$$

which is "don't advertise", and

$$f_2(\text{sells}) = \$.9M, \quad f_2(\text{bombs}) = \$-.1M,$$

which is the act "advertise".

But this won't work – it doesn't matter what are p and u so long as u is increasing – in (4.2) with this formulation, "advertise" is always worse than "don't." The problem is obvious: presumably the action of advertising increases the chances of the item selling – something the Savage representation, in which the likelihood of the states are independent of the acts, cannot accommodate.

In this case, the cure is easy – change the state space to S = $\{s_1, s_2, s_3\}$, where s_1 is the state that the product sells whether you advertise or not, s_2 is the state that the product sells only if you advertise, and s_3 is the state that the product bombs regardless of what you do. Then the two feasible acts are

don't advertise: $f_1(s_1) = \$1M, f_1(s_2) = \$0, f_1(s_3) = \$0$, and advertise: $x_2(s_1) = \$.9M, x_2(s_2) = \$.9M, x_2(s_3) = \$ - .1M$.

But in other examples of this sort of thing, the cure may not be so apparent – cf. the Martian problem given at the end of this chapter.

ANSCOMBE-AUMANN

A strength of the Savage setup is that *none* of the uncertainty is objective – probabilities are completely subjective. But this strength comes at a price – obtaining the representation is (as you'll discover) quite a hard task. There isn't much doubt that the NM formulation, with objective probabilities only, is not good enough for all the applications of which we can think. Suppose I asked you to choose between:

if Yankees win next World Series, you win \$1000, and otherwise you get \$0; or

you win \$1000 if a fair coin that I flip comes up heads four times in a row, and otherwise you win \$0.

The uncertainty in the first gamble is certainly not objective, and I expect that some of you (quite rationally) would take the gamble, while others would select the sure thing. Note that this can't have anything to do with your utility function for money (assuming that you like more money to less); all that is important is whether you think the Yankees have a better than 1 in 16 chance of winning the World Series next year. In order to deal with decision making under uncertainty for such problems, we certainly do need a theory that deals with subjective uncertainty.

But is it necessary to go as far as Savage and have all uncertainty objective? Can't we agree (if only as a "thought experiment") that there are objective randomizing devices such as fair coins, perfect dice, balanced roulette wheels, urns filled with colored ping pong balls, etc.? If we can, then a lot of the difficulty that Savage encounters can be eliminated using a "middle of the road" formulation and development due to Anscombe and Aumann. The setup starts the same as the Savage setup – we are given:

(a) a state space S, which we will assume is finite for simplicity – this represents the subjective uncertainty, just as in Savage; and

(b) a set of prizes Z, also assumed to be finite for simplicity.

But now instead of looking *only* at acts which are functions from states to prizes, we imagine that acts are functions from states to *probability distributions on prizes*. The idea is that the subjective uncertainty will resolve, and depending on how it resolves Totrep will get an objectively uncertain prospect with prizes out of Z. Thinking of S as the results of a horse race (subjective uncertainty) and the resulting gamble being based on something objective such as the spin of a balanced roulette wheel, we will refer here to this theory as the horse race–roulette wheel theory.

Formalizing this is easy. Let P be the set of probability distributions on Z – since Z is finite we mean all the probability distributions. And for the choice space, take $H = P^S$, or H is the set of all functions from outcomes of the horse race to probability distributions over prizes.

The representation we seek is: There exist functions $\pi : S \to [0,1]$ with $\sum_{s \in S} \pi(s) = 1$ and $u : Z \to R$ such that

$$h \succ h' \text{ if and only if}$$

(4.5) $$\sum_{s \in S} \pi(s)[\sum_{z \in Z} h(s)(z) \cdot u(z)] > \sum_{s \in S} \pi(s)[\sum_{z \in Z} h'(s)(z) \cdot u(z)].$$

(In order to interpret this, remember that $h(s)$ is a probability distribution on Z, so $h(s)(z)$ should be read as the probability that $h(s)$ gives to the prize z.)

Note that in the special case where h is such that each $h(s)$ gives some prize with certainty, this specializes to exactly the Savage representation. What A-A have done is to enlarge the domain of choice in the Savage formulation in the hope (as it turns out well-founded) that this will make matters easier.

Of course, this makes the A-A setting as vulnerable as the Savage setting to the sorts of problems that we just discussed – that will be something to watch out for.

PROBLEMS

(1) As an alternative to the Savage style representation (4.2), I suggested the "state-dependent expected utility representation" (4.3).

Suppose that for a given finite state space S and finite prize space Z Totrep's preferences $\succ$ conform to this sort of representation: There is a probability distribution p on Z and a function $U : Z \times S \to R$ such that (4.3) holds. For precisely what other probability distributions p' is there a $U' : Z \times S \to R$ such that this sort of representation of $\succ$ holds for the pair (p', U')?

(2) You are engaged in a game of chance with Leonard Savage and a Martian. The game is simple – in the room is a closed steel box which either contains nothing or \$100. You may have either the contents of the box (no looking!!!) or \$5. Whichever you choose, we open the box. Moreover, if you choose the box, Savage will offer you a bet of \$1 to win \$1000 that it is empty, while if you choose the \$5, Savage will offer you a bet of \$1 to win \$1000 that the box has the \$100 in it.

To help you try to decide what to do, Savage suggests that you should use the following formulation, which fits into his framework.

Z – prize space – \$1100, \$1005, \$100, \$5, \$4, \$0, \$-1
S – state space – s_1 – \$100 in box, s_2 – box empty

In this case the four "feasible" acts are:

x_1 – take box and bet $x_1(s_1) = \$1100$, $x_1(s_2) = \$-1$;
x_2 – take box, no bet $x_2(s_1) = \$100$, $x_2(s_2) = \$0$;
x_3 – take \$5 and bet $x_3(s_1) = \$4$, $x_3(s_2) = \$1005$;
x_4 – take \$5 and no bet $x_4(s_1) = \$5$ $x_4(s_2) = \$5$.

Here is the catch. This Martian claims that she can foretell the future. She has already foretold whether you would pick the box or not, and has either not placed or placed the \$100 accordingly, so as to guarantee that Savage will win any wager you make with him. If you find this hard to believe, Savage and the Martian can show you affidavits from 5000 people with whom they have previously played this game, each testifying that the Martian correctly predicted what the person would do. (Moreover, you can be sure that the Martian and Savage have played this game exactly 5000 times.)

If you believe these affidavits (better still, if you now assess probability .97 that the Martian can and does foretell the future), will the formulation that Savage has suggested lead to a Savage style representation of your preferences? (By a Savage style representation I mean the sort of representation given in (4.2).) Why not? (Don't bother to try and explain why – the answer to my first question is no.)

Can you suggest another Savage style formulation that will result in a Savage style representation? (I am specifically interested in the case where you believe that the Martian can probably foretell the future, but you aren't certain of this.) Spell out this alternative formulation.

(3) Suppose that you and I are about to play the following game with the help of John Nash (a famous game theorist). The props are a silver dollar, 1 red marble, 1 blue, 1 green, 1 orange, and two cards which are marked as follows:

	green	orange
red	10,-1	1,1
blue	-1,10	1,1

H card

	green	orange
red	-1,10	1,1
blue	10,-1	1,1

T card

You hold the red and blue marbles, I hold the green and orange. Prof. Nash takes the coin and the two cards and leaves the room. He flips the coin – if it comes up heads he returns with the card H; if tails he returns with the T card. He places the card face down on the table. (There are no distinguishing marks on the backs of the cards.) Prof. Nash invites you to look and see which card he has brought in – I am not allowed to see which card he brought in whether you look or not, but I am allowed to see whether you looked (in fact, I *must* be given this information). Finally, you select either the red or the blue marble, I select either the green or the orange, and we reveal our selections simultaneously. Payoffs are made according to the two numbers in the relevant cell – you get the first number in the cell, I get the second. So, for example, if Nash brings in the T card, you select the red marble and I select the green marble, you get $-1 and I get $10. (This game is being funded by the NSF.) Of course, negative payoffs are losses. You must decide:

(a) Whether or not to look at the card.

(b) If you look, what to do next (which color to play).

(c) If you don't look, what to do next.

This book is supposed to be about choice theory, so it ought to have something to say about your choice problem. Does it (so far)? Can you fit this decision problem into any of the frameworks we have discussed so far? Begin by deciding what you will do in this case. Then formulate the problem according to some one or more of our models, and see if what you've chosen to do can be "rationalized" by the representation we have suggested for the form of model you've chosen.

5

von Neumann-Morgenstern Expected Utility

In our development of von Neumann-Morgenstern (or NM) expected utility theory, we'll begin with the easiest case, where the set of possible prizes is a finite set.

Let Z be a finite set and let P be the set of probability measures on Z. That is P is the set of functions $p : Z \to [0,1]$ such that $\sum_{z \in Z} p(z) = 1$. (Throughout this section, all sums are over Z unless otherwise specified.) The *choice set* in this formulation is P – Totrep is presumed to be making pairwise comparisons between members of P, indicating strict preference by the binary relation $\succ$. (Note well, P is an uncountably infinite set if Z has more than one element, so using the results of Chapter 3 will not be easy.)

If p and q are both in P and $a \in [0,1]$, then there is an element $ap + (1-a)q$ in P which is defined by taking the appropriate convex combinations of the probabilities of each prize separately, or

$$(ap + (1-a)q)(z) = ap(z) + (1-a)q(z).$$

It may help you to think of $ap + (1-a)q$ as representing a compound lottery: First an experiment with two outcomes (say Blue and Orange) is carried out, where the probability of Blue is a. If Blue transpires, then the lottery p is performed. If Orange transpires, then q is performed. But while you may wish to think of the lottery $ap + (1-a)q$ in this fashion, doing so may lead you into some interpretational difficulties; see the remarks later on and the development in Chapter 12.

Now for some axioms about Totrep's preferences on P.

Axiom (5.1). $\succ$ is a preference relation.

We discussed this axiom in Chapter 2, and we said there that negative transitivity might be troublesome. This richer setting doesn't make it any less troublesome, but we won't worry further about it.

Axiom (5.2). For all $p, q, r \in P$ and $a \in (0, 1]$, $p \succ q$ implies $ap + (1 - a)r \succ aq + (1 - a)r$.

This is commonly called the *substitution* or the *independence* axiom. The motivation for it (thinking in terms of compound lotteries) is: The difference between $ap + (1 - a)r$ and $aq + (1 - a)r$ is what happens if Blue transpires (and as $a > 0$, there is positive probability that Blue will transpire). So how Totrep feels about $ap + (1 - a)r$ vs. $aq + (1 - a)r$ should be determined by how he feels about p vs. q.

Axiom (5.3). For all $p, q, r \in P$, if $p \succ q \succ r$ then there exist $a, b \in (0, 1)$ such that $ap + (1 - a)r \succ q \succ bp + (1 - b)r$.

This is called the *Archimedean* or *continuity* axiom. It roughly says that there is no gamble p so good that for $q \succ r$, a small probability b of p and a large probability $1 - b$ of r is always better than q. Similarly, there is no gamble r so bad that for $p \succ q$, a large probability a of p and a small probability $1 - a$ of r is always worse than q. It is called the Archimedean axiom because of the resemblance to Archimedes' principle: No matter how small is $x > 0$ and how big is $y > 0$ there is an integer n such that $nx > y$. The reason that it is called the continuity axiom will become clear in a little bit.

Most people, viewing the substitution axiom for the first time, think it looks pretty convincing on first principles as a normative precept for choice under uncertainty. The idea is a straightforward and compelling one: When comparing two (complex) entities, you should disregard those places in which the two are the same and focus your attention on the differences. Of course, there is more to this axiom than that, in that the way in which the things are the same is (according to the axiom) not to matter. Put it this way: Suppose that you are comparing two dinner menus. In the first, you start with smoked salmon, continue on to a steak, and finish with apple pie. In the second, you start with smoked salmon, then have grilled salmon, and then finish with apple pie. Now these two differ only in the entree, steak vs. grilled salmon. And you may have a general preference for grilled salmon over steak. (You may not, but suppose you do.) Still, having an appetizer of smoked salmon may well tip the balance towards the first menu. The point of this is that your preferences are defined over the entire "package" of the meal, and it isn't so sensible in this setting to restrict attention to individual pieces.

The substitution axiom, however, is saying that you can look at individual pieces when comparing two packages. Why is this sensible in this setting? Sometimes the reason is put as some sort of independence of irrelevant alternatives. In the comparison of $ap + (1 - a)r$ with $aq + (1 - a)r$, either the a outcome happens or the $1 - a$. If the former happens, then what you would have gotten in the $1 - a$ outcome is irrelevant – it didn't happen, and you may as well ignore it. On the other hand, if the $1 - a$ outcome does happen, then it is irrelevant which of the two you selected. So, the story goes, it is sensible to ignore the $1 - a$ part, which is irrelevant for purposes of comparison, and focus on the comparison of the two a pieces.

This is, though, just a story. From the point of view of normative theory, it is up to the decision maker (you?) to decide whether you think this is a sensible axiom to follow. And, as we'll see in Chapter 14, there are a number of well-known and well-honed cases in which the substitution axiom, as a description of how people do choose, is falsified empirically.

The Archimedean axiom is, typically, the one that causes most people to express doubts. Consider the following example: p is a gamble in which you get \$1000 for sure; q is a gamble in which you get \$10 for sure; and r is a gamble in which you are killed for sure. Most people would express the preference $p \succ q \succ r$. And so, the axiom holds, there must exist a probability $a \in (0, 1)$, presumably close to 1, such that $ap + (1 - a)r \succ q$. That is, you are willing to risk a small (but nonzero) chance of your death, to trade up from \$10 to \$1000. This, many people say, is rather dubious. One hears such lovely sentiments as "no amount of money is worth my health," and so on. But consider: Suppose I told you that you could either have \$10 right now, or, if you were willing to drive five miles (pick some location five miles away from where you are), an envelope with \$1000 was waiting for you. Most people would get out their car keys at such a prospect, even though driving the five miles increases ever so slightly the chances of a fatal accident. So perhaps the axiom isn't so bad normatively as may seem at first.

Regardless of how you feel about them, together these three axioms yield the following result.

Theorem (5.4). A binary relation $\succ$ on P satisfies Axioms (5.1-3) if and only if there exists a function $u : Z \to R$ such that

(5.5) $$p \succ q \text{ iff } \sum_z u(z)p(z) > \sum_z u(z)q(z).$$

Moreover, if u represents $\succ$ in the sense of (5.5), then a function $u' : Z \to R$ also represents $\succ$ in this sense if and only if there exist real numbers $c > 0$ and d such that $u'(\cdot) = cu(\cdot) + d$.

Note that this gives both necessary and sufficient axioms for the representation (5.5) (which is called an expected utility, or von Neumann-Morgenstern, or cardinal utility representation). It gives as well the uniqueness result for the representation. This uniqueness result is often paraphrased as: u is unique up to a positive affine transformation.

Note also that if we have $u : Z \to R$ and define $f : P \to R$ by

$$f(p) = \sum_z u(z)p(z),$$

then (5.5) becomes $p \succ q$ iff $f(p) > f(q)$. That is, f gives an ordinal representation of the preference relation $\succ$ (in the sense of (3.1)). Since P is uncountable, we know from Chapter 3 that there is a countable $\succ$-order dense subset of P. Somehow, this is implied by some one or more of our three axioms We'll later discover that it is mostly (5.3) that is doing this.

To prove this result, we need the following lemmas.

Lemma (5.6) If $\succ$ on P satisfies Axioms (5.1-3), then:
(a) $p \succ q$ and $0 \le a < b \le 1$ imply $bp + (1 - b)q \succ ap + (1 - a)q$.
(b) $p \succeq q \succeq r$ and $p \succ r$ imply there exists a unique $a^* \in [0, 1]$ such that $q \sim a^*p + (1 - a^*)r$.
(c) $p \sim q$ and $a \in [0, 1]$ imply $ap + (1 - a)r \sim aq + (1 - a)r$ for all $r \in P$.

Remarks. Part (b) of the lemma sometimes appears directly as an axiom, in which case it is called the calibration or solvability axiom.

Also, this part of the lemma is what causes (5.3) to be called a continuity axiom. To see why, recall from calculus the intermediate value theorem, which says that if f is a continuous function which takes on a value y_1 at some argument x_1 and another value y_2 at x_2, then for any value y_3 between y_1 and y_2 there is some argument between x_1 and x_2 at which the function takes on the value y_3. In part (b) of the lemma, we are seeing that along the "line segment" joining p and r, for any q that is between p and r in terms of preference, there is some convex combination $ap + (1 - a)q$ which is indifferent to q. In other words, preference is continuous in probability. As we will see, the proof of part (b) relies enormously on (5.3). Finally, part (c) sometimes appears as an axiom and, just like (5.2), is called the substitution or the independence axiom.

Proof. (a) First consider the special case $a = 0$. Then $p \succ q$ and $0 < b \leq 1$ with Axiom (5.2) imply $bp + (1 - b)q \succ bq + (1 - b)q = q = ap + (1 - a)q$. Now let $r = bp + (1 - b)q$ and suppose $a > 0$. Then $(a/b) < 1$, and $r \succ q$ and (5.2) together imply that

$$r = (1 - (a/b))r + (a/b)r \succ (1 - (a/b))q + (a/b)r$$
$$= (1 - (a/b))q + (a/b)(bp + (1 - b)q) = ap + (1 - a)q.$$

(b) Since $p \succ r$, part (a) ensures that if a^* exists it is unique. If $p \sim q$, then $a^* = 1$ works. If $q \sim r$, then $a^* = 0$ works. So we need only consider the case $p \succ q \succ r$. Define

$$a^* = \sup\{a \in [0, 1] : q \succeq ap + (1 - a)r\}.$$

Since $a = 0$ is in the set, we aren't taking a sup over an empty set.

By the definition of a^*, if $1 \geq a > a^*$, then $ap + (1 - a)r \succ q$. Moreover, by (a), if $0 \leq a < a^*$, then $q \succ ap + (1 - a)r$. To see this, note that if $0 \leq a < a^*$, then there exists a' such that $0 \leq a < a' \leq a^*$ and $q \succeq a'p + (1 - a')r$ by the definition of a^*. And $a < a'$ implies $q \succeq a'p + (1 - a')r \succ ap + (1 - a)r$.

There are three possibilities to consider.

Suppose $a^*p + (1 - a^*)r \succ q \succ r$. Then by (5.3) there exists $b \in (0, 1)$ such that $b(a^*p + (1 - a^*)r) + (1 - b)r = ba^*p + (1 - ba^*)r \succ q$. But $ba^* < a^*$, so by the previous argument $q \succ ba^* + (1 - ba^*)r$. Contradiction.

Suppose $p \succ q \succ a^*p + (1 - a^*)r$. Then by (5.3) there exists $b \in (0,1)$ such that $q \succ b(a^*p + (1 - a^*)r) + (1 - b)p = (1 - b(1 - a^*))p + (b(1 - a^*))r$. Since $(1 - b(1 - a^*)) > a^*$, we have from above that $(1 - b(1 - a^*))p + (b(1 - a^*))r \succ q$. Contradiction.

This leaves us with the third possibility (which is what we want), namely that $a^*p + (1 - a^*)r \sim q$.

(c) This result is trivial for case where, for all $s \in P$, $p \sim q \sim s$. So suppose that there is some $s \in P$ with $s \succ p \sim q$. Suppose as well that $ap+(1-a)r \succ aq+(1-a)r$. An application of (5.2) shows that for all $b \in (0,1)$, $bs+(1-b)q \succ bq+(1-b)q = q \sim p$, and hence a second application of (5.2) shows that $a(bs+(1-b)q)+(1-a)r \succ ap+(1-a)r$ for all $b \in (0,1)$. Since (by assumption) $ap+(1-a)r \succ aq+(1-a)r$, (5.3) implies that there exists for each b some $a^*(b) \in (0,1)$ such that $ap+(1-a)r \succ a^*(b)(a(bs+(1-b)q)+(1-a)r)+(1-a^*(b))(aq+(1-a)r)$. Fix, say, $b = 1/2$, and let $a^*(1/2)$ be written a^*; then we have that

$$ap + (1 - a)r \succ [a^*a/2]s + [a^*a/2 + (1 - a^*)a]q + [1 - a]r.$$

But the term on the right hand side is

$$a[(a^*/2)s + (1 - a^*/2)q] + (1 - a)r,$$

and since $a^*/2 > 0$, this must $\succ ap + (1 - a)r$, a contradiction. The other cases are handled similarly.

Before giving the next lemma, we need a bit of notation. For any $z \in Z$, let δ_z denote the probability distribution degenerate at z, i.e.,

$$\delta_z(z') = \begin{cases} 1 & \text{if } z' = z \\ 0 & \text{if } z' \neq z \end{cases}$$

Lemma (5.7). If $\succ$ on P satisfies Axioms (5.1-3), then there exist z° and z_0 in Z such that $\delta_{z^\circ} \succeq p \succeq \delta_{z_0}$ for all $p \in P$.

The proof is left as an exercise, with the hints that you should use induction on the size of the support of p, and that part (c) of Lemma (5.6) and Axiom (5.2) play major roles in the proof. Finally, we are ready for:

Proof of Theorem (5.4). Suppose such a function u exists. Then showing that (5.1-3) all hold is a straightforward exercise and is omitted. (If you try to supply the proof and you get to the point of showing that (5.3) is implied by the representation, don't forget our discussion of the intermediate value theorem.)

Suppose that $\succ$ satisfies (5.1-3). Apply Lemma (5.7) to produce z° and z_0. If $\delta_{z^\circ} \sim \delta_{z_0}$, then $u \equiv c$ for some constant c satisfies (5.5), as neither $p \succ q$ nor $\sum u(z)p(z) > \sum u(z)q(z)$ is possible. Moreover, it should be clear that u constant is the only possible function for this representation in this case, so u' is any other representation iff $u' = eu + d$ for constants $e > 0$ and d. So for the rest of the proof we consider the case $\delta_{z^\circ} \succ \delta_{z_0}$.

For $p \in P$ define

$$f(p) = a \text{ where } a\delta_{z^\circ} + (1-a)\delta_{z_0} \sim p.$$

By the lemmas, such an a exists and is unique, so f is well defined. Moreover,

$$f(p) \succ f(q) \text{ iff } f(p)\delta_{z^\circ} + (1-f(p))\delta_{z_0} \succ f(q)\delta_{z^\circ} + (1-f(q))\delta_{z_0} \text{ iff } p \succ q$$

by part (a) of the lemma and standard properties of preference and indifference relations. Hence $f(\cdot)$ is a representation of $\succ$ in the sense of Chapter 3. (We've already gotten the result that there is a countable $\succ$-order dense subset in P. How did that happen?)

Next, for all $p, q \in P$ and $a \in [0, 1]$, by repeated application of part (c) of the lemma,

$$ap+(1-a)q \sim a[f(p)\delta_{z^\circ}+(1-f(p))\delta_{z_0}]+(1-a)[f(q)\delta_{z^\circ}+(1-f(q))\delta_{z_0}].$$

Thus by the definition of f,

(5.8) $$f(ap + (1-a)q) = af(p) + (1-a)f(q).$$

If you like fancy math-speak, (5.8) says that the function f is an *affine* function. Remember this step in the development, as we'll come back to it in a bit. In fact, put an X in the margin of the page right here (in pencil, please), so that you'll be able to find this spot quickly later on.

Now for $z \in Z$ define

$$u(z) = f(\delta_z).$$

By virtue of the above, we'll have the representation (5.5) as soon as we show that

(5.9) $$f(p) = \sum_z u(z)p(z),$$

for all $p \in P$. The method is to use (5.8) and induction on the size of the support of p. (The support of p is the set $\{z \in Z : p(z) > 0\}$.) If the support of p has one element, say z', then $p = \delta_{z'}$ and (5.9) follows trivially.

So suppose inductively that (5.9) is true for ps with support of size $n - 1 \geq 1$. Take any p with support of size $n > 1$, and let z' be in the support of p. Then if q is defined as

$$q(z) = \begin{cases} 0 & \text{if } z = z' \\ p(z)/(1 - p(z')) & \text{if } z \neq z' \end{cases},$$

q has support of size $n - 1$ and $p = p(z')\delta_{z'} + (1 - p(z'))q$.

By (5.8) and the induction hypothesis applied to q,

$$f(p) = p(z')f(\delta_{z'}) + (1 - p(z'))f(q)$$

$$= p(z')u(z') + (1 - p(z')) \sum_{z \neq z'} [p(z)/(1 - p(z'))]u(z) = \sum_z p(z)u(z).$$

This establishes (5.9) by induction, since Z is finite.

It is left to you to establish the uniqueness result, namely, if u and u' are two utility functions representing $\succ$ in the sense of (5.5), then each is a positive affine transformation of the other.

Before moving on to the NM representation for more complicated settings, I would like to close this section with a few comments about the role of compound lotteries in this theory.

In a number of books, the theory above is described and motivated with compound lotteries, as we did above. Typically, there are pictures that look like figure 5.1, which is supposed to represent, say, drawing a ball out of an urn with one blue and three orange balls, and then, if a blue ball is drawn, rolling a perfect die, etc. This is *presumably* distinct from the lottery depicted in figure 5.2, which represents drawing a ball from an urn with 154 balls: 14 blue, 14 orange, 14 red, 18 pink, 36 purple and 66 mauve, with outcomes z_1 if blue comes up, etc. And when motivating the substitution axiom, it is figure 5.1 that is drawn to represent the convex combination of lotteries depicted in figure 5.3 and and not figure 5.2.

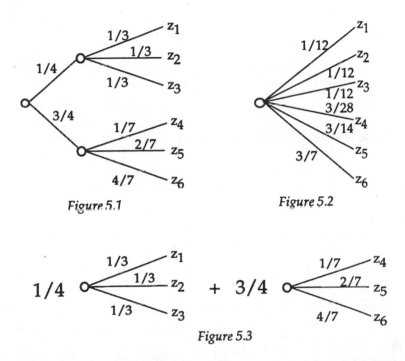

Figure 5.1   Figure 5.2

Figure 5.3

The point is that the *theory* given above is a mathematical theory of preference among objects which are depicted by figure 5.2, and not by figure 5.1. It is figure 5.2 that is meant by the convex combination in figure 5.3. Now there is nothing inherently wrong with depicting the lottery in figure 5.2 as we have done in figure 5.1, as long as you are willing to agree that they are the same object. But insofar as there is any difference between figures 5.1 and 5.2, in that Totrep might like one better than the other, this is not a difference that our theory can ever record, because our theory has no way (yet) to make a distinction between the two. Carrying things a bit further, our theory identifies any two lotteries that attach the same probabilities to the same prizes, even if the randomizing devices are different. The theory is a theory of choice among probability distributions – and when we seek to apply it to real phenomena that involve randomizing devices, or collections of randomizing devices used in sequence, there is an implicit axiom zero that all that matters to Totrep are the probabilities and prizes – the randomizing devices and their order are inconsequential to him.

This doesn't mean that one can't have a theory of preference where Totrep distinguishes between "compound" and "simple" lotteries (between figures 5.1 and 5.2) – only that the theory developed above is incapable of such distinctions. To build a theory that makes this sort of distinction, we'll first need mathematical way of distinguishing compound and simple lotteries. Problem 6 in Chapter 12 gets you started on doing this, if you so desire.

THE MIXTURE SPACE THEOREM

The next order of business is to obtain the NM representation for cases where Z is infinite and probability measures are more complicated. The method we'll take to do this is a little indirect, but this indirection will pay a large dividend later on – we look at a purely mathematical result called the mixture space theorem. (The original reference for this theory is Herstein and Milnor (1953).) This theorem concerns an abstract object, called a *mixture space*.

Definition (5.10). A *mixture space* is a set of objects Π, with typical elements π, ρ, μ, and v, and a family of functions $h_a : \Pi \times \Pi \to \Pi$ for $a \in [0,1]$ such that:
(a) $h_1(\pi,\rho) = \pi$,
(b) $h_a(\pi,\rho) = h_{1-a}(\rho,\pi)$, and
(c) $h_a(h_b(\pi,\rho),\rho) = h_{ab}(\pi,\rho)$.

The use of Greek letters is supposed to suggest to you that this is an abstract object – in examples, I'll use standard Roman letters, to indicate that I have in mind something specific.

Example 1. Let Z be a countable set and let P be the set of all probability measures on Z. For $p,q \in P$, define $h_a(p,q) \in P$ by $h_a(p,q) = ap + (1-a)q$. It is easy to verify that $(P, \{h_a\}_{a\in[0,1]})$ so defined satisfies the conditions of Definition (5.10) and so is a mixture space.

Example 2. Let Z be any arbitrary set and let P_S be the set of *simple* probability measures on Z. That is P_S is the set of functions $p : Z \to R$ such that there is a finite subset supp(p) of Z with $p(z) = 0$ for $z \notin Y$ and $\sum_{z \in \text{supp}(p)} p(z) = 1$.

Another way to say the same thing is to say that P_S is the set of probability measures on Z that have finite support. For $p, q \in P$ define $h_a(p, q) = ap + (1-a)q$. (Note that supp($h_a(p,q)$) = supp(p)$\cup$ supp(q), for $a \in (0, 1)$. Don't move on until this makes sense to you.) Again the conditions of the definition all hold, and we have a mixture space.

Example 3. Let $Z = R$ and let P_D be the set of probability distributions on Z which have continuous densities. That is, P_D is the set of probability distributions (or measures) p such that $p(Y) = \int_Y f(r)dr$ for all sets $Y \subseteq R$, where f is a continuous function and such that $\int_R f(r)dr = 1$. (If you know enough to worry about such things, I really only want this to hold for measurable sets Y.) For $p, q \subset P_D$ define $h_a(p, q) = ap + (1 - a)q$ – that is, $h_a(p, q)$ is the probability distribution whose density is $af + (1 - a)g$ where f is the density of p and g is the density of q. Again the conditions of the definition can be verified – we have a mixture space.

Example 4. So far, all examples have been sets of probability measures. Here is an example that is different. Let S be a finite set, and let Z be another. Let P be the set of all probability distributions on Z, and let $H = P^S$. That is, an element h of H is a function from S into P – for each $s \in S$ there is a corresponding probability measure $h(s) \in P$ on Z. Define $h_a(p, q) = ap + (1 - a)q$ pointwise. That is, $(h_a(p, q))(s) = ap(s) + (1 - a)q(s)$. Once again, you can verify that the conditions of the definition are satisfied, and thus we have a mixture space.

In each of the above examples, we wound up writing $h_a(p, q) = ap + (1-a)q$ – where addition here eventually resolves into addition of real numbers. Indeed, there are some standard reference books (and I'm thinking here of Fishburn (1970)) that use the notation $ap + (1 - a)q$

from the start. I don't do so to keep you aware of the fact that the mixture space theory is an abstract theory, stated without reference to any particular context having to do with addition of real numbers. (But on this point, see the discussion near the end of this section.)

Theorem (5.11). Suppose Π is a mixture space and $\succ$ is a binary relation on Π. Then

(a) $\succ$ is a preference relation,

(b) $\pi \succ \rho$ and $a \in (0,1]$ implies $h_a(\pi,\mu) \succ h_a(\rho,\mu)$ for all $\mu \in \Pi$, and

(c) $\pi \succ \rho \succ \mu$ imply that there exist $a, b \in (0,1)$ such that $h_a(\pi,\mu) \succ \rho \succ h_b(\pi,\mu)$,

if and only if

(d) there exists a function $F : \Pi \to R$ such that

    (di) $\pi \succ \rho$ iff $F(\pi) > F(\rho)$, and

    (dii) $F(h_a(\pi,\rho)) = aF(\pi) + (1-a)F(\rho)$.

Moreover, if F represents $\succ$ in the sense of (d), F' is another representation (in this sense) if and only if $F' = aF + b$ for constants $a > 0$ and b.

This is quite a mouthful. Note the general flow: Properties (a), (b), and (c) are necessary and sufficient for the representation (d), and the representation (d) is unique up to a positive affine transformation.

    This begs for comparison with the von Neumann-Morgenstern expected utility theorem, Theorem (5.4), that we proved in the previous section. Of course, (a), (b), and (c) look just like the three axioms (5.1,2 and 3). All that is different is that ps and qs have changed to πs and ρs. As for (d), remember that in the proof of Theorem (5.4), I told you to put a big X in the margin. At just that point, we had reached a conclusion that looks just like (d). (Don't erase the X just yet.) So, except for the uniqueness result, which looks the same as in Theorem (5.4), we have here a part of Theorem (5.4), up to the point where we used induction in order to show (in the proof of (5.4)) that if f is affine, then it has an expected utility representation. Nothing like that here, but otherwise this mixture space theorem looks like just what we had before.

    And the proof of this looks pretty much like the proof of the theorem. To provide all the details, we would begin with a lemma analogous to Lemma (5.6). Let me set aside for the moment commentary on how the analogous lemma would be proved and proceed on the basis of the assumption that we have obtained such a lemma for general mixture spaces.

Once we have the result analogous to Lemma (5.6), we are almost in business. The next step in the proof of Theorem (5.4) was to state and prove Lemma (5.7), which established (well, claimed, since it was left to you to do) that there was a best and worst prize. Note how we used that lemma in the proof of the theorem: We could calibrate (using part (b) of the first lemma) every gamble p in terms of a simple convex combination of the best and worst prize: If $p \sim a\delta_{z^o} + (1 - a)\delta_{z_o}$, then we defined $f(p) = a$. Now in general, we can't establish that there will be a best and worst element in the mixture space − in some applications, that just simply won't be true. So we'll have to do without Lemma (5.7).

How? It is really not too complicated. In the first place, consider the case where $\pi \sim \rho$ for every π and ρ in Π. Not a very interesting case and simple to deal with: $\succ$ is represented by any constant function. So we pass on to there case where there is at least one pair (π, ρ) with $\pi \succ \rho$. Fix any such pair, calling the better element π^o and the worse element π_o. Define F on these two elements by $F(\pi^o) = 1$ and $F(\pi_o) = 0$.

Now we have to define F for all the other $\pi \in \Pi$. There are three cases to consider. First, suppose that $\pi^o \succeq \pi \succeq \pi_o$. Then, just as in the proof of the theorem, we can apply part (b) of the "analogous lemma" (that is, Lemma (5.6) stated for mixture spaces) to generate some unique a such that $\pi \sim h_a(\pi^o, \pi_o)$. Define $F(\pi) = a$. Second, it might be that $\pi \succ \pi^o$. In this case there is a unique a such that $\pi^o \sim h_a(\pi, \pi_o)$. And in this case define $F(a) = 1/a$. (How do we know that $a \in (0, 1)$?) Finally, there is the case that $\pi_o \succ \pi$. Then there is a unique a such that $\pi_o \sim h_a(\pi^o, \pi)$. Define $F(\pi) = a/(a-1)$ for this a.

What's going on here? Is is simpler than it looks. We set a scale from π^o to π_o and then we calibrate everything else on that scale. The scale is set so that π_o is at the level zero, and π^o at the level one. For anything that falls between them, we calibrate as in the proof of Theorem (5.4) − nothing new here. What about things which are better than π^o? For these we find where π^o would fall on a scale from π_o up to the element π that we are measuring. Then if F is to be affine, since $\pi^o \sim h_a(\pi, \pi_o)$, it will have to be that

$1 = F(\pi^\circ) = aF(\pi) + (1-a)F(\pi_\circ) = aF(\pi)$ (since $F(\pi_\circ) = 0$). Solve this equation, and you have $F(\pi) = 1/a$, which is just what we did. (Now you show why we did what we did for the case where π falls below $\pi_\circ$.)

This defines a function F. Does it represent $\succ$, and is it really affine? The answers are yes to each, although showing this is a tedious affair of algebra. I leave the details to you. Also left to you are the very simple details of showing that (d) in the theorem implies (a) through (c), and also showing that the representation is unique up to positive affine transformations. If you don't want to do the algebra yourself, any of the standard reference books will provide the details for you.

So we are done. Except that we still have to obtain a result analogous to Lemma (5.6) in this setting. Will the proof we gave before work in this general setting? Not quite. In all the applications that we've discussed, $h_a(p, q) = ap + (1-a)q$ where the addition is eventually addition of real numbers. Thus things like

$$ap + (1-a)bq + (1-a)(1-b)r$$

are well defined in applications – it is $ap + (1-a)(bq + (1-b)r)$ or $h_a(p, h_b(q, s))$. But because addition of real numbers is associative, in all applications this is the same as

$$(a+b-ab)\left(\frac{a}{a+b-ab}p + \frac{(1-a)b}{a+b-ab}q\right) + (1-(a+b-ab))r,$$

or

$$h_{a+b-ab}(h_{a/(a+b-ab)}(p, q), r).$$

The question is: Is "this" true in general – for a general mixture space is it the case that

$$h_a(\pi, h_b(\rho, \mu)) = h_{a+b-ab}(h_{a/(a+b-ab)}(\pi, \rho), \mu)?$$

No, this isn't implied by the definition of a mixture space that we gave above. And, if you go back and review carefully the proof that we gave of Lemma (5.6), you'll see that this property was assumed.

So what do we do? There are two options. We can add this property to our definition of a mixture space. After all, this property is satisfied by the examples we gave, and, as you will see, it will be satisfied by all the examples of mixture spaces that we will have in this book. Hence, for purposes of the applications in this book, the proof of Lemma (5.6) that we gave will suffice. Alternatively, we can go looking for a proof of the lemma which doesn't use this property. Such proofs do exist – you will find one in Fishburn (1970), if you look.

By either of these means, we have an abstract result which looks a lot like our NM theorem for a finite prize space (at least as far as the X you put in the margin). We move on now to applications.

SIMPLE PROBABILITY DISTRIBUTIONS

For our first application, we look at the set of *simple probability distributions* over an arbitrary set Z. Recall from Example 2 above that a probability distribution p on an arbitrary set Z is a simple probability distribution if it has finite support (or, in other words, if it gives positive probability to a finite number of outcomes in Z). This is, as we noted, a mixture space, with component-wise addition of probabilities the mixing operation. Parts (a), (b) and (c) of the mixture space theorem are just Axioms (5.1), (5.2) and (5.3) in this case, and so we have the following instant corollary to the mixture space theorem:

Corollary (5.12). For arbitrary set Z and P_S the space of simple probability distributions on Z, a binary relation $\succ$ on P_S satisfies Axioms (5.1-3) if and only if there is a function $F : P_S \to R$ such that, for all $p, q \in P_S$ and $a \in [0,1]$,

$$p \succ q \text{ if and only if } F(p) > F(q), \text{ and}$$

(5.13) $$F(ap + (1-a)q) = aF(p) + (1-a)F(q).$$

Moreover, F in the representation is unique up to a positive affine transformation.

How does this compare with the von Neumann-Morgenstern expected utility representation that was obtained in Theorem (5.4) for finite Z? It is weaker than that theorem, because in Theorem (5.4) we had a bit more; we concluded that the function F that represents $\succ$ could be written as

(5.14) $$F(p) = \sum_{z \in Z} u(z)p(z),$$

for some function $u : Z \to R$. It is easy to see that any function F on P_S that can be written as in (5.14) satisfies (5.13). But it isn't obvious that any function F on P_S that satisfies (5.13) can be written in the form (5.14).

But while this isn't obvious, it is true. Look back at the proof of Theorem (5.4), beginning just after the point where you put the X in the margin. Essentially, we got to the point of the corollary above, and then we used an argument by induction on the size of the support of p to show that, for $u(z) = f(\delta_z)$, (5.14) would hold. Pretty clearly, we can do exactly the same thing here, because it isn't the finiteness of Z that is critical, but the finiteness of the support of each p. And in this case, where we are looking only a simple probability distributions, the finiteness of the support of each p is ensured. So if we define $u(z) = F(\delta_z)$ for the function F given to us by the corollary, and we repeat the argument in Theorem (5.4), we have the following:

Theorem (5.15). For arbitrary Z, a binary relation $\succ$ defined on the set P_S of simple probability distributions on Z satisfies Axioms (5.1-3) if and only if there is a function $u : Z \to R$ such that, for all $p, q \in P_S$,

$$p \succ q \text{ iff } \sum_z p(z)u(z) > \sum_z q(z)u(z),$$

where the two sums in the display are over all z in the respective supports of p and q. Moreover, another function u' gives this representation if and only if u' is a positive affine transformation of u.

There is one comment to make before we move on: In the case of a finite set Z, we know (more precisely, you were supposed to show) that there are a best and a worst prize. For the set of all simple probability distributions on an arbitrary set, this is certainly not the case. (Provide a counterexample. You should be able to do so in at most thirty seconds, if you understand that the representation in (5.15) is necessary and sufficient for the three axioms.) So in this case we really do need the fancier technique of the mixture space theorem, which is proved without the assumption of a best and worst prize.

NON-SIMPLE PROBABILITY MEASURES AND THE SURE-THING PRINCIPLE

What happens when we try to extend our previous results to non-simple probability measures? To see what might happen, consider the following example.

Let P° be the set of all probability distributions on the real line R that are convex combinations of simple probability distributions and probability distributions with continuous density functions. To be precise, let P_S be the set of all simple probability distributions on the real line, and let P_D be the set of probability distributions on the real line that have continuous density functions. That is, for every $p \in P_D$ there exists a continuous function $f : R \to [0, \infty)$ such that $\int_R f(r)dr = 1$. The probability that this p gives to a subset B of R is $\int_B f(r)dr$. Note that any such p gives zero probability to any single point or any finite collection of points. A standard example of such a probability distribution is the Normal distribution, with density function $\exp(-r^2)/\sqrt{2\pi} = f(r)$. (I'm relying on your knowledge of such probability distributions being sufficient to follow what will ensue. I think that this will make sense from all possible states of knowledge.) In fact, there is a one-to-one correspondence between elements p of P_D and functions f as above. So by abuse of notation, I will write f as the element of P_D really meaning the probability distribution with density function f.

An element of P° is then a probability distribution $p = ap_s + (1-a)f$ for given $a \in [0,1]$, $p_s \in P_S$ and $f \in P_D$. If $p = ap_s + (1-a)f$ and $q = bq_s + (1-b)g$ are two elements of P°, then for $c \in [0,1]$ we can define $cp + (1-c)q \in P^\circ$ by

$$cp + (1-c)q = (ac + b(1-c))[\frac{ac}{ac + b(1-c)}p_s + \frac{b(1-c)}{ac + b(1-c)}q_s]$$

$$+ \quad (1 - ac - b(1-c))[\frac{c(1-a)}{1 - ac - b(1-c)}f + \frac{(1-c)(1-b)}{1 - ac - b(1-c)}g].$$

(Can you verify that this is indeed an element of P°? What is involved in that verification?) With this definition and with $h_c(p, q)$ defined to be $cp + (1 - c)q$, it can be shown that $P°$ is a mixture space.

There is nothing mysterious in this construction. $P°$ is merely the set of probability distributions on the real line "gotten" by doing some two outcome (blue vs. orange) experiment, then if blue comes up, doing an experiment with finitely many real valued outcomes, while if orange comes up, doing an experiment that produces a real number according to some continuous probability distribution. And the convex combinations defined above are just the obvious mixing of two such probability distributions.

So we can imagine Totrep contemplating a choice among such probability distributions, where the prizes are, say, dollar prizes. Actually, it will make things a little smoother if we assume that the prizes lie in some finite interval of real numbers – say 0 to 10^{100}. (So we want in $P°$ only convex combinations of simple probability distributions on this range and probability measures with continuous densities f that are zero outside this range.) Letting Totrep express his preferences among such lotteries by the binary relation $\succ$ as usual, we posit the standard three von Neumann-Morgenstern axioms:

$\succ$ is a preference relation;

if $p, q \in P°$ are such that $p \succ q$, then for all $r \in P°$ and $a \in (0, 1]$ it follows that $ap + (1 - a)r \succ aq + (1 - a)r$; and

if $p, q, r \in P°$ are such that $p \succ q \succ r$, then there exist $a, b \in (0, 1)$ such that $ap + (1 - a)r \succ q \succ bp + (1 - b)r$.

Before going any further, stop and think – is there any new reason to suppose that these axioms are not reasonable (normatively) in this expanded setting?

Directly from the mixture space theorem:

Corollary (5.16) A binary relation $\succ$ on $P°$ satisfies the three mixture space axioms given above if and only if there exists a function $F : P° \rightarrow R$ such that

$$p \succ q \text{ iff } F(p) > F(q) \quad \text{and} \quad F(ap + (1 - a)q) = aF(p) + (1 - a)F(q).$$

Moreover, such functions F are unique up to positive affine transformations.

Not bad, but is this an expected utility representation? Not really – an expected utility representation would read something like:

Pseudo-theorem (5.17) A binary relation $\succ$ on $P°$ satisfies the three axioms if and only if there exists a function $u : [0, 10^{100}] \rightarrow R$ such that

(5.18) $\qquad\qquad p \succ q$ iff $E_p[u] > E_q[u]$.

Moreover, such functions u are unique up to positive affine transformations.

In this pseudo-theorem, $E_p[u]$ means the expectation of u taken with respect to p; if $p = ap_s + (1 - a)f$, then

$$E_p[u] = a \sum_z p_s(z)u(z) + (1 - a) \int_0^{10^{100}} u(z)f(z)dz,$$

where the summation is taken over all z in the support of p_s. If you are worried about whether u is an integrable function, stifle your concern. Or, if you are both a chronic worrier and well enough trained to know what this means, rewrite the theorem to read in line 0 "if and only if there exists a bounded and measurable function $u : [0, 10^{100}] \rightarrow R$ such that..." As we'll see in a minute, this pseudo-theorem will fail for reasons unrelated to the restriction that u is bounded and measurable.

Can this stronger result be deduced from the corollary? It was possible when instead of $P°$ we had P_S – then defining $u(z) = F(\delta_z)$ and the induction argument did the trick. But the induction argument will hardly work here.

Just because our old argument doesn't suffice to prove this pseudo-theorem doesn't mean that it is false. But, as it happens, it is false. Here is a counterexample:

For $p = ap_s + (1 - a)f$ where $p_s \in P_S$ and $f \varepsilon P_D$ define

$$F^*(p) = (1 - a) + a \sum_{z:p_s(z)>0} zp_s(z).$$

Then F^* is a well-defined function from $P°$ into R. (How do I know this? What do I need to show in order to really prove this?) Moreover, it can be shown (by you for homework perhaps) that F^* satisfies

$$F^*(ap + (1 - a)q) = aF^*(p) + (1 - a)F^*(q).$$

So if I define a binary relation $\succ$ on P° by

$$p \succ q \text{ if } F^*(p) > F^*(q),$$

then Corollary (5.16) ensures that $\succ$ satisfies the three axioms. And yet, for $\succ$ so defined, no function u exists that will satisfy (5.18).

To see this takes two steps: First, suppose such a u did exist. Let $u(10^{100}) = u^\circ$ and $u(0) = u_o$. Pick any number $z \in [0, 10^{100}]$, and note that $F^*(\delta_z) = z = F^*[(z/10^{100})\delta_{10^{100}} + (1 - z/10^{100})\delta_0]$. Thus $\delta_z \sim (z/10^{100})\delta_{10^{100}} + (1 - z/10^{100})\delta_0$. Then by the assumption that such a u does exist, we would have $u(z) = (z/10^{100})u^\circ + (1 - z/10^{100})u_o$, which implies that $u(z) = az + b$ for some constants $a > 0$ and b. What are we doing here? It is really quite simple. We know that $u(z) = z$ represents $\succ$ restricted to simple probability distributions, because that is how $\succ$ is defined. So by the uniqueness result for expected utility representations on simple probability distributions, we know that any other utility function will have to be a positive affine transformation of $u(z) = z$. All that the details in this paragraph do are to verify that fact.

Now compare the following two lotteries – a uniform distribution on the interval $[0, .5]$, call this p', and the degenerate distribution at $3/4$, call this p''. Since p' is purely a continuous density distribution, we have that $F^*(p') = 1$. And p'' is purely simple, so $F^*(p'') = \sum_{z:p''(z)>0} z p''(z) = 3/4$. Thus $p' \succ p''$ by the definition of $\succ$. But under the supposition that a u exists, and the fact that such a u must have the form $u(z) = az + b$, we would have

$$E_{p'}[u] = \int_0^{.5} (az + b)2dz = (a/4) + b < (3a/4) + b = E_{p''}[u].$$

This contradicts $p' \succ p''$, and we have the desired counterexample.

It isn't hard to see what is going wrong in this counterexample. Looking at p' and p'', we have two distributions where the first (p') is *certain* to give us a prize (between 0 and 1/2) that we like less than the prize we are certain to get from the second. And yet the first is preferred to the second. The example shows that such anomalies are not ruled out by the three mixture space axioms, so we'll have to add an axiom that rules them out.

Axiom (5.19). If $r, q \in P^\circ$ and $B \subseteq [0, 10^{100}]$ are such that $r(B) = 1$ (that is, both the simple and continuous density parts of r are zero outside of B) and $\delta_z \succ q$ for every $z \in B$, then $r \succ q$. And if $r, q \in P^\circ$ and $B \subseteq [0, 10^{100}]$ are such that $r(B) = 1$ and $q \succ \delta_z$ for every $z \in B$, then $q \succ r$.

In words, if r is concentrated on a set, and if every prize in that set is as good as q, then r is as good as q. And vice-versa. This seems a perfectly sensible axiom, and it is this axiom that the example violates. This sort of axiom is typically called a "sure-thing" principle, for obvious reasons.

So, it is natural to ask, will this axiom joined to the other three be enough to guarantee the sort of expected utility representation that we want? The answer is: almost, but not quite. There are some technical niceities that must be assumed as well. To go into them would make things too complex for this first pass through the subject, so I will leave off the story here, leaving it to the diligent reader to chase down the complete story in some standard reference book. As usual, my recommendation is Fishburn (1970). But you can take it more or less on faith that an executive summary of this state of affairs runs as follows: In order to get an expected utility representation theorem for other than non-simple probability measures, necessary and sufficient conditions are (a) the three mixture space axioms, (b) the sort of sure-thing principle sketched above, and (c) some technical conditions. (If you insist on seeing a complete treatment of expected utility for other than simple probability distributions, go to the final section of this chapter – one way to proceed with something extra in the bargain is sketched there.)

BOUNDED UTILITY

An important point about von Neumann-Morgenstern expected utility for non-simple probability distributions should be made. Most treatments that you will find in the literature have as part of the big theorem that the utility function u must be bounded. Especially when the prize space is the real line, this isn't very nice. (Why isn't this very nice? Because, for example, we'll want to talk about "risk averse" utility functions on the real line – these are concave – and there are no strictly increasing, concave and bounded functions on the real line.)

Why do utility functions necessarily come out being bounded? Roughly, the reason is as follows. In most treatments, the allowed probability distributions include all those with countable support and lots more besides. Probability distributions with countable support are just like a simple probability distributions, except that the support can be countably infinite. Suppose then that the utility function u was unbounded. It will then be unbounded either above or below – let's suppose below. Then there are prizes $z_1, z_2, \ldots$ such that $u(z_k) \leq -2^k$. Now let $p°$ be the probability distribution assigning probability $1/2^k$ to prize z_k. We have

$$E_{p°}[u] = \sum_{k=1}^{\infty} u(z_k)p(z_k) = -\infty.$$

The expected utility of $p°$ is $-\infty$. This will screw up the Archimedean Axiom, for one thing – if p' and p'' are such that $\infty > E_{p'}[u] > E_{p''}[u] > -\infty$, then $p' \succ p'' \succ p°$, yet for $a \in (0,1)$, $E_{ap°+(1-a)p'}[u] = -\infty$, or $p'' \succ ap° + (1-a)p'$. That is, this is true supposing that we allow $-\infty$ as an expected utility in our representation. If we don't allow this, then we're sunk as soon as $p°$ is produced. The only way this can be avoided, and the axioms satisfied, is if u is bounded ...

... or if we don't allow probability distributions like $p°$. For example, we could look at sets of probability distributions with bounded support. Then all that would be needed is that u is bounded on bounded sets – not a very onerous condition. Of course, it needs to be shown that a representation theorem for this sort of set of probability distributions is possible. And you will have a hard time finding this sort of result in standard reference books. But it can be done. For one way, although it takes a bit of math, see the next section of this chapter.

My point is that most standard references have bounded utility functions in their von Neumann-Morgenstern expected utility theorems, and this causes some grief in applications. But this isn't necessary – it certainly isn't necessary when you're looking at simple probability distributions only, and it can be done without for larger classes of probability distributions. In general, what is needed is that the utility function must be such that plus and minus infinity are not possible expected utilities for the class of probability distributions under consideration. In general, you will need this sort of restriction, but nothing more.

CONTINUITY

The material in this section is likely to be inaccessible to readers without a good background in mathematics. Sorry.

We said way back at the start that the Archimedean axiom is sometimes referred to as the continuity axiom. Roughly, this is because this axiom says that preferences are continuous in probabilities. If $p \succ q$, for any r at all, we tend to think that $\lim_{a \to 1} ap + (1-a)r = p$, and so we would want, for a sufficiently close to one, to find that $ap + (1-a)r \succ q$. (And similarly on the other side.)

But there is another way to define continuity. For the sake of this discussion, assume that Z is the real line. Let P_S denote all simple probability distributions on Z and let P be all (Borel) probability distributions on Z. If you don't know what the space of Borel probability distributions is, don't worry about it. On the other side of the spectrum, if you know all about such things and are wondering why I've restricted to the case that Z is the real line, you can proceed directly to the case of Z a connected subset of some Euclidean space, or even just a separable metric space. I'll talk in terms of Z being the real line, but it is easy to see how all this extends, if you know the requisite math.

There is something called the *weak topology* defined on P. Let me remind the reader who may have seen it: This topology is defined by saying that $p_n \to p$ if for every bounded and continuous function f on the real line, $\int_R f(z)dp_n(z) \to \int_R f(z)dp(z)$. This topology is metrizable, by the so-called Prohorov metric, when restricted to probability distribution functions.

For those of you who have never seen this sort of thing, let me give you three examples of convergent sequences in this topology. First, consider the sequence of degenerate probability distributions $\{\delta_{1+1/n}\}$. That is, in the nth distribution, you get the prize $1 + 1/n$ with certainty. Now as anyone can clearly see, this has as "limit" the probability distribution which gives the prize 1 with certainty, or δ_1. And, indeed, this sequence does converge to this limit in the weak topology. Second, consider the sequence of probability distributions $\{p_n\}$ where p_n gives prizes $\{0, 1/n, 2/n, ..., (n-1)/n, 1\}$, each with probability $1/(n+1)$. This sequence, in the weak topology, has as limit the uniform distribution on $[0,1]$. Finally, consider the sequence of probability distributions $\{p_n\}$ where the nth distribution is Normal with mean 4 (say) and variance $1/n$. This sequence converges in the weak topology to the distribution which is degenerate at the value 4.

I want to add to the three von Neumann-Morgenstern axioms one more:

Axiom (5.20). The binary relation $\succ$ is continuous in the weak topology.

Recall from Chapter 3 what it means for preferences to be continuous. Now one thing is immediate: Since $\lim_{a \to 1} ap + (1-a)r = p$ and $\lim_{a \to 0} ap + (1-a)r = r$ in the weak topology, this axiom supercedes the Archimedean axiom. But it says something much stronger than the Archimedean axiom, as the following results establish.

Theorem (5.21). A binary relation $\succ$ defined on P_S satisfies Axioms (5.1), (5.2) and (5.20) if and only if there is a bounded and continuous function $u : Z \to R$ such that preferences are represented in the usual sense by expected utility calculated with u. Moreover, this representation is unique up to positive affine transformations, something I'll hereafter neglect to say as we move along.

What is added in this theorem over Theorem (5.15) is the continuity and boundedness of the utility function u. Since we didn't have continuity or boundedness in Theorem (5.15), they are not implied, for simple probability distributions, at least, by the three standard mixture space axioms. (So, with particular reference to continuity, when we call the Archimedean Axiom a continuity axiom, we should be careful to say in what topology we mean continuity.)

How is this proven? Let me sketch one part of the proof. Assume that the three axioms hold. Now since (5.20) implies (5.3), we know (see Theorem (5.15)) that there is an expected utility representation, and moreover the representing function u is unique up to positive affine transformations. So suppose it isn't continuous at, say, the value

z. Suppose, to take one possible case, that $u(z) > \liminf_n u(z_n)$ for some sequence $\{z_n\}$ with limit z. There is a point z_m far enough along the sequence so that for $n > m$, z_n for sure is worse than a gamble which gives z_m with probability 1/2 and z with probability 1/2, which in turn is worse than z for sure. (Fill in the many blanks – this is just a sketch.) This, then, would violate weak continuity of $\succ$. I leave it to you to show that u must be bounded. (You won't have a chance of doing this if you don't know about the weak topology.) On the other side, suppose that u is bounded and continuous. Then continuity in the weak topology for preferences given by expected utility is virtually a matter of definition.

And we can quickly extend this to all of P:

Corollary (5.22) A binary relation $\succ$ on P satisfies Axioms (5.1), (5.2) and (5.20) if and only if there is a bounded and continuous utility function $u : Z \to R$ such that $\succ$ is represented in the usual sense by expected utility computed using u.

Wow! We got expected utility for all sorts of probability distributions without anything like the sure-thing axiom stated above. (In truth, continuity in the weak topology is a lot stronger than the wimpy sure-thing axiom stated previously.) How is this proven? Going from the repesentation to the axioms is virtually a matter of definitions. As for the other direction, I leave it to you – if you're still reading this, you probably have the math skills needed to prove this – with the hint that simple probability distributions are dense in the space of all (Borel) probability distributions in the weak topology. Have fun!

One thing you may not like about what just happened is that the utility function wound up being bounded. Continuity of u is actually somewhat desirable, but bounded utility will be a real pain in applications. How to cure this? Well, there is one very cheap way to do it. Simply restrict attention to the case where Z is a bounded set (say, some bounded subinterval of the real line). Then you wouldn't be worried about u being bounded – if it's continuous, it has to be bounded.

But that is rather too cheap. We'd like to get rid of bounded u and, at the same time, keep Z all of R. The way to do this is to strengthen somewhat the requirements for convergence in the continuity axiom; if it is harder to converge, then the continuity axiom will have less bite. For example, and it is only an example, consider the following construction. First, let P_K be the set of all Borel probability distributions with compact support. (Note that $P_S \subseteq P_K$.) Suppose that $\succ$ is defined on P_K only, and replace Axiom (5.20) with the following:

Axiom (5.23). If $p \succ q$, and if $\{p_n\}$ is a sequence of probability distributions that approach p in the weak topology and that have supports that are uniformly bounded, then $p_n \succ q$ for all sufficiently large n. And vice versa, for $q \succ p$.

I'm being sloppy, but you get the point. Note that Axiom (5.23) implies Axiom (5.3) for the case of $\succ$ defined on P_K. (Proof?) So we know that Axioms (5.1), (5.2) and (5.23) will give us an expected utility representation on P_S. Well, to make a long story short, they do even better than that:

Theorem (5.24). A binary relation $\succ$ defined on P_K (or just on P_S, if you prefer) satisfies axioms (5.1), (5.2) and (5.23) if and only if there is a continuous function $u : Z \to R$ such that $\succ$ is represented in the usual sense by expected utility computed with u.

Bingo. Continuous but not bounded utility. I leave the proof in your hands, which are, no doubt, quite capable if you've persevered in reading this section. And I close with a puzzle. What I really want for some applications is to have unbounded utility (I'd really like utility functions that are exponential, for reasons that you'll see in the next chapter) and probability distributions that include the family of all Normal distributions. Can you now see how to do it?

PROBLEMS

(1) Planners in the war room of the state of Freedonia can express the quality of any war strategy against arch-rival Sylvania by a probability distribution $(p_1, p_2, 1-p_1-p_2)$ on the three outcomes: Freedonia wins; draws; loses. Rufus T. Firefly, Prime Minister of Freedonia, expresses his preferences over such probability distributions by the lexicographic

preferences:

$$(p_1, p_2, p_3) \succ (q_1, q_2, q_3) \text{ if } p_3 < q_3 \text{ or } [p_3 = q_3 \text{ and } p_2 < q_2].$$

By the methods of Chapter 3, it is easy to show that these preferences cannot be represented by an ordinal utility function, let alone by an expected utility representation. So some one or more of the three von Neumann-Morgenstern axioms must be violated here. The question is: Which of the three axioms does this binary relation satisfy (if any), and which does it violate? Of course, you should prove any statement that you make.

(2) Let Z be any set, let P_S be the set of simple probability distributions on Z, and let $\succ$ be a binary relation on P_S satisfying the three von Neumann-Morgenstern axioms. Then $\succ$ has an expected utility representation. Since this encompasses an ordinal representation of $\succ$, we know that there exists a countable $\succ$-order dense subset Q of P_S. The problem: Produce one such Q. If you find this too hard, you should try it assuming that Z is finite.

(3) Prove that the three von Neumann-Morgenstern axioms (in the setting, say, of a finite set of prizes Z and all the probability distributions P on Z) form an independent set of axioms.

(4) Provide a proof for Lemma (5.7).

(5) In the theorems of this chapter, we always left it to you to show that if an expected utility representation holds, then the three axioms hold. Show this now. Specifically, show first that, in the setting of arbitrary Z and P_S the set of simple probability distributions on Z, if we are given a function $u : Z \rightarrow R$ and we define from it a function $F : P_S \rightarrow R$ by $F(p) = \sum_{\text{supp}(p)} p(z)u(z)$, then F satisfies the second half of (5.13). Then show that, in the general context of Theorem (5.11), if a binary relation on Π and a function $F : \Pi \rightarrow R$ satisfy part (d) of the theorem, then the binary relation satisfies (a), (b) and (c).

(6) Give the details (for any of the representation theorems) for proving the uniqueness result.

(7) In the definition of a mixture space, Definition (5.10), it is not assumed that $h_a(\pi, \pi) = \pi$ for all a and π. But this property was used (implicitly) in several places. Is this implied the the three properties in (5.10), or do we need to add this property to the list of properties that defines a mixture space?

(8) Fill in the many blanks in the final section of this chapter.

(a) Give all the details for showing that if preferences over simple lotteries on the real line are represented by expected utility for a discontinuous utility function, then these preferences are not continuous in the weak topology.

(b) And show that if the utility function is unbounded, preferences aren't continuous in the weak topology.

(c) Provide the details for extending Theorem (5.21) to Corollary (5.22).

(d) Provide a proof of Theorem (5.24).

(e) Provide a theory along the lines of this last section which will allow you to have all Normal distributions among the probability distributions you may consider, and which will not rule out the utility function $U(z) = -\exp(-\lambda z)$, for λ a positive constant. (Good luck.)

6

Utility Functions
for Money

In common applications of von Neumann-Morgenstern expected utility theory, the prize space is some subset Z of the real line, with the interpretation that the prizes are money amounts, say reckoned in dollars. To make things as concrete as possible, suppose for the time being that Totrep is entering into gambles involving his net worth (bank balance) – these gambles are based on randomizing devices with objective probabilities, and the outcomes are independent of anything else affecting Totrep, such as other income he may earn. (We'll see why this assumption is necessary in Chapter 12.) Moreover, all gambles under consideration are described by simple probability distributions, and Totrep happily ascribes to the three mixture space axioms in this context, so that we know his preferences can be represented by expectation of a utility function $u : Z \rightarrow R$. Interpret the outcome z as Totrep's bank balance after the gamble is conducted, and not as his net winnings from the gamble. The question is: What can be said about this function u?

BASIC PROPERTIES AND DEFINITIONS

To keep things simple, I'll assume throughout that Z is an open interval $(z_o, z^o) \subseteq R$. The cases $z_o = -\infty$ and $z^o = \infty$ are not ruled out. P_S will denote the set of simple probability distributions on Z, with typical elements p, q, r. Totrep's preferences over P_S will be denoted by the binary relation $\succ$ as usual. For the lottery degenerate at the (real) value z I'll write δ_z. And for any function $f : Z \rightarrow R$, the expectation of f taken with respect to p will be written $E[f; p]$. I'll use $e(p)$ to denote the expected value of p, and $v(p)$ to denote the variance of p.

An almost trivial property of u (and one that is normatively unobjectionable) is strict monotonicity.

Proposition (6.1). The utility function u is strictly increasing if and only if

$$\delta_z \succ \delta_{z'} \text{ iff } z > z'.$$

The proof should be clear to you. I'll assume from here on out that u is strictly increasing.

Next comes the property of *risk aversion*. Preferences $\succ$ are said to be *risk averse* if $\delta_{e(p)} \succeq p$ for all $p \in P$. Preferences $\succ$ exhibit *strict risk aversion* if $\delta_{e(p)} \succ p$ for all $p \in P$ such that $v(p) > 0$. $\succ$ exhibits *risk neutrality* if $\delta_{e(p)} \sim p$ for all $p \in P$. $\succ$ exhibits *risk seeking* behavior if $p \succeq \delta_{e(p)}$ for all $p \in P$, and it exhibits *strict risk seeking behavior* if $p \succ \delta_{e(p)}$ for all $p \in P$ such that $v(p) > 0$

I rather expect that you know these things, but let me give here a few definitions from mathematics: A function $f : Z \to R$ is *concave* if $f(az + (1-a)y) \geq af(z) + (1-a)f(y)$ for all $z, y \in Z$ and $a \in [0,1]$ It is *strictly concave* if this holds with strict inequality for $z \neq y$ and $a \in (0,1)$. It is *affine* if $f(z) = az + b$ for some constants a and b. It is convex if the weak inequality is reversed, and it is strictly convex if we have a strict (reversed) inequality for all $z \neq y$ and $a \in (0,1)$.

Let me also state a couple of elementary propositions concerning concave and convex functions: For p a simple probability distribution on Z, $f(e(p)) \geq E[f; p]$ if f is concave, with a strict inequality if f is strictly concave and $v(p) > 0$. If f is affine, the inequality is an equality. If f is convex, the weak inequality reverses, and if f is strictly convex, the weak inequality is strict running the other way for p such that $v(p) > 0$. These inequalities are proved (by you for homework) by induction on the size of the support of p. They generalize to the case where p is any probability distribution with, let us suppose, compact support, in which case they are known (variously) as *Jensen's inequality*.

Some other elementary propositions that will come in handy are: If a concave function u is defined on an open interval in the real line, u is continuous, and it is continuously differentiable almost everywhere. (For those of you who followed the last section Chapter 5, what is the implication of this in terms of continuity of preferences and risk aversion?) It has well defined left-hand and right-hand derivatives everywhere. Ignoring the points where the derivative is not defined, u', the derivative, is nonincreasing, and at points where u is not differentiable, the left hand derivative is the limit of u' from the left, and the right hand derivative is the limit of u' from the right. Finally, if u is concave and twice continuously differentiable, then u'' (the second derivative of u) is nonpositive. Affine functions are certainly differentiable, and their derivatives are constant – you didn't need me to tell you that. For convex functions, the mirror-image results to those stated above are true.

The results stated in the paragraph two before this one make almost immediately obvious the following:

Proposition (6.2). $\succ$ exhibits risk aversion if and only if u is concave. $\succ$ exhibits strict risk aversion iff u is strictly concave. $\succ$ exhibits risk neutrality iff u is affine. $\succ$ exhibits risk seeking behavior iff u is convex, and strict risk seeking behavior iff u is strictly convex.

It is typical in most economic applications to assume that all agents are risk averse, not excluding the extreme case of a risk neutral agent. How does risk aversion do as a descriptive property? The answer is: moderately well, although gambles with negative prizes and gambles with small probabilities of enormous gains tend to screw this up. As to whether risk aversion is any good as a normative property – what do *you* think?

To take the next step, fix the preference relation $\succ$, and for $p \in P$, define $C(p)$ by

$$C(p) = \{z \in Z : \delta_z \sim p\}.$$

That is, $C(p)$ is the set of *certainty equivalents* for p – the set of "for certain" monetary amounts that Totrep rates as just as good as p. In general, $C(p)$ may be empty and it may be multivalued. But:

Proposition (6.3). (a) If u is strictly increasing, then $C(p)$ is at most a one element set.
(b) If u is continuous, then $C(p)$ is nonempty.
(c) If u is concave (if preferences exhibit risk aversion), then $C(p)$ is nonempty.

The proofs of (a) and (b) are left as easy exercises. For (c), use the fact that any concave function on an open interval of R is continuous.

Assume for the remainder of this chapter that u is strictly increasing and concave. Then $C(p)$ is a singleton set, and I'll denote the single element of $C(p)$ by $c(p)$.

Next define the *risk premium* associated by gamble p by

$$rp(p) = e(p) - c(p).$$

Since preferences are risk averse and monotone increasing, it is easy to see (do you?) that $rp(p)$ is nonnegative for all p. This is called the risk premium because it denotes the amount that Totrep would pay to replace p by its expected value. That is, as $c(p) = e(p) - rp(p)$, Totrep is indifferent between p and the amount of money $e(p) - rp(p)$ for sure.

DECREASING, INCREASING, AND CONSTANT RISK AVERSION

Recall that the prizes z are supposed to be Totrep's net wealth after the gamble is conducted. In general, this will be the sum of Totrep's wealth prior to the gamble and his net winnings from the gamble. Letting w be Totrep's wealth prior to the gamble and letting q be a (simple) probability distribution representing his net winnings from the gamble, I will write $w + q$ to denote the (simple) probability distribution that describes Totrep's final wealth position. That is, Totrep seeks to maximize $E[u; w + q]$ through his choice of the net gamble q that he chooses.

How does Totrep's attitude towards various gambles change as his wealth changes? For example, suppose Totrep has a choice between a gamble represented by q and a sure net payment (positive or negative) in the amount z. That is, at wealth level w he can have either $q + w$ or $z + w$. His choice (clearly) depends on whether

$$E[u; q + w] >, =, \text{ or } < u(w + z).$$

The question I'm asking is, how does this change with changes in Totrep's initial wealth w? (Another way to interpret the same mathematical question is – how does Totrep's attitude towards risk change as gambles are "shifted" towards greater terminal wealth positions? That is, how will his choices be affected if I increase *all* the prizes by a constant amount?)

Definition (6.4). Totrep (characterized by his preferences $\succ$ or, equivalently in this chapter, by his utility function u) is said to be *decreasingly* (absolute) *risk averse* if for all $q \in P, z \in R, w$ and $w' \in R$ such that $q + w, q + w', w + z$, and $w' + z$ all lie in Z and $w' > w$,

(6.5)   if $E[u; w + q] > u(w + z)$, then $E[u; w' + q] > u(w' + z)$.

The motivation behind this definition is: *If* Totrep prefers the risky gamble q to the sure thing z at wealth level w, then if we increase his wealth to w' he doesn't become "more risk averse" and prefer the sure thing. My use of "decreasingly" here would more properly be termed "nonincreasingly" – I'm not insisting on any "strict decrease" in risk aversion. A parallel definition can be given for *increasing risk aversion* – change the direction of implication in (6.5) and for *constant risk aversion* – make the implication in (6.5) two sided). Finally, "absolute" is sometimes used here to distinguish this from "relative" risk aversion – see ahead.

An alternate and equivalent definition of decreasing risk aversion is given as follows.

Proposition (6.6). Totrep (and his u) is decreasingly risk averse if and only if for all $q \in P$ the function $w \to rp(q + w)$ is nonincreasing in w.

Remember, we assume throughout that u is strictly increasing and concave. The obvious modifications are made for increasing and constant risk aversion. I hope that the interpretation is obvious. The proof, which is something of a matter of marshalling definitions, is left as an easy exercise.

Before going any further, what do you think of decreasing, increasing, and constant risk aversion as normative properties? In particular, what do you think of constant risk aversion as a normative property when all the gambles being contemplated are small in comparison with the amount of money you are comfortable handling?

Later on I'll try to convince you that you should be very comfortable with constant risk aversion in this sort of situation.

In order to keep the analysis simple, I'm now going to make what economists call a "purely technical and innocuous" assumption, that u is twice continuously differentiable. I'll write u' for the first derivative of u and u'' for the second derivative. By our previous assumptions, $u' > 0$ because u is strictly increasing, and $u'' \leq 0$ because u is concave.

Theorem (6.7). Totrep (his utility function u) is decreasingly risk averse if and only if the function

$$\lambda(z) = -\frac{u''(z)}{u'(z)}$$

is nonincreasing in z. Totrep is increasingly risk averse if and only if $\lambda(z)$ is nondecreasing. Totrep has constant risk aversion if and only if $\lambda(z)$ is constant, in which case there exist constants $a > 0$ and b such that

$$u(z) = \begin{cases} az + b & \text{if } \lambda(z) \equiv 0, \text{ or} \\ -ae^{-\lambda z} + b & \text{if } \lambda(z) \equiv \lambda > 0. \end{cases}$$

The proof will be given eventually (or rather, a sketch will be given). But for now, some discussion may help. The function $\lambda(z)$ is called the *Arrow-Pratt measure of* (absolute) *risk aversion.* Note that if I replace $u(z)$ by the equivalent (in terms of $\succ$) $au(z) + b$, the value of the function $\lambda(z)$ does not change – it is a property of $\succ$ and not of the representing function u chosen. $\lambda(z)$ is certainly well defined, because $u'(z) > 0$. And as $u''(z) \leq 0$ we have $\lambda(z) \geq 0$. (The function λ could be defined as long as $u' > 0$, even if u'' was not restricted in sign. In this case positive λ would correspond to "local risk aversion," negative λ to "local risk seeking," and zero λ to "local risk neutrality.")

You can picture λ as a local measure of risk aversion as follows: Suppose that I have two utility functions u and v with corresponding measures of risk aversion λ and ρ. Then $\lambda(z^\circ) > \rho(z^\circ)$ roughly means that u is more risk averse for prizes close to z° than is v. The picture you should carry in your head is to pick constants $a > 0$ and b so that

$$u(z^\circ) = av(z^\circ) + b \text{ and } u'(z^\circ) = av'(z^\circ).$$

Then, because $\lambda(z^\circ) > \rho(z^\circ)$, if we graph u and $av + b$ together we get the picture shown in figure 6.1. That is, $av + b$ is "more flat" or "more linear" or "closer to risk neutral." (How do I know that this is the picture? Those of you who know some math should work out an answer to this question.)

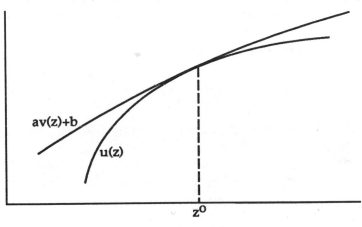

Figure 6.1

COMPARISON OF THE RISK AVERSION OF TWO TOTREPS

As a step in proving the theorem, and because it is of independent interest, I want to take a small detour at this point and pursue the story begun just above. Suppose we have two utility functions u and v, giving the preferences of two Totreps whom we'll refer to as Totrep I and Totrep II, respectively. Both u and v are assumed to be twice continuously differentiable, concave and strictly increasing. For simplicity, suppose the two functions have the same domain of definition Z.

Definition (6.8). Totrep I (with utility function u) is said to be *at least as risk averse as* Totrep II (with v) if, for all simple lotteries p on Z, the risk premium that Totrep I would pay for p is at least as large as that Totrep II would pay. Equivalently, Totrep I's certainty equivalent for any p is no larger than Totrep II's, for every $p \in P$.

The notation is not nice, but I'll use $rp_u(p), rp_v(p), c_u(p)$ and $c_v(p)$ to denote, respectively, the risk premiums of Totrep I and II and the certainty equivalents of Totrep I and II for the gamble p. Then Totrep I is at least as risk averse as Totrep II if for all $p \in P$, $rp_u(p) \geq rp_v(p)$ or, equivalently, $c_u(p) \leq c_v(p)$.

There is no reason to believe that this "ordering" of Totreps is complete – that is, it may be (and is) that there are two utility functions u and v neither of which is at least as risk averse as the other.

A little more notation: Define

$$\lambda(z) = -\frac{u''(z)}{u'(z)} \text{ and } \rho(z) = -\frac{v''(z)}{v'(z)}.$$

That is, λ is Totrep I's Arrow-Pratt measure of risk aversion, and ρ is Totrep II's.

Lemma (6.9). If u and v are such that $\lambda(z) \geq \rho(z)$ for all $z \in Z$, then $u(z) = f(v(z))$ for some concave, strictly increasing function f from the range of v to R.

Proof. The existence of a strictly increasing f with $u(z) = f(v(z))$ is derived as follows. Since v is continuous and strictly increasing, there is a strictly increasing and continuous function v^{-1} from the range of v into Z satisfying $v^{-1}(v(z)) = z$. Then defining $f(\cdot) = u(v^{-1}(\cdot))$ produces a strictly increasing function with $u(z) = f(v(z))$. It remains to show that f is concave. Differentiating $u = f \circ v$ (and using the chain rule) gives $u'(z) = f'(v(z))v'(z)$, or $f'(v(z)) = u'(z)/v'(z)$.

Differentiating again yields

$$f''(v(z))v'(z) = u''(z)/v'(z) - v''(z)u'(z)/(v'(z))^2, \text{ or}$$

$$f''(v(z)) = [u'(z)/v'(z)^2][u''(z)/u'(z) - v''(z)/v'(z)] \text{ or}$$

$$f''(v(z)) = [u'(z)/v'(z)^2][\rho(z) - \lambda(z)].$$

Now f is a concave function if and only if its second derivative is everywhere nonpositive – since $u'(z)/v'(z)^2$ is positive and $\rho(z) \leq \lambda(z)$, this follows immediately from the expression above. (I cheated you. How did I know that f is differentiable, let alone twice differentiable?

If you know enough math to be bothered by this, provide a clean proof of this lemma.)

Proposition (6.10). Totrep I is at least as risk averse as Totrep II if and only if, for all $z \in Z$, $\lambda(z) \geq \rho(z)$.

In words, for Totrep I to be at least as risk averse as Totrep II it is necessary and sufficient that Totrep I's Arrow-Pratt measure of risk aversion be everywhere at least as large as Totrep II's.

Proof. Suppose $\lambda(z) \geq \rho(z)$ holds for all z. Then $u(z) = f(v(z))$ for some strictly increasing concave function f. Pick any $p \in P$. Then

$$u(c_u(p)) = E[u(z); p] = E[f(v(z)); p]$$
$$\leq f(E[v(z); p]) \text{ (for justification see below)}.$$
$$= f(v(c_v(p)) = u(c_v(p))$$

Thus by the fact that u is strictly increasing, $c_u(p) \leq c_v(p)$, which is the desired conclusion. The key step in this chain is the inequality $E[f(v(z)); p] \leq f(E[v(z); p])$. This follows from the concavity of f; cf. our discussion a while back concerning properties of concave functions.

Now to go the other way. Suppose $rp_u(p) \geq rp_v(p)$ for all $p \in P$, but that for some $z \in Z$ it is the case that $\lambda(z) < \rho(z)$. Consider the simple probability distribution p^δ that gives prize $z + \delta$ and $z - \delta$ each with probability 1/2. (Since Z is an open interval, for small enough δ, p^δ has support in Z.)

Now $E[u; p^\delta] = (u(z + \delta) + u(z - \delta))/2$. Using a Taylor series expansion of u around z, this is

$$E[u; p^\delta] = (u(z) + \delta u'(z) + \delta^2 u''(z)/2 + o(\delta^2)$$
$$+ u(z) - \delta u'(z) + \delta^2 u''(z)/2 + o(\delta^2))/2$$
$$= u(z) + \delta^2 u''(z)/2 + o(\delta^2),$$

where $o(\delta^2)$ are terms that are "small" relative to δ^2 in the sense that as $\delta^2 \to 0$, $o(\delta^2)/\delta^2 \to 0$.

Also, $e(p^\delta) = z$, so $u(z - rp_u(p^\delta)) = E[u; p^\delta]$, or, again using the Taylor series expansion,

$$u(z) - u'(z)(rp_u(p^\delta)) + o(rp_u(p^\delta)) = E[u; p^\delta], \text{ and thus}$$

$$u(z) - u'(z)(rp_u(p^\delta)) + o(rp_u(p^\delta)) = u(z) + \delta^2 u''(z)/2 + o(\delta^2).$$

If I can show that $rp_u(p^\delta)$ is of order no greater than δ^2, I'm entitled to conclude that

$$rp_u(p^\delta) = -\delta^2 u''(z)/2u'(z) + o(\delta^2) = \delta^2 \lambda(z)/2 + o(\delta^2).$$

In fact, I can show that $rp_u(p^\delta)$ is of order no greater than δ^2, although I'll leave this to you (if you are so inclined). So this is a valid conclusion.

Similarly, I can show that

$$rp_v(p^\delta) = \delta^2 \rho(z)/2 + o(\delta^2).$$

So by my assumption that $\rho(z) > \lambda(z)$, for small enough δ I have that $rp_v(p^\delta) > rp_u(p^\delta)$, contradicting my hypothesis that u is at least as risk averse as v.

PROOF OF THEOREM (6.7)

Now I'm ready to prove Theorem (6.7). Actually, I won't try to give a formal proof, but rather to sketch what I'd say in a formal proof. If you have doubts about what I'm about to say, it would be a good idea to try and fill in the outline with details.

Step 1. Suppose $\lambda(z)$ does increase over some range. That is, there exist w and w' with $w' > w$ yet $\lambda(w') > \lambda(w)$. Then consider the gamble q that gives prizes δ and $-\delta$, each with probability $1/2$, and compare risk premia of $w' + q^\delta$ and $w + q^\delta$. Using almost exactly the argument in the second half to the last proposition, you'd be able to show that $rp(w' + q^\delta) > rp(w + q^\delta)$, showing that this u is *not* decreasingly risk averse.

Step 2. Suppose $\lambda(z)$ is nonincreasing. Fix w and w' with $w' \geq w$. Then in comparing $rp(w' + q)$ with $rp(w + q)$ (for given q), think of the former as $rp_{v^\circ}(q)$ where $v^\circ(z) = u(w' + z)$ and think of the latter as $rp_{v_\circ}(q)$ where $v_\circ(z) = u(w + z)$. Since $w' \geq w$ and λ is nondecreasing, the Arrow-Pratt measure of risk aversion for v° is everywhere no larger than that of $v_\circ$ (at least where their domains overlap), and thus by the previous proposition $rp_{v^\circ}(q) \leq rp_{v_\circ}(q)$.

But this is just $rp(w' + q) \leq rp(w + q)$, hence u is decreasingly risk averse by Proposition (6.6).

Steps 1 and 2 together prove the first statement of the theorem. The second is proved by symmetrical argument, and the third by intersecting the first two and integrating $-u''/u' = $ constant.

In these proofs, I've made abundant use of my assumption that u is twice continuously differentiable. Without getting into details here, let me assert that this assumption is really unnecessary. If u has constant risk aversion, then it can be shown that u is twice continuously differentiable. While for u to be, say, decreasingly risk averse, continuity of the second derivative isn't necessary, but there is a sense in which a second derivative must exist. Some of the problems will let you hassle with this.

RELATIVE RISK AVERSION

In the story on (absoluto) risk aversion, the basic question involved how risk attitude changes with changes in the initial wealth position, without changes in the size of the gamble. A variation on this theme concerns changes in risk attitude as initial wealth and the scale of the gamble change together proportionally.

For simplicity, fix a Totrep who is choosing among simple probability distributions on the set $Z = (0, \infty)$. This Totrep has strictly increasing, concave utility function u, which happens to be twice continuously differentiable.

Let w denote Totrep's initial wealth, and imagine that the gamble he is contemplating calls for an investment of all his wealth – let q be a simple probability distribution on Z – then if Totrep takes q, he will wind up with final wealth wz with probability $q(z)$. That is q gives the distribution of return per dollar invested. I'll use wq to denote this probability distribution on final wealth.

Suppose Totrep has a choice between the gamble q and a sure thing investment that will leave him with wealth $wz°$. He chooses between the two according to whether

$$u(wz°) >, =, \text{ or } < E[u; wq].$$

Definition (6.11). Totrep (and his utility function u) is *increasingly relative risk averse* if for all $w' > w$ and q and $z°$.

$$E[u; w'q] > u(w'z°) \text{ implies } E[u; wq] > u(wz°).$$

He has *decreasing relative risk aversion* if this holds with the implication reversed. He has *constant relative risk aversion* if the implication holds in both directions.

Question: What do you think *normatively* of increasing, decreasing, and constant relative risk aversion?

Proposition (6.12). Totrep (or u) has increasing relative risk aversion if and only if the function

$$w \to -\frac{wu''(w)}{u'(w)}$$

is a nondecreasing function (of w); u has decreasing relative risk aversion iff this function is nonincreasing; and u has constant relative risk aversion iff this function is a constant, in which case there exist constants $a > 0$ and b such that either $u(z) = a\ln(z) + b$ or $u(z) = a\gamma z^\gamma + b$ for some $\gamma \in (-\infty, 0) \cup (0, 1)$.

For proof, see either a reference book on choice under uncertainty, or see the classic article by Pratt (1964).

NORMATIVE USES OF THESE PROPERTIES

After all this work, it is natural to wonder why any of this is useful. We'll look at some of the normative uses in this section, and discuss (very briefly) one aspect of the descriptive uses in the next.

To discuss the normative uses of the developments of this chapter requires us to go back one step, to the normative uses of expected utility theory itself. Let me illustrate these uses by recounting a speech that is often made to "clients" of these techniques. In this case, it is an abridgment of a speech that is made to MBA students at Stanford University in a course on Decision Making Under Uncertainty.

"Suppose that you (the student) had choose among the four gambles depicted in figure 6.2.

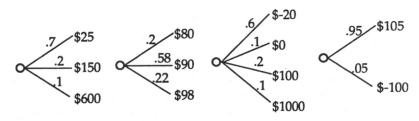

Figure 6.2

"The probabilities depicted on the chance nodes will be objectively determined – the gambles are all based on things like the spin of a smooth roulette wheel, etc.

"It is very likely that you won't find it very easy to make a choice. At least, I myself have a hard time making a selection, because I find it hard to think about probabilities such as .22 and to think about gambles with four possible prizes. But *if* in this choice situation I subscribe to the three axioms of von Neumann and Morgenstern, then I know that my choice *should be* based on maximizing the expectation of a utility function. And, having considered the matter, I see nothing wrong with those axioms in this setting, although there are settings in which there are problems with the axioms. [To readers of this book: We'll discuss those problems in Chapter 12.] So I want my choice behavior among the four gambles to conform to expected utility maximization. All that I need to do is to discover my own utility function, and I'm in business: I'll compute the expected utility of each of the four gambles, and choose whichever comes out highest.

"Since I don't have handy my utility function, you may consider that this conclusion is quite useless. But that is not correct. I can discover (or, more accurately, I can assess) my utility function by making some judgments easier than what is called for in a direct choice among the four gambles above.

"First, I ask myself: What is my certainty equivalent for the gamble that gives me probability one-half of getting $1000 and probability one-half of getting $-100? Note that this gamble, depicted overleaf, is selected so that its two prizes bracket all the prizes in the four gambles from which I must choose, and it gives probability 1/2 to each.

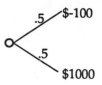

It isn't a trivial judgment to make, but it is not so hard, because I'm asking myself to compare sure things with a gamble having only two prizes and a simple 50-50 probability structure. In any event, right at the moment I assess that I'm roughly indifferent between the gamble above and $400 for sure.

"So next I ask myself: what is my certainty equivalent for the gamble:

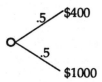

Note that this gamble has top prize equal to the upper prize from my previous question, and bottom prize equal to my previously assessed certainty equivalent. And I answer: Approximately $675.

"Next question: What is my certainty equivalent for the gamble:

Answer: Approximately $100.

"The point of this is that, if I am able to answer these questions, then I'll have five points on my utility function in the range $-100 to $1000 – assigning $-100 utility level 0 and $1000 utility level 1, (these two utility levels are arbitrary, as long as $1000 gets a higher level than $-100, although the zero-to-one scale is convenient), the answers that I gave above tell me that the utility level .5 goes with $400, utility level .75 goes with $675, and utility level .25 goes with $100. With those five values, I can rough in a pretty good approximation of my utility function and compute expected utilities for the four original gambles, making my choice accordingly. Even if my approximation is off, if it is close to my "true utility" the choice according to the approximation will be nearly as good as the best gamble using my "true utility." This sort of approximation result is easy to formalize and to prove. [To mathematically inclined readers of the book: Give it a shot. If you need some hints as to how to proceed, problem 8 will get you started.]

"Of course, I'm making some judgment calls above, and I may not be doing so well. But the data above allow me to run consistency checks, such as: What is my certainty equivalent for:

It should be $400. Why? Because, if I am conforming to the axioms, this is a gamble whose prizes have utilities .25 and .75, so it has expected utility .5, and the certain amount of money that has utility .5 is $400. As it turns out, my assessed certainty equivalent for this gamble is approximately $375, but now I can go back to my original assessments and try to fudge them enough so I have five consistent values.

"Why is this procedure better than just choosing one of the original four gambles? Because the numerical judgments that I'm asking myself to make are for the easiest conceivable cases that aren't trivial – two prize lotteries with equally likely outcomes. I'm quite ready to believe that I'm better at processing that sort of gamble than I am at the four more complicated gambles with which we started.

"Is this benefit coming for free? *No* – I also had to make a *qualitative* judgment that in *this* choice situation, the three axioms are good guides for choice behavior. But because I know where the pitfalls in those axioms can be found [to the reader: as will you after Chapter 12], I am confident that, in this case, the axioms are a sound guide to behavior."

This is where the speech stops with MBA students. When I've made this speech to them, they tell me that it convinces them, although they probably (at least in part) are telling me what they think I want to hear. (If so, they're certainly correct about what I want to hear.) The hard part, they claim, is that they still are called upon to assess some certainty equivalents – isn't there anything that I can do to make that part easier?

This is where the material from this chapter would come in handy (if it was something that I could make MBA students understand). For example, I'm happy with the following statements concerning my preferences in this choice situation:

(a) I like more money to less.

(b) I'm risk averse in the range of prizes being considered.

(c) I'm *decreasingly* absolute risk averse over this range, and at that only slightly. In my current bank balance/permanent income position, a loss of $100 and a gain of $1000 are not big deals. At 10% rate of interest, $1000 is the same as a perpetual stream of $100 per year. That isn't much, in the scale of decisions that I have to make. I'd be surprised if a decrease in my lifetime income of even $500 per year made much of a difference in my choice over lotteries.

So when I assess my utility function:

(a) It will be strictly increasing.

(b) It will be concave.

(c) It will have $-u''/u'$ decreasing slightly, and will be virtually a function of the form $u(z) = -\exp(-\lambda z)$ for z in the range of these gambles (where z here represents my net winnings from these gambles, which is added to or subtracted from my bank account).

This last bit is especially helpful – I can look for my certainty equivalents for the two gambles depicted on the next page and know that they *ought* to be $100 different. This is helpful because I'm probably better at assessing my certainty equivalent for the first gamble than for the second – this has to do with the "framing" of the question on which the assessment is based. Specifically, I'm not very good at making assessments for gambles that entail losses, even when, given

my current state of financial health, the losses are relatively insignif-
icant. Framing is a topic that we'll take up in Chapter 14, but the
idea is that I'm better at judging/processing questions framed in one
manner than in another. And having judged that my utility is virtually exponential in the range $- 100 to $1000, I can assess the relevant
single parameter λ with each of several well-framed questions, checking the consistency of my answers by checking whether the certainty
equivalents that I give lead me to the same rough estimate of this
parameter λ.

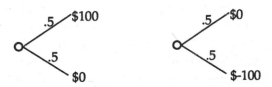

In particular, when I went back to gambles that I used to assess
my utility function over the range $-100 to $1000, I discovered why I
didn't pass the consistency check. The problem was in the third step,
when I assessed my certainty equivalent for the 50-50 gamble with
prizes $-100 and $400. Recall that my assessment at the time was
that my certainty equivalent was $100. But if I reframe the question,
asking for my certainty equivalent for a 50-50 gamble with prizes $0
and $500, I come up with the assessment of $230 or $235 or so. I'm
decreasingly risk averse, but not quite that much! What is going on
is that the minus sign on the prize $-100 is getting too much weight
in my considerations. By reframing the question and relying on the
fact that I know I'm nearly constantly risk averse over this range, I
come up with a much better utility curve. By the way, in case you're
checking me, the implied value of my coefficient of risk aversion λ is
around .0004.

Of course, all this would be less helpful if I multiplied all prizes in
this section by a factor of 100, because then, while I do think I'm still
risk averse over this larger range and I do think I'm decreasingly risk
averse, the decrease in my coefficient of risk aversion (over this range)
is probably quite significant. Certainly an assumption of constant risk
aversion over this larger range is unwarranted. Still, knowing that my
utility function should exhibit decreasing risk aversion may be a help.

That is, as the range increases, the properties discussed in this

chapter are harder (normatively) to subscribe to, and one gets corre-
spondingly less out of them. But for problems such as the one with
which this section started, they can be quite useful.

ON DESCRIPTIVE APPLICATIONS AND
"STRONGER MEASURES OF RISK AVERSION"

These properties for utility functions on money have also been
used descriptively in economic theory. It is typically assumed that
economic agents are described by decreasing absolute risk aversion.
Based on this assumption, we might be able, for example, to derive
some implications for the demand of individuals for risky assets as
their wealth increases. Or we might assume that people of one sort or
from one economy are less risk averse then people of/in another, and
derive comparisons of how they will act as individuals and what will
be the consequences of that behavior on market equilibrium.

I will not take you into such applications, per se. They belong
to a course on the economics of uncertainty, and this book is limited
to choice theory. But there is one question to raise concerning those
applications, asked first (to my knowledge) by Ross (1981). We can
approach this question by asking either of the following two:

(a) Suppose we have two Totreps with utility functions u and v, and
we have two probability distributions p and q on their final wealth
such that p has higher average return than does q, but p is also
riskier than q. If Totrep I is at least as risk averse as Totrep II, and if
Totrep I prefers p to q, then does Totrep II also prefer p to q? Put
another way, shouldn't "at least as risk averse as" be defined in a way
that makes the answer to this question yes?

(b) Suppose Totrep is decreasingly risk averse, and he has a choice
between two gambles whose payoff (not including his initial wealth)
are given by simple probability distributions p and q. As before,
suppose p has higher average return than does q but that p is riskier
than q. If Totrep chooses p over q when his initial wealth is w,
then does he also choose p over q at all higher wealth levels w'?
Put another way, shouldn't "decreasing risk aversion" be defined in a
manner that makes the answer to this question yes?

If in the above questions, q is a degenerate (single prize) lottery, then with the definitions of "as risk averse as" and "decreasingly risk averse" given above, the answers to the questions are yes – in fact, this is virtually the definitions of the two terms. But the two questions above are posed for the case where q is not necessarily degenerate, and that could conceivably make a difference. Of course, to handle such cases we must first tackle a preliminary task: We must formalize what it means for p to be riskier than q.

For any simple probability distributions p and q with the same expectations, I'll say that p is *as risky as* q if, for $\{z_1, \ldots, z_n\}$ the support of q, there exist simple probability distributions $q_1, \ldots, q_n$ with

(i) $e(q_j) = 0$ for $j = 1, \ldots, n$, and

(ii) $p(z) = \sum_{j=1}^{n} q(z_j) q_j(z - z_j)$ for all z.

An example may helpful illustrate this definition. Suppose q is

Let q_1 and q_2 be

Then setting $p(z) = \sum_{j=1}^{2} q(z_j) q_j(z - z_j)$, we obtain the probability distribution that is computed by compounding q with q_1 if the outcome of q is z_1 and with q_2 if the outcome of q is z_2, and then adding the outcomes. (See overleaf for the picture.) In general, the definition comes down to this: p is as risky as q if, on some probability space, you can find joint random variables X and Y such that Y has the distribution q, X has distribution p, and $E[X \mid Y] = Y$. The idea is that we get p by running the gamble q and "adding noise". The precise distribution of the noise can depend on the outcome of q, but it is called "noise" because its conditional expectation, conditional on the outcome of q, is zero.)

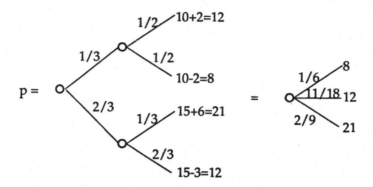

Why is this a good definition of "as risky as?" The intuition is that p is sort of fair odds garbling of q – to carry out p, first do q and then, depending on the outcome of q, run one of several even money gambles. Since the second round of gambles are even money gambles, any risk averse person would (weakly) prefer to stop after the first round. We have

Proposition (6.14). If p and q have the same expectation and p is as risky as q, then no risk averse Totrep would ever strictly prefer p to q.

And, conversely:

Proposition (6.15). Given two distributions p and q with the same expectation, p is as risky as q if every risk averse Totrep weakly prefers q to p.

For p and q with different expectations, simply say that p is as risky as q if $p - e(p)$ is as risky as $q - e(q)$. In the construction of p from q as above, this corresponds to

Step 1: Run q and make the appropriate payoffs.

Step 2: Run some "even money" gamble, depending on the outcome in step 1 and make the appropriate payoff.

Step 3: No matter what happened in steps 1 and 2, make the payoff $e(p) - e(q)$.

If this can be done so the entire payoff has distribution p, then p is as risky as q.

So suppose we have two gambles p and q with p as risky as q. By Proposition (6.14), p could never be strictly preferred to q if $e(p) \leq e(q)$ (proof?), so assume $e(p) > e(q)$. Now go back to questions (a) and (b) above. For such p and q:

(a) If Totrep I is at least as risk averse as Totrep II in the sense of Definition (6.8), and if Totrep I strictly prefers p to q, then does Totrep II strictly prefer p to q?

(b) If Totrep has decreasing risk aversion as defined in Definition (6.6), and if he strictly prefers p to q at wealth level w, then does he strictly prefer p to q at all higher wealth levels w'?

The answer to each of these questions is no. (As you could have guessed. Why would I be saying all this otherwise?) Ross (1981) gives examples, and he goes on to develop stronger definitions of "at least as risk averse as" and "decreasing risk aversion" based on a stronger "measure" of risk aversion. (And he does the same thing for relative risk aversion.) These stronger definitions are essentially set up so that the answers to (a) and (b) are yes – the point of Ross' paper is: What are necessary and sufficient conditions on Totrep I and II's utility functions/on Totrep's utility function so that the answers are yes? You should consult Ross (1981) for answers if you are so inclined (and anyone using this book as a supplement to a course on the economics of uncertainty should certainly be so inclined).

Since I'm not going to give you the answers, you may well ask: Why did we bother with all this? We did so to make the following point.

From a descriptive point of view, it may be important that "as risk averse as" and "decreasingly risk averse" are defined so that the answers are yes. In descriptive applications of this theory one typically looks at how choices between two risky situations, one more risky than the other, and not at the choice between a risky situation and one that is risk free. This is so because the choices we see people make (and that we would wish to make predictions about) are only part of the overall choices they are making. There is uncertainty in their lives that they cannot control (entirely), or that is outside the scope of the current analysis. Insofar as descriptive theory is about pieces of a larger puzzle, the "two risky gamble" choice situations are the interesting ones, and the old, weak definitions do not give very strong results – they only work in the "one risky, one safe" choice situation. This is a theme to which we will return in Chapter 12, when we look at whether the von Neumann-Morgenstern axioms themselves can be safely applied to pieces of a larger problem. But since you are apt to see the measures of risk aversion developed in this chapter used descriptively on parts of larger choice situations, I thought it a good idea to sound an alarm now.

A final bibliographic note. My definition of "p is as risky as q" is loosely transcribed from a large economics literature on the subject. The concept sometimes appears in the literature under the rubric "second degree stochastic dominance." If you're interested in it, standard references are Rothschild and Stiglitz. "Increasing Risk, I, II, and Addendum," found in the *Journal of Economic Theory*, (1970-3). Once again, I'm dodging this subject because it doesn't quite belong in a book on choice theory per se. But it would be the next thing to do in developing economic implications of the von Neumann-Morgenstern expected utility model, and you may wish to go chase it down if you haven't already.

PROBLEMS

(1) Show that if f is a concave function and p is a simple probability distribution, then $f(e(p)) \geq E[f;p]$. Show that the inequality is strict if f is strictly concave and $v(p) > 0$.

(2) (This takes a little mathematical expertise. Although if you have the mathematical expertise it requires, then there is a good chance that you've already done all these finger exercises. Even if so, quickly remind yourself of how they go.) Show that if f is a concave function on an open interval of the real line, then f is a continuous function. (What happens if f is defined on an interval which may not be open?) Show that if u is concave, then u is differentiable almost everywhere, and has right hand and left hand derivatives everywhere. Show that if we plot the function u' (leaving it blank at points where u is not

differentiable, then u' is a decreasing function. Prove that the right and left hand derivatives at points of nondifferentiability of u are the right and left hand limits, respectively, of u'. Show that if u is twice continuously differentiable at some point, this second derivative must be nonpositive. Finally, what can you say about the second derivative of u? (That is, if u is concave, must it be twice continuously differentiable everywhere?; almost everywhere?; somewhere?)

(3) (A bit more math expertise is needed:) Use the results in problem (2) to show that the results given in (1) extend to the case where, say, p is a probability distribution given by a continuous density function on a compact subinterval of the open interval on which f is defined. (If you know more math, generalize the statement as far as you can. What happens if f doesn't have compact support?)

(4) (Only if you know a lot of mathematics:) Suppose I defined a concave function as a function f such that $f((z + z')/2) \geq (f(z) + f(z'))/2$. That is, we have the definition given early in this chapter, but only for the special case of $a = 1/2$. Suppose that I tell you that the function f (defined on some open interval in the real line) is concave in this sense and is (Borel) measurable. Is it then the case that f is concave according to the original definition? Either give a proof or a counterexample.

(5) Prove Proposition (6.3).

(6) Prove Proposition (6.6).

(7) Suppose a decision maker you know has constant absolute risk aversion over the range $-100 to $1000. We ask this decision maker for her certainty equivalent for a 50-50 gamble with prizes $0 and $1000, and she says that her certainty equivalent for this gamble is $488. What, then, should she choose, if faced with the choice of: (a) a gamble with prizes $-100, $300, and $1000, each with probability 1/3, (b) a gamble with prize $530 with probability 3/4 and $0 with probability 1/4, or (c) a sure thing payment of $385?

(8) Suppose that Totrep is choosing among a set of five complicated gambles, each of which has a finite number of prizes. This five gam-

bles have prizes that range from a maximum of \$10,000 to a minimum of \$0. Totrep, having heard the speech given to MBA students at Stanford University, decides that he subscribes to the three von Neumann-Morgenstern axioms in this case, and so he will assess a utility function over this range and then apply it to see which gamble has the highest utility. Totrep always sets the scale of his utility function so that \$10,000 has utility level one and \$0 has utility level zero.

Totrep is, however, worried that the assessments he makes in coming up with a utility function may be "off." "Suppose," he asks himself, "I come up with a function u on this range that I use for the decision, when my 'true' utility function is some function U. How bad a mistake will I make if I use u?"

We will measure the size of mistakes that Totrep might make in what seems rather natural units – dollar equivalents. Precisely, suppose that Totrep is choosing among a set of gambles $\{p_1, p_2, ..., p_n\}$. He is doing this using the utility function u, and we suppose that p_N is the one that seems to be best. Suppose that, if Totrep used his "true" utility function U, he would have concluded that p_M is best. If we let $c_U(p)$ be the certainty equivalent of a gamble p computed with the utility function U, we say that Totrep has just made an error of size $\$(c_U(p_M) - c_U(p_N))$.

Design a theory that leads to a result such as: If u is within δ of U, then the largest size error that Totrep could make in using u (instead of U) is $f(\delta)$ (or less). (You will want to have a theory where $f(\delta) \to 0$ as $\delta \to 0$.) The things you have to work out are: How will we measure distance between u and U? What is the "modulus of continuity" function f? You may assume throughout that Totrep knows that he likes more money to less, so that both u and U are strictly increasing functions. Can you improve your theory if you know that u and U are both concave? Can you improve it further if you know that both u and U exhibit decreasing (absolute) risk aversion?

(9) Prove Proposition (6.14). This shouldn't present a problem for you. On the other hand, try to prove Proposition (6.15). For this, you may want to do a little library research.

(10) Consider the set of all simple probability distributions on the real line that have expectation 150. Let ARA be the binary relation "as risky as," defined on this set as in this chapter. Prove or give a counterexample to each of the following assertions:

(a) ARA is reflexive.

(b) ARA is antisymmetric.

(c) ARA is transitive.

(d) If $pARAq$ and $rARAq$, then for all $a \in [0,1]$, $(ap+(1-a)r)ARAq$.

(e) (Good luck!!!) Suppose that $pARAq$. Write $\{z_1,\ldots,z_n\}$ for the support of q, and let $q_1,\ldots,q_n$ be the simple probability distributions described in the definition on page 89. Fix a constant $a \in (0,1)$ and let $r_1,\ldots,r_n$ be the probability distributions defined by

$$r_j(z) = q_n(z/a) \text{ for } j = 1,\ldots,n.$$

That is, r_j is q_j "shrunk" by a factor a. Now define r by

$$r(z) = \sum_{j=1}^{n} q(z_j)r(z - z_j) \text{ for all } z.$$

That is, r is q followed by "shrunk" versions of the q_j. If there is any justice in the world, we should have $pARAr$ - - at least we should if one's intuition about "as risky as" is correct. So prove or provide a counterexample to:

Suppose $pARAq$. Construct r as above. Then $pARAr$. (Hint: Try a few examples before setting out to look for a proof. You might find part (d) handy.)

(Regarding this last part: You might find the whole thing relatively easy *if* you use Proposition (6.15). But if you like a challenge, try to produce a direct proof, without using this result. It can be done, but it isn't easy.)

(11) Suppose that I have a single gamble and a vast number of Totreps, all having the same risk averse utility function. We will say that the gamble is acceptable for sharing among N Totreps if there is some way to divide the outcome of the one gamble N ways so that each of the

N Totreps prefers his or her share to getting zero for sure. Show that for a gamble to be acceptable for N Totreps for any N, the gamble must have nonnegative expected value. Under what conditions on the gamble and the Totrep's utility function is it true that the gamble is acceptable for N Totreps, as long as N is sufficiently large? What can you say if the Totreps can have different utility functions?

(12) Now suppose that we have a given gamble, and N identical Totreps. We will say that the gamble is acceptable for self-insurance among N Totreps if there is some way to divide up the outcome of N independent copies of the gamble N ways such that each of the Totreps prefers his or her share to getting zero for sure. What can you say about when a gamble is acceptable for self-insurance among all large enough numbers of Totreps?

(13) When (and if) you ever teach expected utility to MBA students (and probably in other contexts as well), you are likely to encounter the following bit of nonsense, concerning one Totrep and N independent copies of a given gamble:

Suppose that I offered you, absolutely for free, a gamble where, with probability .4 you win $1000, and with probability .6 you lose $500. You might well choose not to take this gamble (if the alternative is zero) if you are risk averse – although this gamble has a positive expected value of $100, it also has substantial risk. But if I offered you, say, 100 independent trials of this gamble, then you would certainly wish to take them, because the law of large numbers says that you will wind up ahead. That is, risk aversion is perhaps sensible when a single gamble or just a few are being contemplated. But it is senseless when we are looking at many independent copies of the same gamble. Then the only sensible thing is to go with the long-run averages.

Is this nonsense? Can you produce a particular consumer who is rational according to the von Neumann-Morgenstern axioms and who would turn down any number of independent copies of this gamble, no matter how many or how few? Or is it the case that any von Neumann-Morgenstern expected utility maximizer would take these gambles if offered enough independent copies?

Some hints: You should get one answer if you assume that the consumer is allowed to take any number of these gambles, with the number depending on the outcomes, and the consumer needn't be solvent except when he or she decides to stop. And you should get another answer if the number of copies of the gamble must be fixed in advance. In this second variation, you can assume that the consumer is never bankrupt – his or her utility function is specified for all levels of wealth, positive and negative, and he or she must make good on any losses. Or you can assume that this consumer must prespecify the number of gambles, but if the gambles go against the consumer and the consumer reaches a point where he or she couldn't cover another loss, the consumer is restrained from any further gambling. And if you are up for a real challenge, suppose that the rules are in the second option in the second variation. The consumer prespecifies a number of gambles, but the gambling ends if ever the consumer's wealth falls so far that he or she can't cover another loss. Then can you give sufficient conditions on the consumer's utility function so that, for N sufficiently large, the consumer will always take N or more copies of the given gamble? Can you give conditions on the utility function sufficient to guarantee that for all N large, the consumer will turn down N copies? Can you make your conditions necessary and sufficient?

7

Horse Race Lotteries and Roulette Wheels

In the story of Chapters 5 and 6, all uncertainty came with objective probability numbers attached. This isn't a theory that works in applications where it isn't clear "what the odds are." For example, if I'm going to bet on the outcome of a horse race in which three horses, say Kelso, Swaps and Trigger are running, the theory in the previous chapters doesn't help me decide between the gambles depicted in figure 7.1. To choose between two gambles, I have to decide how likely are the three outcomes and then combine those judgments with my attitude towards the risk involved.

Figure 7.1

It isn't clear at the outset that there is any way to quantify likelihood, that such quantification if possible can be combined with risk attitude as given in Chapter 5 by a utility function, or that such quantification can be done independently of the risks involved. But all this is possible *if* my preferences for this sort of gamble satisfy certain axioms – the representation that we are shooting for is to have a probability number associated with every outcome of the race (and with all events, or collections of outcomes, satisfying the laws of probability theory) that is independent of the prizes in the gambles, and to have a utility function u on prizes, so that choice is according to

the expectation, now subjective, of the utility function. In this chapter
we take a first shot at such a representation theorem, assuming that
Totrep has at his disposal some objective randomizing devices that he
can employ, such as fair coins, color wheels, roulette wheels, etc. (In
the following two chapters, we'll try to do without these extraneous
randomizing devices.) This development is due to Anscombe and
Aumann, in the classic paper listed among the references.

THE CHOICE SET

There is given a finite set of *states of the world* S. A typical
state will be denoted by s. I'll assume that the states are numbers,
so that $S = \{1, 2, \ldots, n\}$. In the horse race example, the states
would be all possible outcomes of the horse race, such as (Trigger
first, Swaps second, Kelso third). Counting ties, there are thirteen
possible outcomes.

Also given is an arbitrary set Z of prizes. If you want something
concrete, interpret $Z = R$ and the prizes z as money to be won/lost
by betting on the horse race.

A *simple act* (or *horse race lottery*) is a function $f : S \to Z$.
The interpretation is that in the lottery f, Totrep wins the prize
$f(s)$ if s is the outcome of the horse race. I'll write $f(s)$ and f_s
interchangeably. The set of all such simple acts will be denoted F.
Then Totrep's problem is to choose one horse race lottery from a set
of available lotteries.

To make this problem easier, we envision that Totrep has at his
disposal extraneous randomizing devices. Formally, let P be the set
of all simple probability distributions on Z, and let H be the set of
all functions $h : S \to P$. I'll write $h(s)$ and h_s interchangeably, so
that every $h \in H$ has the form

$$h = (h_1, \ldots, h_n)$$

where $h_s \in P$ for $s = 1, \ldots, n$. I've suppressed the subscript S on
P, standing for "simple", since now S means something else.

The interpretation of this is that Totrep can imagine *compound
lotteries* involving both the horse race and the extraneous randomizing
devices. Each $h \in H$ is such a compound lottery – the horse race is

run, and if the outcome is s the randomizing devices are used to construct the simple probability distribution h_s.

In a formal sense, F can be identified with a particular subset of H, namely the subset of compound lotteries where, after the horse race is run, the roulette wheel lottery that ensues is degenerate. That is, there is a compound lottery h in H that consists of conducting the degenerate simple lottery $\delta_{f(s)}$ if the outcome of the horse race is s. I'll abuse the notation and write $f \in H$, meaning this particular compound lottery.

We shall assume that Totrep's preferences are defined on all of H – in other words, Totrep has preferences on H (given by a binary relation $\succ$), and his preferences on F are simply $\succ$ restricted to F. Some words about the philosophy of this construction seem in order. In most applications of this theory, Totrep's actual available choices will come only from F. What we are doing here is to enrich the choice set with imaginary objects – in this case compound lotteries. And we shall try to get the representation on this expanded choice set. The motive behind this is that axioms stated on a richer set of objects are stronger axioms since they must be true for more cases – at least, if the axioms are of the "for all" and not the "there exist" type – thus axioms posed on the expanded choice set will make it easier to get the representation.

This procedure of enriching the set of items to which preference must apply is quite standard. It makes perfectly good sense in normative applications, *as long as* the Totrep involved is able to envision the extra objects and agree with the axioms applied to them. This need be no more than a thought experiment for Totrep, so long as he is willing to say that it is a valid (i.e., conceivable) thought experiment. But this is a very dicey and perhaps completely useless procedure in descriptive applications. In descriptive applications, axioms are supposed to concern behavior that is observable, so what sense does it make to pose axioms about preferences/choices that are never observed, because the items concerned don't exist? Therefore, insofar as these compound lotteries are just imaginary constructions, and don't correspond to any objects that we might observe Totrep choosing, I think we have to view the theory to follow as being as close to purely normative as anything that we do in this book.

H AS A MIXTURE SPACE

For h and g from H and for $a \in [0,1]$, define $ah + (1-a)g$ by

$$(ah + (1-a)g)(s) = ah(s) + (1-a)g(s) \text{ for } s \in S.$$

That is, two compound lotteries are "mixed" by mixing the objective lotteries that comprise them. For example, if $S = \{1,2\}$ and I depict two compound lotteries h and g as in figure 7.2(a) and (b), then $.6h + .4g$ is the compound lottery in figure 7.2(c).

Then defining $h_a(h,g) = ah + (1-a)g$, we have (with a little bit of checking) a mixture space. (Guesses on what comes next?)

Axiom (7.1). $\succ$ on H is a preference relation.

Axiom (7.2). $h \succ h'$ and $a \in (0,1]$ imply that $ah + (1-a)g \succ ah' + (1-a)g$ for all $g \in H$.

Axiom (7.3). $h \succ h' \succ h''$ imply that there exist $a, b \in (0,1)$ such that $ah + (1-a)h'' \succ h' \succ bh + (1-b)h''$.

These are the same old axioms, but since they are in a very different setting, you might want to give them some additional thought. Do they still make sense normatively? Of course, we know what we will conclude if they are assumed. There is going to be a function $F : H \to R$ that represents $\succ$ and that satisfies $F(ah + (1-a)g) = aF(h) + (1-a)F(g)$. From this corollary to the mixture space theorem, we derive in this setting a very nice result.

Proposition (7.4). Axioms (7.1,2 and 3) are necessary and sufficient for there to exist functions $u_1, \ldots, u_n$, each mapping Z into R, such that

$$(7.5) \qquad h \succ g \text{ iff } \sum_{s=1}^{n} \sum_z u_s(z) h_s(z) > \sum_{s=1}^{n} \sum_z u_s(z) g_s(z).$$

Moreover, if $u'_1, \ldots, u'_n$ is another collection of functions satisfying (7.5), then there exist constants $a > 0$ and b_s such that $au_s + b_s = u'_s$ for each s.

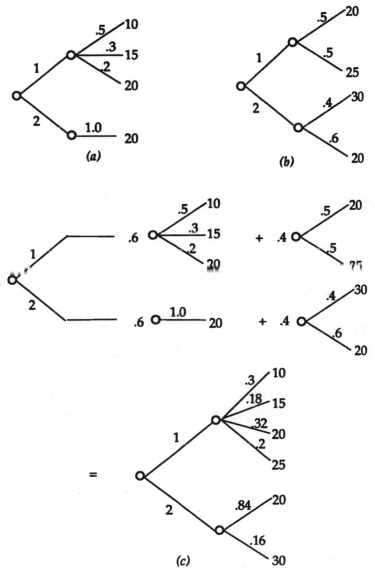

Figure 7.2

Note: In the representation, $\sum_z$ means the sum over all $z \in Z$ such that $h_s(z)$ or $g_s(z)$ are nonzero – that is, sum over the supports of the objective probability distributions.

Proof. That such a representation implies the three axioms is left as an exercise.

Assume that the three axioms hold. Repeating what we said just a minute ago, by the mixture space theorem there exists a function $F : \Pi \to R$ such that

(7.6) $$h \succ g \text{ iff } F(h) > F(g), \text{ and}$$

(7.7) $$F(ah + (1-a)g) = aF(h) + (1-a)F(g).$$

Moreover, this F is unique up to positive affine transformations.

Let F be any function satisfying (7.7). We will now show that it has the form

$$F(h) = \sum_{s=1}^{n} \sum_z u_s(z) h_s(z)$$

for some functions $u_1, \ldots, u_n$. To do this, fix some h^* in H. For any $h \in H$ let $h^1 = (h_1, h_2^*, \ldots, h_n^*), h^2 = (h_1^*, h_2, h_3^*, \ldots, h_n^*)$, etc. That is, h^s is h^* but with h_s replacing h_s^*. Get out your pencil, and observe that

$$\frac{1}{n}h + \frac{n-1}{n}h^* = \sum_{s=1}^{n} \frac{1}{n}h^s.$$

(The reason for getting your pencil is: Put an X in the margin here.) Thus by (7.7) and the standard induction argument on (7.7),

(7.8) $$\frac{1}{n}F(h) + \frac{n-1}{n}F(h^*) = \frac{1}{n}\sum_{s=1}^{n} F(h^s).$$

For $s = 1, \ldots, n$, define $F_s : P \to R$ by

(7.9) $$F_s(p) = F(h_1^*, \ldots, h_{s-1}^*, p, h_{s+1}^*, \ldots, h_n^*) - \frac{n-1}{n}F(h^*).$$

Thus for $h \in H$, this definition gives

$$F_s(h_s) = F(h^s) - \frac{n-1}{n}F(h^*).$$

Summing this last equation over s and dividing by n yields

$$\frac{1}{n}\sum_{s=1}^{n} F_s(h_s) = \frac{1}{n}\sum_{s=1}^{n} F(h^s) - \frac{n-1}{n}F(h^*).$$

Comparing this with (7.8), we have

(7.10)
$$F(h) = \sum_{s=1}^{n} F_s(h_s).$$

Now (7.9) combined with (7.7) yields

$$F_s(ap + (1-a)q) = aF_s(p) + (1-a)F_s(q).$$

For $z \in Z$, let $u_s(z) = F_s(\delta_z)$ – then the usual induction argument, using the fact that the support of distributions in P is finite, shows that
$$F_s(p) = \sum_z p(z)u_s(z).$$

This, combined with (7.6) and (7.10), establishes the desired representation.

The uniqueness result is left as an exercise – it follows from the uniqueness result for F.

FIRST ROULETTE AND THEN THE HORSES

That is all pretty slick and amazing. In fact, it is a bit too slick, because the details of the proof do not really tell you just what is going on. Let me defend that assertion by asking a question: Suppose that, instead of having the horses run first and the roulette wheel lottery spun after, we first spin the roulette wheel and then run the horses. Formally, we start with Z and S, but instead of constructing $H = P^S$ (with F a "subset" of H), we construct F and then Π, which will be the set of all simple probability distributions on F. Informally, the idea is that the roulette wheel pays off in betting tickets (elements of F), which prescribe what in Z will be won as a function of the outcome of the horse race (the state s).

In this setting, we can again pose the mixture space axioms, but applied to Π. Since Π is a set of simple probability distributions, it is of course a mixture space. Before reading further, take a guess: Will this different treatment of the problem matter? Is it important whether we run the horses or spin the roulette wheel first?

It certainly does matter. If we apply the three mixture space axioms to Π, the conclusion is that there is a function $V : F \to R$ such that $\succ$ on Π is represented by expected utility, computed using V. This is much weaker than what we got in Proposition (7.4). This function V doesn't have to be additive over states at all. It could be, for example (if X is some set of real numbers) $V(f) = \max_s f(s)$. It could be $V(f) = (\sum_s f(s))^{1/2}$. Any function V that we can imagine on F will give preferences $\succ_V$ on Π by computing expected utility that will necessarily satisfy the three mixture space axioms on Π. (Remember that those axioms are necessary and sufficient for an expected utility representation on a space of simple probability distributions.)

Why is it that running the horses first makes the mixture space axioms so much more powerful? When you understand the answer to this question, you will understand the magic in the proof of Proposition (7.4).

To get to the answer, consider the question: What sort of correspondence is there between H and Π? That is, how do elements of the horse-race-first construction correspond to elements of the spin-the-wheel-first construction. Given any $\pi \in \Pi$, there is a natural embedding in H: We let

$$h_s(z) = \sum_{\{f \in \text{supp}\pi : f(s) = z\}} \pi(f).$$

That is, for given π, the chances of getting z in state s are the chances of getting a betting ticket f (from π) that gives the prize z in state s. (Is this induced h uniquely defined? Is there any other candidate for the element h that corresponds to a given π?)

Now try to go the other way. Given an $h \in H$, what is the corresponding $\pi \in \Pi$? Here things are not so easy. To see why, let me give you a very concrete example. Suppose, for simplicity, that there are two states, 1 and 2. Suppose that $Z = R$. Consider the element $h \in H$ which is: if the state is 1, you get a 50-50 chance at prizes 10 and 0; and if the state is 2, you get a 50-50 chance at prizes 0 and 10. Now consider two elements of Π: each is a 50-50 gamble; in the first, the prizes are 10 regardless of the state and 0 regardless of the state; and in the second the prizes are (a) 10 in state 1 and 0 in 2 and (b) 0 in 1 and 10 in 2. Both these elements of Π correspond to the element h we just described: Each gives equal chances of 10 and 0 no matter which state prevails. So which of these two elements of Π will we associate with h?

There is no correct answer to this last question, so don't try to find one. The important point is that these two elements (and others besides) in Π all correspond to a single element in H. Now when we define $\succ$ on Π, there is no reason to believe that Totrep is indifferent between any of these elements of Π. At least, unless we pose this as an axiom, it won't follow; it certainly doesn't follow from the mixture space axioms on Π. But when we use H as the basic choice set, we are implicitly assuming that Totrep is indifferent among these many "different" items, since they are all the same as elements of H. In other words, thinking in terms of $\succ$ on Π, by saying that $\succ$ can be induced from preferences on H we are implicitly establishing large indifference classes in Π. Doing so makes the mixture space axioms much more powerful, leading to the additive representation (7.5).

Where do we see this in the proof of the proposition? Go back to where you were told to leave an X in the margin. At that point, essentially, we constructed the same element in H in two different ways in terms of elements in Π. You'll have to do a bit of thinking about all this before that last sentence makes sense to you. But when it does, you've gotten the intuition in the proof. The way on the right-hand side is, of course, extremely convenient, because it allows us to look at the state-by-state components of the given h one at a time, in a sum form. From there, it is all a matter of bookkeeping.

Are the implicit indifference relations that come from defining $\succ$ on H reasonable normatively? To give a complete answer, you'll need at least to understand what those implicit indifference relations are precisely, and I'm leaving that for homework. So I will leave this one as well for you to puzzle at, saying only that the essence of the implicit indifference relations is that all that matters to Totrep in any compound gamble is, conditional on each state s, the marginal distributions over prizes that is entailed in the compound gamble. The joint distributions of the various roulette lotteries with each other are immaterial. In the spirit of the independence axiom (see the discussion in Chapter 5), this seems reasonable. (However see Chapter

14 concerning the Ellsberg paradox.)

There is one further technical question. Suppose we took the three mixture space axioms on Π and added as an axiom those implicit indifference relations. Would we then get the representation (7.5)? More homework.

STATE DEPENDENT AND STATE INDEPENDENT UTILITY

Proposition (7.4) isn't too bad a proposition, but it isn't quite what I had in mind in the introduction. I want there to be a single utility function $u : Z \to R$ and a probability distribution μ on the states of the world $S = \{1, \ldots, n\}$ such that

$$(7.11) \quad h \succ g \text{ iff } \sum_{s=1}^{n} \mu(s)[\sum_z u(z)h_s(z)] > \sum_{s=1}^{n} \mu(s)[\sum_z u(z)g_s(z)].$$

This may seem a bit opaque to you, but it will probably be clearer when I specialize to the case of pure horse lotteries. Then (7.11) becomes

$$(7.12) \quad f \succ f' \text{ iff } \sum_{s=1}^{n} \mu(s)u(f(s)) > \sum_{s=1}^{n} \mu(s)u(f'(s)).$$

By comparison, in this special case, (7.5) is the weaker statement that

$$(7.13) \quad f \succ f' \text{ iff } \sum_{s=1}^{n} u_s(f(s)) > \sum_{s=1}^{n} u_s(f'(s)).$$

You should convince yourself that (7.13) is indeed weaker than (7.12). Representation (7.13) is called an *additively separable representation*. (You will sometimes find it called a "state dependent expected utility" representation. Since the probability distribution over which one is taking expectation is almost completely arbitrary, this is not very good terminology.) In (7.12), the utility does not depend on the state except via the scale factor of the probability of the state, and so (7.12) is called a subjective expected utility representation.

Since we want (7.11) and we have only (7.5), and since (7.5) is necessary and sufficient for the three mixture space axioms, we need to go looking for more axioms. First rule out the trivial case where $h \sim g$ for all $h, g \in H$.

Axiom (7.14). There exist h and g from H such that $h \succ g$.

Next a definition: State s is said to be *null* if $h \sim g$ for all pairs h and g such that $h_{s'} = g_{s'}$ for all $s' \neq s$. That is, if we can't find compound lotteries that differ only in the sth component and that are not indifferent to each other, then the sth state of nature can be ignored and is called null.

Corollary (7.15). Let $\succ$ satisfy Axioms (7.1,2 and 3) and let $\{u_s, s = 1, \ldots, n\}$ represent $\succ$ in the sense of (7.5). Then state s is null if and only if u_s is constant on X. Moreover, Axiom (7.14) implies that there is some non-null state.

The proof is left as an exercise. It is so easy that I won't even list it among the problems at the end.

The key to getting (7.11) from (7.5) is the following axiom.

Axiom (7.16). If $h \in H$, $p, q \in P$ are such that

$$(h_1, \ldots, h_{s-1}, p, h_{s+1}, \ldots, h_n) \succ (h_1, \ldots, h_{s-1}, q, h_{s+1}, \ldots, h_n),$$

for some s, then for all non-null s'

$$(h_1, \ldots, h_{s'-1}, p, h_{s'+1}, \ldots, h_n) \succ (h_1, \ldots, h_{s'-1}, q, h_{s'+1}, \ldots, h_n).$$

That is, if p is better than q in state s, then p is better than q in *all* non-null states s'. Note that in the presence of Axioms (7.1,2 and 3), if Axiom (7.16) holds for any fixed h, then it holds for all h'.

This is a very strong axiom, and it will fail to hold in many applications. For example, suppose that the states are possible weather types instead of the results of horse races and prizes are bundles of picnic equipment. To be more exact, suppose $S = \{\text{shine, rain}\}$, and $p = \delta_z$, $q = \delta_{z'}$, where z and z' are identical bundles of equipment except that z has an umbrella and z' doesn't. Presumably Totrep strictly prefers to have bundle z to z' in state 2 (rain), but is at best indifferent in state 1. Indeed, in state 1 Totrep may strictly prefer z', if the umbrella is heavy and must be carried around. Of course, in this example you wouldn't (or rather, shouldn't) expect a state independent expected utility representation – tastes are quite clearly state dependent. (Recall our discussion about potential "fixes" for this problem in Chapter 4.)

Theorem (7.17). Axioms (7.1,2,3,14 and 16) are necessary and sufficient for there to exist a nonconstant function $u : Z \to R$ and a probability distribution μ on S such that

$$(7.18) \quad h \succ g \text{ iff } \sum_{s=1}^{n} \mu(s)[\sum_{z} u(z)h_s(z)] > \sum_{s=1}^{n} \mu(s)[\sum_{z} u(z)g_s(z)].$$

Moreover, the probability distribution μ is unique, and u is unique up to a positive affine transformation in this representation.

Proof. That the representation implies the axioms and the uniqueness statements are left as exercises.

Suppose that the axioms hold. Then by the first three, there is a representation in the form of (7.5). Moreover, by (7.14) there is at least one non-null state – let $s°$ be one such. Take $p, q \in P$ and let s be any non-null state. Then by the representation, for arbitrary h,

$$\sum_{z} u_s(z)p(z) > \sum_{z} u_s(z)q(z) \text{ iff}$$

$$(h_1, \ldots, h_{s-1}, p, h_{s+1}, \ldots, h_n) \succ (h_1, \ldots, h_{s-1}, q, h_{s+1}, \ldots, h_n)$$

if and only if (by Axiom (7.16))

$$(h_1, \ldots, h_{s°-1}, p, h_{s°+1}, \ldots, h_n) \succ (h_1, \ldots, h_{s°-1}, q, h_{s°+1}, \ldots, h_n)$$

if and only if (by the representation (7.5) again)

$$\sum_{z} u_{s°}(z)p(z) > \sum_{z} u_{s°}(z)q(z).$$

By the uniqueness result for von Neumann-Morgenstern utility for simple lotteries, this says that there are constants $a_s > 0$ and b_s such that

$$a_s u_{s°}(\cdot) + b_s = u_s(\cdot).$$

For null states such constants exist as well – but with $a_s = 0$, since s is null if and only if u_s is constant. So if we define $u(z) = u_{s^\circ}(z)$ (and $a_{s^\circ} = 1$ and $b_{s^\circ} = 0$), (7.5) becomes

$$h \succ g \text{ iff } \sum_{s=1}^{n}\sum_{z}(a_s u(z) + b_s)h_s(z) > \sum_{s=1}^{n}\sum_{z}(a_s u(z) + b_s)g_s(z),$$

which simplifies to

$$h \succ g \text{ iff } \sum_{s=1}^{n}b_s + a_s[\sum_{z}u(z)h_s(z)] > \sum_{s=1}^{n}b_s + a_s[\sum_{z}u(z)g_s(z)].$$

If we cancel the identical b_s terms and then divide both sides of the inequality by the strictly positive term $\sum_{s=1}^{n}a_s$, and then define $\mu(s) = a_s/(\sum_{s'=1}^{n}a_{s'})$, we have (7.18).

This gives the basic development by Anscombe and Aumann. Extensions have been given in the literature to cases where there are different prize sets for different states of nature and to cases where $\mathcal{Z}$ is infinite, in particular. (See Fishburn (1970)) In addition, there has recently been some work using this basic setting to explore lexicographic probabilities, as a step in studying solution concepts in noncooperative game theory.

PROBLEMS

(1) Prove that if the representation (7.5) holds, $\succ$ satisfies the three mixture space axioms in this setting.

(2) Give the details of the proof for the uniqueness result in Proposition (7.4).

(3) After the proof of Proposition (7.4), we discussed what would happen if we had put the roulette lotteries first, so that $\succ$ is defined on Π. We gave there a map from Π into H, which I'll denote ϕ. That is, $\phi : \Pi \to H$ is defined by

$$(\phi(\pi))_s(z) = \sum_{\{f \in \text{supp}(\pi): f(s)=z\}} \pi(f).$$

Consider the three mixture space axioms on Π, to which we add $\pi \sim \pi'$ if $\phi(\pi) = \phi(\pi')$. Do these four axioms give the representation in (7.5)? Provide a proof or a counterexample. If you give a counterexample, can you salvage this result (by adding yet another axiom)? Finally, give as complete a characterization as you can of ϕ-equivalence classes: sets $\{\pi \in \Pi : \phi(\pi) = h\}$ for given h.

(4) Prove that Axioms (7.1,2,3,14 and 16) are necessary for the representation in Theorem (7.17). Prove the asserted uniqueness results in that theorem.

(5) What happens to all this theory if the prize space Z changes with the state? That is, suppose that in state s_n the possible prizes are given by a set Z_n. How much of the development above can you adapt to this setting? If you know that there are at least two prizes that lie in each of the Z_n, how much of this chapter's development can you carry over?

(6) Here is a variation on the results of this section. For the sake of concreteness, let $S = \{1,2\}$ and $Z = [0,1]$, so that compound lotteries look like $h = (p,q)$, where p and q are simple probability measures on Z. Let p° and $p_\circ$ denote, respectively, the degenerate simple probability measures with prizes 1 and 0.

An individual, Macsman (Most Acutely Cautious MAN), makes pairwise comparisons between elements of H – given by the binary relation $\succ$. This binary relation satisfies:

(a) $\succ$ is a preference relation.

(b) $(p,q) \sim (q,p)$ for all $p,q \in P$. (P denotes the set of simple probabilities on $[0,1]$.)

(c) $(p^\circ,q) \succeq (p,q) \succeq (p_\circ,q)$ for all $p,q \in P$.

(d) If $(p^\circ,p) \succeq (p^\circ,q)$, then $(p',p) \succeq (p',q)$ for all $p' \in P$.

(e) If $(p^\circ,p) \succ (p^\circ,q)$, then $(p^\circ,ap + (1-a)r) \succ (p^\circ,aq + (1-a)r)$ for all $a \in (0,1]$ and $r \in P$.

(f) If $(p^\circ,p) \succ (p^\circ,q) \succ (p^\circ,r)$, then there exist a and b in (0,1) such that $(p^\circ,ap + (1-a)r) \succ (p^\circ,q) \succ (p^\circ,bp + (1-b)r)$.

(g) $(p^\circ, p^\circ) \succ (p_\circ, p_\circ)$.

(h) If $(p^\circ, p) \succeq (p^\circ, q)$, then $(p, q) \sim (q, p) \sim (q, q)$.

Using (a) through (g), show that there exists a function $u : [0, 1] \to [0, 1]$ and a complete and transitive ordering $\succeq^*$ on $[0, 1] \times [0, 1]$ such that

$$(p, q) \succeq (p', q') \text{ iff}$$

$$[\sum_z u(z)p(z), \sum_z u(z)q(z)] \succeq^* [\sum_z u(z)p'(z), \sum_z u(z)q'(z)].$$

Next show that (h), together with (a) through (g), imply that

$$(p, q) \succeq (p', q') \text{ iff}$$

$$\min[\sum_z u(z)p(z), \sum_z u(z)q(z)] \geq \min[\sum_z u(z)p'(z), \sum_z u(z)q'(z)].$$

Finally, which of the axioms (7.1,2,3,14 and 16) does $\succ$ satisfy?

8

Subjective Probability

This chapter is something of a break from preference theory, although it plays an important role in the next chapter. We consider subjective probability theory, or how to quantify judgments of likelihood. The story will go roughly as follows: There will be a set S of states of the world. A will denote a collection of subsets of S – for now think of A as the set of *all* subsets of S. Notation $a \in A$ and $a \subseteq S$ will be used.

Totrep, who for the time being is a social scientist, will compare a and b from A and say things like

> "I judge a to be more likely than b."

This will be written $a \succ b$. That is, he will make paired comparisons between *events* (subsets of S) saying when one event is, in his judgment, more likely than a second.

We want to quantify these likelihood judgments with a *probability measure*: a function $p : A \to [0, 1]$ satisfying

$$p(S) = 1 \quad \text{and} \quad p(a \cup b) = p(a) + p(b) \text{ if } a \cap b = \emptyset.$$

This quantification p should be related to $\succ$ by the condition

(8.1) $\qquad\qquad a \succ b$ if and only if $p(a) > p(b)$.

The question is: What conditions on $\succ$ are necessary and sufficient for there to be a p such that (8.1) holds? Note that in this story, Totrep has no stake, financial or otherwise, in the eventual outcome – he is an outside observer who is simply trying to give statements about how likely things are.

PROBABILITY MEASURES

Up to this point, we've dealt almost entirely with simple probability distributions. The few times we spoke of nonsimple probability distributions, we weren't very exact about it. As long as all I care about are simple probabilities on a set S, I can describe the probability as a function p on S that is nonzero on only finitely many elements. But for this chapter, we'll need to go beyond simple probability distributions, and to begin we need to cover some basic definitions and concepts. (For more details on these definitions and concepts, consult a good book on probability theory, such as Chung (1974), or Fishburn (1970, Chapter 10), from which this material is loosely abridged.)

Begin with a set S. A collection of subsets of S, denoted by A, is called a (Boolean) *algebra* if
(a) $S \in A$,
(b) $a \in A$ implies that $a^c \in A$, where a^c denotes $S \setminus a$, the complement of a, and
(c) if a and b are in A then so is $a \cup b$.

It is easy to establish that for an algebra A:
(d) $a_i \in A$ for $i = 1, \ldots, n$ implies that $\bigcup_{i=1}^n a_i \in A$, (or A is closed under finite unions), and
(e) $a_i \in A$ for $i = 1, \ldots, n$ implies that $\bigcap_{i=1}^n a_i \in A$ (or A is closed under finite intersections).

If in addition to (a), (b) and (c) (thus (d) and (e)) the algebra A satisfies
(f) $a_i \in A$ for $i = 1, 2, \ldots$ implies that $\bigcup_{i=1}^\infty a_i \in A$ (A is closed under countable unions)
then A is called a *σ-algebra* or *σ-field*. Moreover, if A is a σ-algebra, it is closed under countable intersections.

Example 1. For any set S, the set of all subsets of S is a σ-algebra.

Example 2. Let $S = [0,1]$ and let A be the set of all subsets of $[0,1]$ that are finite unions of subintervals of $[0,1]$. A is an algebra but is not a σ-algebra.

If S is a set and A is an algebra of subsets of S, then a *probability measure* on (S, A) is a function $p : A \to [0,1]$ such that
(a) $p(S) = 1$, and
(b) if $a, b \in A$ satisfy $a \cap b = \emptyset$, then $p(a \cup b) = p(a) + p(b)$.

It is easy to see from (a) and (b) that

(c) $p(a^c) = 1 - p(a)$ for all $a \in A$.

A probability measure p is called *σ-additive* (or *countably additive*) if, in addition to (a) and (b) (hence (c)), p satisfies

(d) if $a_i \in A, i = 1, 2, \ldots$ are such that $a_i \cap a_j = \emptyset$ for $i \neq j$ and $\bigcup_{i=1}^{\infty} a_i \in A$, then $p(\bigcup_{i=1}^{\infty} a_i) = \sum_{i=1}^{\infty} p(a_i)$.

Some interpretation might be helpful. S is the *outcome* or *state space* of some random experiment. Sets $a \in A$ are *events*, sets of outcomes. $p(a)$ is the *probability* of the set a. Probability is supposed to be a quantification of likelihood, where this will be made precise in a bit. The fact that p may not be defined for all subsets of S (that is, A may be smaller than the set of all subsets of S) can be interpreted as meaning that Totrep is unwilling to make likelihood judgments concerning certain subsets of S; A is the collection of all subsets that Totrep is willing to consider. Having the ability to discuss probability where likelihood judgments need only be expressed for an algebra smaller than the set of all subsets of S makes it a more general, hence a more useful, concept.

One warning: When mathematicians use the term probability, they almost always mean a σ-additive probability measure defined on a σ-algebra. The reason for this is that those extra properties are needed to prove many of the mathematically interesting theorems in probability theory. We'll have need of σ-additive probabilities later in the book, but for now we'll deal with the finitely additive type.

QUALITATIVE PROBABILITY

Back to our main story. Given are a state space S and an algebra of events A. Totrep expresses "is more likely than" by a binary relation $\succ$ on A, and we'd like to get a theorem along the lines of

"The binary relation $\succ$ satisfies —— iff there is a probability measure p on (S, A) such that $a \succ b$ iff $p(a) > p(b)$."

Unhappily, we won't quite achieve this ideal of a single set of necessary and sufficient conditions.

First let's investigate some *necessary* conditions on $\succ$ for there to be representation by a probability measure.

Since p, if it exists, gives a numerical ordering on A, it is necessary that $\succ$ be asymmetric and negatively transitive. (Calling $\succ$ a preference relation would be formally correct, but seems to be inappropriate to the interpretation of this chapter.) Then defining $\succeq$ and $\sim$ in the usual way, these will be complete and transitive and reflexive, symmetric and transitive, respectively.

Since $p(a) \geq 0 = p(\emptyset)$, it is necessary that $a \succeq \emptyset$ for all a.

Since $p(S) = 1 > 0 = p(\emptyset)$, it is necessary that $S \succ \emptyset$.

Suppose $a \cap c = b \cap c = \emptyset$. Then if p exists, $p(a \cup c) = p(a) + p(c)$ and $p(b \cup c) = p(b) + p(c)$. So, in such circumstances, it is necessary that $a \succ b$ iff $a \cup c \succ b \cup c$.

The four conditions give what is called a qualitative probability.

Definition (8.2). A binary relation $\succ$ on A is called a *qualitative probability* if
(a) $\succ$ is asymmetric and negatively transitive,
(b) $a \succeq \emptyset$ for all $a \in A$,
(c) $S \succ \emptyset$, and
(d) $[a \cap c = b \cap c = \emptyset]$ implies $[a \succ b$ iff $a \cup c \succ b \cup c]$.

Then summarizing the above discussion, we have:

Proposition (8.3). A necessary condition for $\succ$ to be represented by a probability measure is that $\succ$ is a qualitative probability.

It is easy to come up with other necessary conditions, such as

$$a \succ b \text{ iff } b^c \succ a^c.$$

(Why is this necessary?) But this can be obtained from the conditions in (8.2). Decompose S into four disjoint sets

$$I = a \setminus b, \quad II = b \setminus a, \quad III = a \cap b, \quad \text{and } IV = (a \cup b)^c.$$

It may help to draw a Venn diagram. Note that $a = I \cup III$, $a^c = II \cup IV$, $b = II \cup III$ and $b^c = I \cup IV$, where each of these is a disjoint union. Then $a \succ b$ iff $I \cup III \succ II \cup III$ iff $I \succ II$ iff $I \cup IV \succ II \cup IV$ iff $b^c \succ a^c$.

Similarly:

Proposition (8.4). If $\succ$ is a qualitative probability, then
(a) $b \subseteq c$ implies $S \succeq c \succeq b \succeq \emptyset$,
(b) $a \sim b$ and $a \cap c = \emptyset$ imply $a \cup c \succeq b \cup c$,
(c) $a \succ b$ and $a \cap c = \emptyset$ imply $a \cup c \succ b \cup c$,
(d) $a \sim b, c \sim d, a \cap c = b \cap d = \emptyset$ imply $a \cup c \sim b \cup d$,
(e) $a \sim b, c \sim d, a \cap c = \emptyset$ imply $a \cup c \succeq b \cup d$, and
(f) $a \succeq b, c \succ d, a \cap c = \emptyset$ imply $a \cup c \succ b \cup d$.

The question is, since it is necessary for a representation that $\succ$ be a qualitative probability, what else will be sufficient? Maybe we'll get lucky and this will be necessary and sufficient. (Well, I already told you that this wouldn't happen.)

In 1959, Kraft, Pratt and Seidenberg showed that for finite S, being a qualitative probability is insufficient. It takes a five element set to show this. Let $S = \{s, t, u, v, w\}$ and abbreviate subsets such as $\{s, t, w\}$ by stw. Define $\succ$ as by

$$suv \succ tw \succ stv \succ sw \succ uv \succ tv \succ stu \succ w \succ$$

$$tu \succ sv \succ v \succ su \succ st \succ u \succ t \succ s \succ \emptyset$$

(with the rest of $\succ$ given by $a \succ b$ iff $b^c \succ a^c$). Then $\succ$ is a qualitative probability (which you can verify), but it cannot be represented by a probability measure p. For supposing that there was a probability representation, then
$tu \succ sv$ implies $p(t) + p(u) > p(s) + p(v)$,
$v \succ su$ implies $p(v) > p(s) + p(u)$,
$sw \succ uv$ implies $p(s) + p(w) > p(u) + p(v)$, and
$suv \succ tw$ implies $p(s) + p(u) + p(v) > p(t) + p(w)$.
Sum the right and left hand sides of these four inequalities, and you get

$$2p(s) + p(t) + 2p(u) + 2p(v) + p(w) > 2p(s) + p(t) + 2p(u) + 2p(v) + p(w),$$

which won't be easy to satisfy.

Kraft, Pratt and Seidenberg go on to show exact necessary and sufficient conditions for there to be a quantitative probability representation of $\succ$, when S is a finite set. We won't pursue these, however, and turn instead to the approach pioneered by Savage.

BASICS OF THE SAVAGE APPROACH

Before launching into the details, however, a few words of introduction. For the remainder of this chapter and in the next, we take up Savage's axiomatization of choice under uncertainty, which begins with an axiomatization of quantitative probability from qualitative probability. Savage's theory, which is the crowning glory of choice theory, has its difficult mathematical moments, although many of the steps are not so hard. In any event, we will not really prove much of anything here. Instead of providing proofs, my objectives for the rest of this chapter and the next is to take you on a guided tour of Savage's theory, as to how it is put together and what are some of the key ideas. For those steps where the proofs are not difficult, I'll so indicate; providing proofs then will become exercises. Those of you who wish to chase down all the details should consult Savage's classic "Foundations of Statistics." As always, Fishburn (1970) gives a very nice and complete treatment.

The first thing to understand is that while the Pratt, etc. methodology is intended for finite S, Savage's techniques are intended precisely for "large" S (infinite and more besides). Indeed, the basic idea won't work otherwise.

This basic idea is built up as follows. Suppose that for every $n = 1, 2, \ldots$, the set S can be partitioned into 2^n equally likely events. That is, for each n there are sets

$$a_1^n, a_2^n, \ldots, a_{2^n}^n$$

all from A, such that $a_j^n \cap a_k^n = \emptyset$ for $j \neq k$, $a_j^n \sim a_k^n$ for all j and k, and $\bigcup_{i=1}^{2^n} a_i^n = S$. One way that this would be possible would be to have a fair coin lying around, which is flipped infinitely many times. Then for each n, the events a_j^n would be the various strings of heads and tails on the first n flips, irrespective of what else happens. If the coin is "fair," then Totrep would say that these events are equally likely.

Note that such a_j^n can exist only if S is large – it certainly must be the case that S is infinite. Moreover, no single state $s \in S$ can have positive probability, since then it would be impossible to have a partition that divides S into pieces of probability all smaller than the probability of this s. However S need not be uncountable; on this point see problem (4).

Of course, if such a_j^n exists, and if p is a probability measure representing $\succ$, then it would have to be the case that $p(a_j^n) = 1/2^n$ for all j and n.

Still supposing such a_j^n exist, we can use them to find $p(b)$ for any other event b. Fix an event b. For each n, there is a smallest k such that

$$\bigcup_{j=1}^{k} a_j^n \succ b.$$

(This excludes the special case where $b \sim S$, but that case is easy to handle.) In view of the dependence on n, let this k be called $k(n)$. Then if p exists, it is clear that

$$(k(n) - 1)/2^n \le p(b) < k(n)/2^n.$$

So consider defining

(8.5)
$$p(b) = \lim_{n \to \infty} k(n)/2^n.$$

Note well the technique. Having these sets a_j^n is like having a set of successively finer measuring rulers – each puts better (more fine) bounds on $p(b)$, and in the limit we get $p(b)$ exactly.

This is a procedure that is bound to work *if* there is a representation p and if these equi-partitions of S exist. Moreover, it is obvious from the procedure that p, when it exists, must be unique – any other representation p' would have to put $p'(a_j^n) = 1/2^n$, thus $(k(n) - 1)/2^n \le p'(b) < k(n)/2^n$, and thus $p'(b) = \lim_n k(n)/2^n$.

But will this work? If $\succ$ is a qualitative probability and if these partitions do exist, will p defined by (8.5) be a probability measure and will it represent $\succ$ in the sense of (8.1)? The answer is almost, but not quite.

Proposition (8.6). If $\succ$ is a qualitative probability and if these partitions exist, then
(a) the limit in (8.5) exists (a technical matter; ignore it if you don't understand it),
(b) p so defined is a probability measure, and
(c) $a \succeq b$ implies $p(a) \ge p(b)$.

The proof of this proposition is really fairly simple. The problem with the result is that (c) isn't quite enough – it may be that $a \succ b$ but $p(a) = p(b)$.

FINE AND TIGHT QUALITATIVE PROBABILITIES

There are two things that can go wrong, so that $a \succ b$ but $p(a) = p(b)$. To exhibit these two things, I'll need a bit of notation. Let $S_1 = [0, 1]$ and let A_1 be the algebra of subsets that are finite unions of subintervals of S_1. For any set $a_1 \in A_1$, let $\ell(a_1)$ be the "length" of a_1 – the sum of the lengths of the disjoint subintervals that make up a_1. Similarly, let $S_2 = [2, 3]$, let A_2 be the algebra of subsets that are finite unions of subintervals of S_2, and for $a_2 \in A_2$ let $\ell(a_2)$ be the length of a_2. Finally, let $S = [0, 1] \cup [2, 3] = S_1 \cup S_2$, and let A be the algebra for all subsets of S such that $a \in A$ if $a \cap S_1 \in A_1$ and $a \cap S_2 \in A_2$. For subsets $a \in A$, I'll generally write a_1 for $a \cap S_1$ and a_2 for $a \cap S_2$, so that $a = a_1 \cup a_2$.

Example 1. For $a = a_1 \cup a_2$ and $b = b_1 \cup b_2$, define $a \succ b$ if $\ell(a_1) > \ell(b_1)$ or if $[\ell(a_1) = \ell(b_1)$ and $\ell(a_2) > \ell(b_2)]$. This is a lexicographic probability. You can verify that $\succ$ so defined is a qualitative probability and that S can be equi-partitioned – take

$$a_j^n = [(j-1)/2^n, j/2^n) \cup [2 + (j-1)/2^n, 2 + j/2^n)$$

except for $j = 2^n$, when you add the two right hand endpoints. It is also straightforward to verify that p defined by (8.5) will satisfy

$$p(a_1 \cup a_2) = \ell(a_1).$$

But this doesn't represent $\succ$: Consider $a = [0, .5] \cup [2, 2.5]$ and $b = [0, .5] \cup [2, 2.4]$. Then $a \succ b$ but $p(a) = p(b) = 1/2$. It is also not hard to show that there is no probability measure p that represents $\succ$. (Although there are easier ways to show this, one way to do so from first principles is to go back to the proof that a lexicographic preference relation cannot have a numerical representation, given in Chapter 3.)

What's gone wrong in this example with our surefire procedure (8.5)? Look at a and b above. We have $a \succ b$ but the difference between them is smaller than any of our equi-partitioning sets. That is, for any n, when we have enough pieces of our equi-partition so that we are (just) larger than b, we are larger as well than a. Hence even though $a \succ b$, for every n the $k(n)$ that "works" for b also works for a.

Example 2. For a and b as above, define $a \succ b$ if $\ell(a_1) + \ell(a_2) > \ell(b_1) + \ell(b_2)$ or if $\ell(a_1) + \ell(a_2) = \ell(b_1) + \ell(b_2)$ and $\ell(a_1) > \ell(b_1)$. Again $\succ$ is a qualitative probability and the same equi-partitions as before will do. Moreover, p defined by (8.5) will give

$$p(a) = [\ell(a_1) + \ell(a_2)]/2,$$

which doesn't represent $\succ$: If $a = [0, .5]$ and $b = [2.2.5]$, then $a \succ b$ yet $p(a) = p(b) = .5$.

How did we screw up this time? This time it's even worse – $a \succ b$ yet there is no space at all "between" a and b. That is, if c is any set such that $b \cup c \succ b$, then $b \cup c \succ a$. So we could hardly expect to be able to squeeze a member of our equi-partitions between a and b.

Definitions (8.6). A qualitative probability $\succ$ is *fine* if for all $a \succ \emptyset$, there is a finite partition of S no member of which is as likely as a. A qualitative probability $\succ$ is *tight* if whenever $a \succ b$, there is some set c such that $a \succ b \cup c \succ b$.

In the first example, we have a qualitative probability that is not fine – the set [2,2.5] is more likely than $\emptyset$, yet any finite partition of S will contain at least one element that is more probable than [2,2.5].

In the second example, we have a qualitative probability that is not tight. The sets $a = [0, .5]$ and $b = [2, 2.5]$ are such that if b is increased by any set c that makes it more likely, then the increased set is at least as likely as (indeed, in the example is more likely than) the other. Yet $a \succ b$.

The usefulness of these definitions comes in

Proposition (8.7). If $\succ$ is a qualitative probability and if the equi-partitions exist, then p defined as in (8.5) satisfies (8.1) if and only if $\succ$ is both fine and tight.

This isn't too hard to prove.

THE SAVAGE THEORY

We're almost done. The trouble with this result is that having
equi-partitions, fineness and tightness are not the most intuitive things
in the world – that is, they are not very good as normative axioms.
Fineness isn't too bad, but tightness is a bit harder to understand.
And the equi-partition thing – well, it makes sense if Totrep has a
fair coin, but this is imposing a little bit of objective probability into
what is supposed to be a totally subjective story.

For the remainder of this chapter, assume that the algebra A of
subsets of S is the algebra of all subsets of S.

Axiom (8.8). If a and b are such that $a \succ b$, then there is a finite
partition $\{c_1, \ldots, c_n\}$ of S such that $a \succ b \cup c_k$ for every $k = 1, \ldots, n$.

Note that the partition $\{c_1, \ldots, c_n\}$ needn't be a partition into
equi-probable sets – just that the "biggest" c_k must be small enough
to fit between a and b. Savage tells the following story: Suppose
Totrep has a silver dollar. It isn't clear (and indeed, it probably
isn't true – whatever that means) that the bias of the silver dollar is
.5 exactly, but most Totreps would be willing to say that the bias is
between, say, .8 and .2. Then if we flip it enough times, the probability
of any particular string of heads and tails gets small – if I flip it, say,
1000 times, the probability of any particular string is no more than
$(.8)^{1000}$. The point is that I, and most any Totrep, would agree that
if $a \succ b$, I can flip the coin enough times so that the occurrence of b
or any one particular string of heads and tails is less likely than the
occurrence of a. This is exactly the axiom above. Note that there is
a bit of objective probability in this story, but only a very small bit.

Although the story in this axiom seems easier to swallow, the
conclusion that it gives remains the same.

Proposition (8.9). If $\succ$ is a qualitative probability, then $\succ$ satisfies
Axiom (8.8) if and only if $\succ$ is fine and tight. And either of these is
sufficient to guarantee the existence of equi-probable partitions of S.

The first statement in this proposition is fairly straightforward.
The second is the one really difficult step in this development. Try
it if you wish, but you can also see Savage. Collecting everything

together, we have the theorem:

Theorem (8.10). $\succ$ is a qualitative probability and satisfies axiom
(8.8) if and only if there exists a probability measure p on (S, A)
such that
(a) $a \succ b$ iff $p(a) > p(b)$, and
(b) for all $a \in A$ and $r \in [0, 1]$ there exists a subset b of a such that
$p(b) = rp(a)$.
Moreover, the representation p is unique.

Note that (b), among other things, guarantees the existence of equi-
probable partitions. Also, Axiom (8.8) requires that S is infinite and
that $\{s\} \sim \emptyset$ for all $s \in S$, thus by finite additivity $\{s_1, \ldots, s_n\} \sim \emptyset$ for
all finite subsets $\{s_1, \ldots, s_n\}$. We still don't have an axiomatization
of probability that works for finite S (or for countably infinite S that
gives σ-additive probability).

PROBLEMS

(1) Prove that (a) through (c) in the definition of an algebra (page
116) imply (d) and (e).

(2) For example 2 on page 116, show that this is an algebra but not
a σ-algebra.

(3) Let $S = [0, 1]$. What is the smallest algebra of subsets of S that
contains all the singleton sets? What is the smallest σ-algebra that
contains all the singleton sets?

(4) (This one takes some mathematical sophistication.) Let $S = \{0, 1, \ldots\}$, and let A be the algebra of all subsets of S. For any
subset $a \subseteq S$, define $f_n(a)$ as the cardinality of $a \cap \{0, 1, \ldots, n\}$
divided by $n + 1$. That is, $f_n(a)$ is the proportion of the first
$n + 1$ nonnegative integers in a. Define $\overline{f}(a) = \lim \sup_n f_n(a)$, and
$\underline{f}(a) = \lim \inf_n f_n(a)$. Is $p^*(a) = (\overline{f}(a) + \underline{f}(a))/2$ a probability measure on A? If not, can you find a probability measure p on A that
satisfies $\underline{f}(a) \leq p(a) \leq \overline{f}(a)$? (For those of you who know some
probability theory, remember that no one said anything here about

σ-additivity.)

(5) Prove Proposition (8.4).

(6) Show that if S has four elements and if $\succ$ is a qualitative probability, then there is a (quantitative) probability representation of $\succ$.

(7) Prove Proposition (8.6).

(8) For the two examples on page 120, verify that in each case we have qualitative probabilities, and verify that the procedure (8.5) will give rise to the two probability measures that are claimed. Verify that in each case there is no probability representation of $\succ$ in the full sense of (8.1). Finally, does example 1 satisfy tightness? Does example 2 satisfy fineness?

(9) Prove the first statement in Proposition (8.9). (If you want to prove both parts of the proposition, be my guest.)

9

Savage's Theory of Choice Under Uncertainty

In the last section we closed with Savage's theory of subjective probability. This is actually part of his theory of choice under uncertainty, which is, as much as anything, the crowning achievement of single-person decision theory. Reviewing developments to date, we began with von Neumann-Morgenstern utility theory, where the uncertainty was objective. After this, and after diddling around with properties of utility functions for money, subjective probability made an appearance in the Anscombe-Aumann theory of choice, where subjective and objective uncertainty were both present, and where the existence of objective uncertainty in the form of extraneous randomizing devices made life relatively easy. The last chapter concerned pure subjective probability theory – no preferences, just "more likely than" judgments, and no objective probabilities. Now we look at *choice* theory, or "preferred to" judgments, with no objective uncertainties.

As in the last chapter, I'm not going to try to give proofs of the major results. Instead, the objective of this chapter is to cover the basic logical flow for obtaining the representation. For the details of the proofs, either provide them yourself or consult Savage or Fishburn.

THE SAVAGE FORMULATION

The basics of the Savage formulation were given in Chapter 4. I'll repeat them here:

There is a set Z of *prizes or consequences*.

There is a set S of *states of the world*. Each $s \in S$ is a compilation of all characteristics/factors about which Totrep is uncertain and which

127

are relevant to the consequences that will ensue from his choice. The set S is to be an exhaustive list of mutually exclusive states – some one s is/will be the state.

The algebra of *all* subsets of S is denoted A.

An *act* or *action* is a function $f : S \to Z$, where $f(s)$ represents the consequences of taking action f if the state of the world is s. The set of all act is the set of all functions from S to Z, denoted by F.

A binary relation $\succ$ gives Totrep's *preferences* over the set F of acts.

For $z, y \in Z$, I'll use notation like $f \succ z$ and $z \succ y$, where z means here the act which always gives the prize z.

THE SEVEN SAVAGE AXIOMS

Axiom (9.1). $\succ$ is a preference relation.

Accordingly, define $\succeq$ and $\sim$.

Axiom (9.2). There exist x and y from Z such that $x \succ y$.

This second axiom is purely structural and should bother no one. Now for a real axiom.

Axiom (9.3). Suppose f, g, f' and $g' \in F$ and $a \subseteq S$ are such that
(a) $f(s) = f'(s)$ and $g(s) = g'(s)$ for all $s \in a$, and
(b) $f(s) = g(s)$ and $f'(s) = g'(s)$ for all $s \notin a$.
Then $f \succ g$ if and only if $f' \succ g'$.

It is easiest to understand this axiom with a picture. Refer to figure 9.1. Note that in comparing f with g and f' with g', we only "need" to be concerned with how they compare on a. This is because they agree (f with g and f' with g') on a^c. And they "ought" to compare the same way on a, because $f = f'$ and $g = g'$ on a. Of course, need and ought are in quotation marks, because the axiom is the force behind those two prescriptions. Note that the "acts don't influence probabilities" assumption is written into this axiom, since if f changed the probabilities inside a in a different way from f'

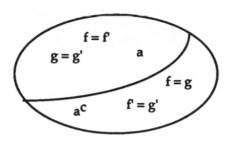

Figure 9.1

(presumably because they differ on a^c) then the axiom wouldn't be reasonable.

Because of this axiom, it makes sense to talk about *conditional preference*.

Definition (9.4). Define $f \succ g$ *given* a if $f' \succ g'$ where $f' = f$ and $g' = g$ on a and $f' = g'$ off of a.

The axiom says that this is a sensible definition, in the sense that it doesn't matter what f' and g' are off of a (as long as they are the same), all that matters are the "on a" parts of f and g.

Lemma (9.5). The relation "$\succ$ given a" is a preference relation if Axioms (9.1 and 3) hold. Also "$\succeq$ given a" and "$\sim$ given a" defined directly from "$\succ$ given a" satisfy
(a) $f \succeq g$ given a iff $f' \succeq g'$ for f' and g' as above, and
(b) $f \sim g$ given a iff $f' \sim g'$ for f' and g' as above.

This proof is very easy, and it is left as an exercise.

Definition (9.6). $a \subseteq S$ is called *null* if for all f and g from F, $f \sim g$ given a.

Null events will turn out to be those with zero probability. The force of Axiom (9.2) is that S is not a null event.

Axiom (9.7). If a is not null, and if $f(s) = x$ and $g(s) = y$ for all

$s \in a$, then $f \succ g$ given a iff $x \succ y$.

This is the "utility is not state dependent" axiom. You can see how it compares with the similar axiom in the Anscombe-Aumann theory.

Axiom (9.8). Suppose $x, y, x', y', f, g, f', g', a$ and b are such that
(a) $x \succ y$ and $x' \succ y'$,
(b) $f(s) = x$ and $f'(s) = x'$ on a, and $f(s) = y$ and $f'(s) = y'$ on a^c, and
(c) $g(s) = x$ and $g'(s) = x'$ on b, and $g(s) = y$ and $g'(s) = y'$ on b^c.
Then $f \succ g$ iff $f' \succ g'$.

This one is quite a mouthful. Its interpretation runs as follows: The acts f and g are pictured in figure 9.2(a). Since $x \succ y$, the act f is a "win" (gives the better prize x) if a happens, while g is a win if b happens. Presumably, then $f \succ g$ if and only if a is judged more likely by Totrep than b. Similarly, as $x' \succ y'$, $f' \succ g'$ if and only if a is more likely than b, since f' wins (gives the better prize) if a happens, and g' wins if b happens. See figure 9.2(b). So the two pairs should compare similarly: $f \succ g$ iff a is judged to be more likely than b iff $f' \succ g'$.

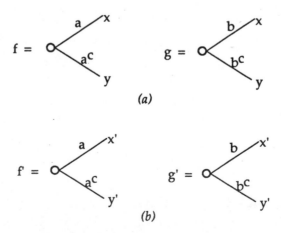

Figure 9.2

This axiom also has some of the "acts don't affect probabilities" flavor to it. What would you think of this axiom if a under f was more likely than b under g, yet a under f' was less likely than b under g'?

Axiom (9.9). For all $a \subseteq S$,
(a) $[f \succ g(s)$ given a for all $s \in a]$ implies $f \succeq g$ given a.
(b) $[g(s) \succ f$ given a for all $s \in a]$ implies $g \succeq f$ given a.

This is the "sure-thing principle," a version of which we saw back in Chapter 5 when we talked about extending von Neumann-Morgenstern utility to nonsimple probability distributions. Its role here is exactly as there.

Axiom (9.10). For all f and g from F such that $f \succ g$ and for all $x \in X$, there is a finite partition of S such that for every a in the partition,
(a) $[f'(s) = x$ for $s \in a, f'(s) = f(s)$ for $s \in a^c]$ implies $f' \succ g$, and
(b) $[g'(s) = x$ for $s \in a, g'(s) = g(s)$ for $s \in a^c]$ implies $f \succ g'$.

The picture to think of is: Cut S up into finitely many (but many) pieces, and for each piece, modify f so that it is identically x on the piece. If the piece is small enough in terms of its likelihood relative to how bad is x and how much better than g is f, then as $f \succ g$, the changed f (which is called f' in the axiom) is still strictly better than g. And for each piece in turn, change g so that it is x on the piece; the changed g (or g') will be strictly worse than f, if the pieces are small in terms of their likelihood relative to how good is x and how much worse than f is g.

The entire force in this axiom comes in the requirement that the partition must be finite – we must be able to break S into *finitely* many pieces each of which is small enough. This is an extremely powerful axiom, that cuts in many ways. Two of the most important are:

(1) It is a restriction on how good or bad a particular prize can be. For suppose there was a super-good prize x°, so good that any positive probability of getting it made the corresponding act better than some act f. Then, so long as there is some g with $f \succ g$, this axiom would fail. Similarly, this rules out super-bad prizes. So this axiom serves as

the Archimedean axiom, when it comes time to get utility functions. (But see problem 5.)

(2) It is a restriction on how small a difference there can be between two acts f and g and still have $f \succ g$. Suppose that $x = \{\$1, \$0\}$. Let $g(s) = 0$ for every state s and let $f(s) = 0$ except on an "impossible event" – say $f(s) = \$1$ for the state s where I flip a coin, it rises to a height of ten feet, stops, then rises to a height of twenty feet, and there breaks out in a chorus of "Dixie." Presumably you cannot partition all the states of the world into finitely many events, each less likely than the one described, so that by the axiom $f \sim g$. The difference between f and g is too small to have $f \succ g$. Again the sense of the axiom is Archimedean, and it will wind up playing the role of the fine and tight assumptions in the part of the overall development that has to do with probability theory.

THE SAVAGE DEVELOPMENT

The first step in the theoretical development is to obtain probabilities from preferences. It seems natural to say that Totrep believes that a is more likely than b if whenever $x \succ y$, $f = x$ on a and $f = y$ on a^c, and $g = x$ on b and $g = y$ on b^c, it follows that $f \succ g$. That is, Totrep thinks that a is more likely than b if he would rather take his chances on getting a good prize if a and a bad one if a^c than on getting the same good prize if b and the same bad one on b^c. Formally, define

Definition (9.11). For a and b in A, say that a is *more likely than* b according to Totrep, written $a \mathrel{\dot\succ} b$, if for all x and y from Z such that $x \succ y$, if f and g are defined by

$$f(s) = \begin{cases} x & \text{for } s \in a \\ y & \text{for } s \notin a \end{cases} \qquad \text{and} \qquad g(s) = \begin{cases} x & \text{for } s \in b \\ y & \text{for } s \notin b \end{cases},$$

then $f \succ g$.

By Axiom (9.8), it doesn't matter which x and y are used to define f and g – whatever answer we get for one we will get for all. In other words, in the definition we could have used "for some x and $y \ldots$" instead of "for all $\ldots$," and so long as the axiom holds, the definition doesn't change. Also, according to Axiom (9.2) there exists at least one pair x and y that can be used to make the comparison.

Proposition (9.12). If Axioms (9.1,2,3,7 and 8) hold, then the binary relation $\overset{\cdot}{\succ}$ as defined above is a qualitative probability.

The proof is fairly easy, so I'll only show one part: If $a \cap d = b \cap d = \emptyset$, then $a \overset{\cdot}{\succ} b$ iff $a \cup d \overset{\cdot}{\succ} b \cup d$. Suppose that a, b, and d are as above. Take $x \succ y$ and let f, g, f' and g' be defined as follows:

	$f =$	$g =$	$f' =$	$g' =$
On $a \setminus b$:	x	y	x	y
On $a \cap b$:	x	x	x	x
On $b \setminus a$:	y	x	y	x
On d:	y	y	x	x
On $(a \cup b \cup d)^c$:	y	y	y	y

By definition of $\overset{\cdot}{\succ}$ and by Axiom (9.8), $a \overset{\cdot}{\succ} b$ iff $f \succ g$, and $a \cup d \overset{\cdot}{\succ} b \cup d$ iff $f' \succ g'$. So we need to show that $f \succ g$ iff $f' \succ g'$.

But $f = f'$ and $g = g'$ on d^c, and $f = g(= y)$ and $f' = g'(= x)$ on d so that $f \succ g$ iff $f' \succ g'$ follows from Axiom (9.3).

Proposition (9.13). If in addition Axiom (9.10) holds, then the qualitative probability $\overset{\cdot}{\succ}$ satisfies Axiom (8.8), so by Theorem (8.10), there exists a probability measure p on (S, A) such that
(a) $a \overset{\cdot}{\succ} b$ iff $p(a) > p(b)$, and
(b) for all $a \subseteq S$ and $r \in [0, 1]$, there exists a subset b of A such that $p(b) = rp(a)$.
Moreover, this p is unique.

Verifying that Axiom (8.8) is implied by (9.10) in this context is trivial.

Before passing on to the rest of the Savage theory, a comment about the philosophy that underlies the above is called for. In the last chapter, we had Totrep making pairwise comparisons between events, telling us when he thought one was more likely than the other. Probability was a quantification of this "more likely than" binary relation. Here, in contrast, "more likely than" judgments are *implicit* judgments, made by making preference judgments between various "win-lose" acts. Most adherents to the subjectivist or personalist school of probability would argue that the second procedure is philosophically correct – "more likely than" judgments make sense only as part of a choice process – they should arise (only) from preferences among actions.

Having obtained probability, we turn to utility. Assume that the Axioms (9.1,2,3,7,8, and 10) hold, so that p is given by the last proposition.

For $f \in F$, define a probability measure p_f on Z (on the algebra of all of the subsets of Z) by, for $Y \subseteq Z$,

$$p_f(Y) = p(\{s \in S : f(s) \in Y\}).$$

That is, $p_f(Y)$ is simply the probability that the outcome falls in Y, if action f is taken. (Notation freaks will doubtless be overjoyed to learn that a mathematician would write this definition $p_f = p \circ f^{-1}$.)

Act f is called a *simple act* if p_f is a simple probability. Write F_s for the set of all simple acts. The first step in the expected utility story is to get an expected utility representation for $\succ$ on F_s. This is done in two steps. First:

Proposition (9.14). Suppose f and g are two simple acts such that $p_f = p_g$. Then $f \sim g$.

That is, we have to begin by proving the implicit "Axiom Zero" for von Neumann-Morgenstern utility – that all that matters is the probability distribution over the prizes and not the particular states in which particular prizes are received. This really is something to prove here – indeed, without Axiom (9.7) this proposition wouldn't stand a chance of being true.

This is not an trivial thing to prove. In Fishburn (1970), for example, it takes about two pages, with two intermediate lemmas. (It is Theorem 14.3 in Fishburn, if you'd like to have a look.) I won't bore you with the details here. But to illustrate how complicated things are, let me do the very first step (which does give some insight into how the proof runs):

Suppose there is some x and two acts f and g such that $p_f(\{x\}) = p_g(\{x\}) = 1$. That is, both f and g give prize x with probability one. Note well, this doesn't mean that f and g are the same – only that they differ on (at most) a set of probability zero. The question is: Does this imply that $f \sim x \sim g$, thus $f \sim g$?

Yes. Suppose conversely that $f \not\succ x$. Also, consider the case where there exists a y such that $x \succ y$. (The other case is done symmetrically.) Then

(a) Let $a = \{s : f(s) \neq x\}$. Since $f \not\succ x$, a is not null.

(b) By Axiom (9.7), if $f' = x$ on a^c and $f' = y$ on a then $x \succ f'$.

(c) By Axiom (9.10), S can be partitioned into finitely many sets $a_1, \ldots, a_n$ such that for each $k = 1, \ldots, n$, if $g^k = x$ on $(a_k)^c$ and $g^k = y$ on a_k, then $g^k \succ f'$. By the definition of $\dot\succ$, this implies that $a \dot\succ a_k$ for each k, or $p(a) > p(a_k)$ for each k.

(d) But $p(a) = 0$ by assumption, and $\sum_{k=1}^{n} p(a_k) = 1$. Contradiction.

See, nothing comes easy. It really does take two pages to establish this Axiom Zero.

Proposition (9.14) says that we can use $\succ$ to define a binary relation $\succ^s$ on the set of all simple probability measures on Z, denoted Q_s. How? If $q \in Q_s$, then judicious use of part (b) of Proposition (9.13) allows me to construct an act $f \in F_s$ such that $q = p_f$. So for q and q' from Q_s, letting f and f' be such that $q = p_f$ and $q' = p_{f'}$, I can define

$$q \succ^s q' \text{ if } f \succ f'.$$

Proposition (9.14) assures me that it doesn't matter which f and f' I take to satisfy $p_f = q$ and $p_{f'} = q'$, hence $\succ^s$ is well defined (doesn't depend on the choice of f and f').

Proposition (9.15). The binary relation $\succ^s$ so defined satisfies the three mixture space axioms, so there exists a function $u : X \to R$ such that for q and q' from Q_s

(9.16) $$q \succ^s q' \text{ iff } \sum_z q(z)u(z) > \sum_z q'(z)u(z),$$

or, equivalently, for f and g from F_s,

(9.17) $$f \succ g \text{ iff } \sum_{z \in \text{supp}(p_f)} p_f(z)u(z) > \sum_{z \in \text{supp}(p_g)} p_g(z)u(z).$$

Moreover, this u is unique up to a positive affine transformation.

Another two page proof. Good luck if you want to give it a try. It isn't impossible. Just tedious. If you do attempt it, note well how Axiom (9.3) is what gives the substitution axiom.

If Z were a finite set, or we were content with looking only at simple acts, we'd be done. But if we want to go whole hog, the last remaining step is extend Proposition (9.15) from simple acts to general ones. To do so requires a general definition of the integral. That is, for $f \in F_s$, "expected utility" is defined quite easily as

$$\sum_{z \in \text{supp}(p_f)} p_f(z)u(z) = \sum_{z \in \text{supp}(p_f)} p(\{s : f(s) = z\})u(z).$$

The question is, how do we extend this definition of expected utility to non-simple acts? I ducked this question back in Chapter 5, and now is no time to stop ducking. See one of the standard reference books if you wish. I will say that this generalization can be done, and in a manner that agrees with standard methods of integration (Riemann, Riemann-Stieltjes, Lebesque). And then, with Axiom 9.9 finally added into the stew, we obtain the classic result:

Theorem (9.16). Axioms (9.1,2,3,7,8,9 and 10) are sufficient for the following conclusions:
(a) $\succ$ as defined above is a qualitative probability, and there exists a unique probability measure p on A such that $a \succ b$ iff $p(a) > p(b)$.
(b) For all $a \in A$ and $r \in [0, 1]$, there exists a subset b of a such that $p(b) = rp(a)$.
(c) For p given above, there is a bounded utility function $u : X \to R$ such that $f \succ g$ iff $E[u(f(s)); p] > E[u(g(s)); p]$, where these are expected utilities, suitably defined.
Moreover, this u is unique up to a positive affine transformation.

PROBLEMS

(1) Prove Lemma (9.5).

(2) Finish the proof of Proposition (9.12).

(3) Consider a problem in the Savage formulation with $Z = [0, 100]$, $S = \{s_1, s_2\}$, and $F = \{$all functions from S to $Z\}$. Define a binary relation $\succ$ on F by

$$f \succ g \text{ if } f(s_1) + [f(s_2)]^2 > g(s_1) + [g(s_2)]^2.$$

Of the seven Savage axioms, which does $\succ$ obey? Provide proofs for those it does obey and counterexamples for those it doesn't.

(4) Suppose $f \succ g$ given A, $f \succ g$ given B, and $A \cap B = \emptyset$. Prove *directly* from the seven Savage axioms that $f \succ g$ given $A \cup B$. (By prove directly I mean: Don't use the representation theorem.) What happens if I omit the premise that $A \cap B = \emptyset$.

(5) In the von Neumann-Morgenstern theory, the Archimedean Axiom read: If $p \succ q \succ r$, then there exist $a, b \in (0, 1)$ such that $ap + (1 - a)r \succ q \succ bp + (1 - b)r$. We claimed above that part of the role of Axiom (9.10) was to give us the Archimedean Axiom. But if you look at Axiom (9.10), you'll see something quite different – there are two "lotteries" and a consequence and not three lotteries, and the whole thing is stated differently. Let us specialize in the von Neumann-Morgenstern theory to the case of an arbitrary set of prizes Z and P_S the space of simple probability distributions on Z. Then what would seem directly analogous to Axiom (9.10) in that specific setting would be the statement: For all $p \succ q$ and $z \in Z$, there are $a, b \in (0, 1)$ such that $ap + (1 - a)\delta_z \succ q$ and $p \succ bq + (1 - b)\delta_z$. Suppose we replaced the Archimedean Axiom in that setting with the statement just given. Would the conclusion (that is, Theorem (5.15) on page 58) still be true? If so, give a proof. If not, give a counterexample.

(6) In the brief commentary following Axiom (9.9), it was claimed that the role played by this axiom is the same as the role played by the sure thing principle back in Chapter 5. Hence, if Z was a finite set, we should be able to dispense with Axiom (9.9). Is this correct? If Z is finite, do the other axioms imply Axiom (9.9)? The answer must be yes given the results we have given above, but I would like a *direct* proof of this fact.

10

Conditional Preference, Conditional Probability, and Contingent Choice

---

This very short chapter continues in development of Savage's theory of choice under uncertainty – the point is to investigate what this theory has to say if anything about the well-known procedure of "taking actions contingent upon new information".

CONDITIONAL PREFERENCE AND CONDITIONAL PROBABILITY

Throughout this chapter, the setup will be exactly as in last chapter. There will be: a set of states of the world S, with A the algebra of all subsets of S; a set Z of consequences – to keep things simple I'll assume Z is finite; from these the set F of acts is formed, the set of all functions from S into Z; and Totrep's preferences among acts, given by $\succ$, which is assumed to satisfy the Savage axioms. This gives us p, Totrep's subjective probability measure over S, and u, Totrep's utility function on Z. Note that because Z is finite, all acts are simple acts. For $f \in F$, I'll write p_f to denote the probability on Z that is induced by p and f. Then if we let $E[u(f(s)); p]$ stand for $\sum_z p_f(z) u(z)$, the representation is

(10.1) $f \succ g$ iff $E[u(f(s)); p] > E[u(g(s)); p]$.

Now recall that in the Savage theory we defined conditional preference by $f \succ g$ given a if $f' \succ g'$ where $f = f'$, $g = g'$ on a and $f' = g'$ on a^c. Axiom (9.3) told us that this is well-defined; it doesn't matter what f' and g' are on a^c, so long as they are the same. I'll write $f \succ_a g$ for $f \succ g$ given a.

139

Proposition (10.2). Suppose a is not null (so that $p(a) > 0$). Define, for $b \subseteq S$,

$$(10.3) \qquad\qquad p(b|a) = \frac{p(a \cap b)}{p(a)}.$$

Then $p(\cdot|a)$ is a probability measure on (S, A), and

$$(10.4) \qquad f \succ_a g \text{ iff } E[u(f(s)); p(\cdot|a)] > E[u(g(s)); p(\cdot|a)].$$

Moreover, $\succ_a$ obeys the seven Savage axioms, so that $p(\cdot|a)$ is the unique probability measure and u is the unique-up-to-a-positive-affine-transformation utility function for which represents $\succ_a$ in the sense of (10.4).

Before proving this proposition, let me be a little clearer about (10.4). By $E[u(f(s)); p(\cdot|a)]$, I mean (recalling that Z is finite)

$$\sum_z u(z)p(\{s : f(s) = z\}|a) = \sum_z u(z)\frac{p(\{s : f(s) = z\} \cap a)}{p(a)}.$$

Abusing notation, I will write $p_f(z|a)$ for $p(\{s : f(s) = z\}|a)$. Then (10.4) is

$$(10.5). \qquad f \succ_a g \text{ iff } \sum_z u(z)p_f(z|a) > \sum_z u(z)p_g(z|a).$$

Proof. (Actually a sketch – lots of details are left out.) That $p(\cdot|a)$ is a probability on A is left as an exercise. Given f and g, let f' and g' be given as in the definition of conditional preference. Then

$$f \succ_a g \text{ iff } f' \succ g' \text{ iff } \sum_z u(z)p_{f'}(z) > \sum_z u(z)p_{g'}(z) \text{ iff}$$

$$\sum_z u(z)[p(a \cap \{f'(s) = z\}) + p(a^c \cap \{f'(s) = z\})] >$$

$$\sum_z u(z)[p(a \cap \{g'(s) = z\}) + p(a^c \cap \{g'(s) = z\})]$$

$$\text{iff } \sum_z u(z)p(a \cap \{f'(s) = z\}) > \sum_z u(z)p(a \cap \{g'(s) = z\})$$

(since $f' = g'$ on a^c, thus $p(a^c \cap \{f'(s) = z\}) = p(a^c \cap \{g'(s) = z\})$ for all z)

$$\text{iff } \sum_z u(z)p(a \cap \{f(s) = z\}) > \sum_z u(z)p(a \cap \{g(s) = z\})$$

(since $f = f'$ and $g = g'$ on a)

$$\text{iff } \sum_z u(z)\frac{p(a \cap \{f(s) = z\})}{p(a)} > \sum_z u(z)\frac{p(a \cap \{g(s) = z\})}{p(a)}$$

(since $p(a) > 0$)

$$\text{iff } \sum_z u(z)p_f(z|a) > \sum_z u(z)p_g(z|a),$$

which is just (10.5), or (10.4) rewritten.

As to the seven axioms, (9.1,3,7,8 and 9) follow directly from the representation (10.4), (9.2) is a consequence of a being non-null, and (9.10) follows from the representation (10.4) combined with the facts that S can be "finely-partitioned" and u is bounded. (This last is especially devoid of necessary details.)

Thus the uniqueness result claimed in the proposition follows from the uniqueness result in the Savage representation.

Conditional preference clearly gives rise to conditional likelihood. Let $x \succ y$ and, for b and d subsets of S, write $b \succeq d$ given a, or $b \succeq_a d$, if $f \succ_a g$, where $f = x$ on b, $f = y$ on b^c, $g = x$ on d, and $g = y$ on d^c. It should be clear that $b \succeq_a d$ iff $b \cap a \succeq d \cap a$, so, for non-null a,

$$b \succeq_a d \text{ iff } p(b|a) > p(d|a).$$

CHOOSING AN ACTION CONTINGENT UPON NEW INFORMATION

All of the above is preparatory for the following story. Totrep is faced with a Savage style decision problem, and he has at his disposal a finite (for simplicity) number of conceivable actions $\{f_1, \ldots f_n\}$. He has formulated his problem in the Savage setup – there are spaces

Z of prizes (finite), S of states, and F of acts, with $f_k \in F$ for $k = 1, \ldots, n$. His preferences over all acts are given by $\succ$, which obeys the seven Savage axioms, and his preferences are thus represented by some given p and u.

The change in the story is as follows. Totrep needn't choose an act from $\{f_1, \ldots, f_n\}$ until after he receives some information about which state prevails. This information comes in the form of a finite partition of S, into $\{a_1, \ldots, a_m\}$. Specifically, Totrep will learn whether the true state is in a_1 or a_2 or $\ldots$ or a_m prior to choosing an action. The question is: How should he choose, contingent on the information he receives? For simplicity, we will assume that each a_j is non-null.

Note that for the first time, we are confronted with a problem that has a dynamic element, in that Totrep isn't choosing until after he gets this information. I don't want to get into this subject too deeply just yet, so I'll revert to the following modification that turns this into a static choice problem: Totrep actually won't make the choice of f_k, because he is going on vacation. Instead his agent will make the choice for him. That is, his agent will learn which cell a_j of the partition pertains and based on this will choose an f_k. Totrep is able to leave detailed instructions for the agent, instructions of the form: If you learn that a_j is the cell that contains the state, then take action f_k – this sort of thing for each $j = 1, \ldots, m$. Now the question is – what instructions should Totrep leave his agent?

For concreteness, suppose $m = 3$ and $n = 5$. You will have no problem seeing how to generalize this, and the notation for the general case is too gruesome to bother with. A typical list of instructions in this specific case is:

If a_1, then choose f_3; if a_2, then choose f_2; and if a_3, choose f_3.

If the true state is s, these instructions give the result $f(s)$ where $f(s)$ is $f_3(s)$ for s in a_1 or a_3 and $f(s)$ is $f_2(s)$ if s is in a_2. Let me denote this particular action f by f_{323}.

In this setting, there are 125 such sets of instructions that Totrep could leave for his agent, where each set of instructions is equivalent to taking an action $f_{kk'k''}$, for k, k' and k'' equal to some element of $\{1, \ldots, 5\}$. The interpretation is that $f_{kk'k''}$ agrees with f_k on a_1, with $f_{k'}$ on a_2, and with $f_{k''}$ on a_3.

Now for a planted axiom. We suppose that Totrep will select

instructions according to whichever of the $f_{kk'k''}$ he thinks is best in terms of his preferences $\succ$. That is, we are assuming that Totrep's preferences over instruction sets is induced from his preferences over the acts that the instruction sets induce, according to the inducement scheme just outlined. (You should be asking yourself: Is this a good description of how individuals act? Is this a good normative prescription for how to choose among instructions to leave with one's agent?)

Whatever you think of this planted axiom, it allows me to say which set of instructions Totrep will leave by answering: Which $f_{kk'k''}$ has highest expected utility for Totrep?

And I have no trouble with this question. Recall that we assume that a_1, a_2, and a_3 are all non-null. Then

$$(10.6) \qquad E[u(f(_{kk'k''}(s)); p] = p(a_1)E[u(f_k(s)); p(\cdot|a_1)]+$$

$$p(a_2)E[u(f_{k'}(s)); p(\cdot|a_2)] + p(a_3)E[u(f_{k''}(s)); p(\cdot|a_3)].$$

You shouldn't take my word for it; verify this equation using the definition of conditional probability introduced above.

Once you've checked that I'm correct about this, we're done. To maximize $E[u(f_{kk'k''}(s)); p]$:

for k, take that i that maximizes $E[u(f_i(s)); p(\cdot|a_1)]$,
for k', take that i that maximizes $E[u(f_i(s)); p(\cdot|a_2)]$,
for k'', take that i that maximizes $E[u(f_i(s)); p(\cdot|a_3)]$.

Paraphrasing this for the general case of a finite partition: For each possible piece of information a_j, find which act f_i maximizes conditional expected utility, using the conditional probability measure $p(\cdot|a_j)$, and leave instructions to take that act if it is learned that a_j pertains.

Now what if Totrep isn't going on vacation, but instead will make the choices himself, once he receives the information? Thinking of this as descriptive theory, how will he act in that situation? Or as normative theory, how should he act? It is a principle of most of choice theory that Totrep should or will act exactly according to the instructions he would leave for an agent, because dynamic choice is the same as the static choice of a strategy. Now as descriptive theory, this is a fairly bold assertion – and when we get to Chapter 13, we will see a way to formalize dynamic choice so that this assertion can be subjected to test. But what about this as normative theory? Should Totrep act in this fashion?

As normative theory there isn't really an issue here. Totrep should wait until he gets the information, consult his preferences at that point, and act accordingly. To create a real issue, let me complicate the story one level further. Suppose that Totrep must choose today either to implement an act from a set $\{f_1, ..., f_m\}$, or to wait for the information and then implement an action from a *different* set of acts $\{f'_1, ..., f'_k\}$. The idea is that by waiting for the information, Totrep's available choices will change. Now there is a real issue for todays choice: In deciding whether to choose an act today or to wait for the information, should Totrep compare his best act (in terms of expected utility) from the first set with the ex ante expected utility from his best *strategy* of choosing an act contingent on the information, where the latter is computed in fashion analogous to what we did above? That is, should Totrep view the set of acts that he has available at the outset as being the first set joined together with all the "strategic acts" that can be created from the anticipated information and the second set of acts?

Savage, and most normative decision theory, asserts that the answer is that this is obviously the correct thing to do. Dynamic choice, it is maintained, amounts to the static choice of an ex ante optimal strategy, using ex ante expected utility computed as illustrated above. Is this right? Do you find this compelling normatively? Before committing yourself irrevocably to an affirmative answer, wait for Chapter 13.

PROBLEMS

(1) Prove that $p(\cdot|a)$ given by (10.3) for non-null a is a probability on A.

(2) Provide the details for the assertion in the proof of Proposition (10.2) that the seven Savage axioms hold for conditional preference.

(3) Verify equation (10.6).

11

Independence, Exchangeability, and de Finetti's Theorem

This is another chapter on refinements of the Savage theory. The subject here is de Finetti's theorem, which is, in my opinion, the fundamental theorem of statistical inference – the theorem that from a subjectivist point of view makes sense out of most statistical procedures. In the course of discussing this theorem and what it pertains to, I'm going to expose you to a very informal and opinionated survey of philosophies of probability. Actually, what I'll do is get in some cheap shots at philosophies other than the subjectivist. You should, if you have any sense at all, agree with me that these other philosophies deserve the treatment they're about to get, but you ought to read a less biased account of them than you'll get here before coming to this conclusion.

SOME BEDTIME READING

Consider an ordinary thumbtack which is to be thrown into the air in the center of a large, smooth wooden floor, say the basketball floor of Madison Square Garden. It can come to rest in one of two ways, called "heads" and "tails", as depicted in figure 11.1.

This experiment will be repeated a great many times, and great care will be taken to make sure that subsequent trials are as identical as possible. As a seeker of wisdom, your narrator is going to ask a number of people the following question:

"What is the probability that there are seven heads in the first ten flips?" It will be up to the people questioned to make whatever sense they can out of this question. If and when they have problems

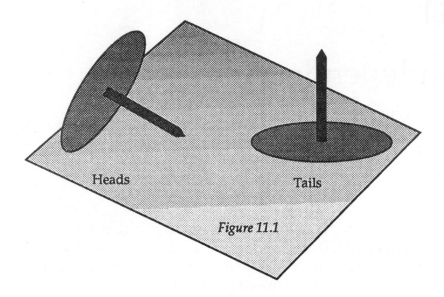

Heads   Tails

Figure 11.1

with that question, I may resort to other, simpler questions.

The first person I meet is the Comte d'Alembert, an 18th century French philosopher and mathematician, who will represent the Classical School of probability. When I put my question to the Comte, he looks at me a little sadly and says:

"Ah, I have no way of telling. There are eleven possible outcomes in your experiment (0 heads, 1, ..., 10), and if I thought that they were equally likely, I would say that the probability of each is 1/11. In doing this, I would be applying the principle of insufficient reason, which says that if I have no reason to suspect that one outcome is more likely than another, then by reasons of symmetry the outcomes are equally likely, and equally likely probabilities may be ascribed to them.

"But I see no reason to apply the principle here – it seems to me to be much less likely that there will be 10 heads than, say, 6. I once made a mistake like this [Narrator's note: See Savage (1972, page 65)], but Bernoulli's arguments have convinced me that there is no symmetry here."

"Well," I reply, "If it is the lack of symmetry between ten heads and six that bothers you, what would you say is the probability of heads on the first toss?"

"Again monsieur, I am unable to answer. This tack, she is not a symmetrical object, so I cannot conclude that heads is as likely as tails, and thus that the probability of each is 1/2. If she were a well balanced coin... But this tack..., no..., it is impossible to say."

The next person I put the question to is Dwight, who describes himself as an unreconstructed "frequentist." Dwight is wearing a white shirt with one of those plastic pocket protectors for holding pencils, pens, etc., and he has a calculator strapped to his belt. When I ask my question, I offer to answer any clarifying questions that he might have, but he cuts me off and crisply announces:

"These are independent and identical Bernoulli trials (each results in one of two distinct outcomes), so the number of heads in 10 trials has a Binomial distribution. That is,

(11.1) $$P(7 \text{ heads out of } 10) = \frac{10!}{7!3!}p^7(1-p)^3,$$

where p is the probability of a head on any given trial."

"And what," I ask, "is p?"

"I just told you – p is the probability of a head on any given trial. Perhaps you want to know how we can get an actual number for p? [I nod.] Well, suppose I define random variables

$$\chi_n = \begin{cases} 1 & \text{if heads on toss \#n} \\ 0 & \text{if tails on toss \#n} \end{cases}$$

Then $\chi_1 + \ldots + \chi_n$ will be the number of heads in the first n tosses. Now one of the most important results in mathematical probability theory is the Strong Law of Large Numbers which, specialized to this situation, says that

$$\lim_{n \to \infty} \frac{\chi_1 + \ldots + \chi_n}{n} = p.$$

That is, the observed long run frequency of heads is exactly the probability of heads on any single toss.

"If you really need a number, we should go to Madison Square Garden and toss the tack a few thousand times. That won't get p

exactly, but it will give us a pretty good idea what it is. And I know some really nifty statistical procedures that will tell us how much confidence we can have in the observed number – tell me how much confidence is necessary and how accurately you want to know p and I can tell you how many times to toss the tack."

Dwight begins to reach for his calculator and a handbook of statistical tables, but this doesn't seem to me to be what I had in mind, so I try one more question. "Would you be willing to enter into the following gamble, Dwight: You get \$100 if there are seven heads out of ten, and you pay \$5 if not?"

"Hmm," responds Dwight, "I can't answer that question until I have a good idea what p is. Can I borrow the tack – and do you know if Madison Square Garden is free right now?"

"No, you misunderstand – I want to know whether you'd take the bet right now."

"That comes down to *guessing* the value of p and so is not a subject amenable to scientific analysis. Probability theory has to do with objective, long run frequencies – haven't you listened to a thing I've said?" With that, Dwight stomps off to a corner of the room and begins making plans to construct confidence intervals for me just as soon as I see the light and lend him the thumbtack. He is present for the next conversation, and several times he breaks into uncontrollable laughter as he overhears various comments.

I next meet a Bayesian statistician named Ralph, who seems pleasant enough but has the weary look of a compromiser. I show him a transcript of the conversation with Dwight, and then ask him my opening question.

Ralph cleans his glasses, sighs, and then begins: "First, let me say that I agree with much of what Dwight said. Suppose we did toss the tack, say 20,000 times, and we observed 11,489 heads. Then I would estimate $p = .57445$ and calculate the probability for seven heads in the next ten tosses according to Dwight's formula (11.1) with this value of p.

"Now if you asked me for the probability of seven heads out of ten without any information (essentially, if you ask me the last question you asked Dwight), then I would represent my uncertainty concerning the true value of p through a *prior probability*. [Ralph actually manages to italicize this phrase in his spoken conversation.] For the sake of discussion, let's suppose that this prior distribution has a continuous density $f(p)$ on $[0, 1]$. [I look somewhat confused, so Ralph elaborates:] This means that I think the probability that the true value of p lies in some interval $[a, b] \subseteq [0, 1]$ is $\int_a^b f(p)dp$. Then I would calculate the probability of seven heads out of ten as being

(11.2)
$$\int_0^1 \frac{10!}{7!3!}p^7(1 - p)^3 f(p)dp.$$

As you can see, this is a (continuous) weighted average of Binomial probabilities, where the weighting is done according to the prior distribution for p. Dwight's formula (11.1) is a special case of (11.2) – it is (11.2) where the prior is concentrated on a single point. So (11.2) is just a generalization of (11.1)."

I have to admit that this is the sort of answer I had hoped to get, but I remember Dwight's remark that this question was not amenable to scientific analysis. I ask Ralph how he responds to that.

"Well, I suppose you could say that if you wanted to." Ralph cleans his glasses again and glances over his shoulder at Dwight, who is hysterical at this point. "The difference between Dwight and me is that in situations like this, I interpret probability as a quantification of personal uncertainty. I'm willing to extend the usage of probability theory into areas where Dwight chooses to make no probabilistic statements at all. But I'd like to emphasize that we are primarily in agreement – I will update my prior distribution on p as sample evidence becomes available (using Bayes' rule of course) and, as the sample size becomes large, my updated or posterior distribution will approach a degenerate distribution concentrated at the empirically observed fraction of heads. There is a very famous theorem in Bayesian statistics which proves that this is so, unless I have a very unusual prior to start with. By the way, I've got some really swell procedures for Bayesian updating on conjugate prior distributions if you're interested."

I tell Ralph that I am interested, so as not to hurt his feelings, but that I don't have the time. I go back to Dwight, who is wiping the tears from his eyes caused by his laughter, and I ask him whether he'd care to comment on Ralph's Bayesian prior procedure.

"I'd love to. Ralph is a nice fellow, but he's out of his mind. The probability of heads on any one toss is a number p, not the result of some random experiment. This prior distribution – what does it mean? Suppose $\int_0^{.5} f(p)dp = 1/3$ – that is, Ralph says that there is 'probability' 1/3 that the bias of the tack is between zero and one-half. By this does he mean that if we tested a whole lot of similar tacks, one-third of them would have bias between zero and one-half? I don't think he does, but that is the closest I can come to attaching any meaning to his statement. Look, the bias of the tack is either between zero and one-half or it isn't, and the 'probability' of this is therefore either zero or one. If Ralph can tell me what experiment or random event he has in mind for this prior distribution, maybe I'll be able to make some sense out of his statement. But it had better be that this random event, whatever it is, can be repeated independently lots of times, so $f(p)$ can be gotten by frequency counts. Of course, Ralph will probably say that he then has a prior on the results of this experiment, with an infinite regress resulting, so I'm not hopeful he can do it."

Ralph reiterates, "I hear what Dwight says, and I can only repeat my earlier statement. The difference between him and me is that I'm willing to use probability to quantify subjective or personal uncertainty and he isn't. And my prior is an example of that."

I turn back to Dwight, expecting a reply, but he's again laughing uncontrollably. So I move on to my fourth and final subject – Totrep. Totrep modestly admits to possessing complete faith in the Savage axioms, which he uses whenever he has a decision problem involving uncertainty. He is the personification of all that is good in the world, and I trust him immediately. [Narrator's note: I may possibly be accused of exercising personal bias in describing various actors in this drama. Compare my description of Totrep with that given by J. M. Harrison in the original version of this drama: "Totrep's arrogance is exceeded only by his lack of worldly knowledge."] I show Totrep transcripts of all my previous conversations and ask him to comment.

"This is a very interesting problem," he begins, "and I must (modestly) admit that I know *all* the answers, including the answers to questions you haven't yet thought to ask. You certainly are lucky to have me around to guide you.

"First off, let me formulate this as a Savage style problem: It will be sufficient for our purposes to take

$$Z = \{\$100, \$0, \$-5\},$$

although Z could be enlarged if you have other questions. Next, for S take

$$S = \prod_{n=1}^{\infty} \{h, t\}.$$

My notation may confuse you [I nod] – what I have in mind is that S is the set of all sequences of the form $s = (hthtthh\ldots)$, where $s = (hthtthh\ldots)$ means heads on flip one, tails on two, heads, tails, tails, heads, heads, etc. Let $\chi_n(s) = 1$ if the nth component of s is an h, and $\chi_n(s) = 0$ if the nth component of s is a t. Then χ_n is a function with domain S – this is what I call a random variable (and Dwight would surely agree with my definition).

"Now it is evident (if you haven't been asleep through the last few chapters of this book) what F is the set of all gambles based on the results of tack tosses with prizes in Z. I have preferences among such acts/gambles, given by the binary relation $\succ$, and I (upon reflection) decide that I want $\succ$ to obey the Savage axioms. In consequence, I get a personal probability measure p on all subsets of S – and note well, $p(a) > p(b)$ if and only if I prefer a gamble which gives prize $100 if a and $0 if a^c to one which gives $100 if b and $0 if b^c. When I say that I assess probability $p(a)$ for some event a, you *know* exactly what I mean, since this number is uniquely determined by my personal preferences on S. (You ought to go ask Dwight, Ralph and the Comte what the term 'probability' means to them. But wait a bit – let me finish my story.)

"Your original question is: 'What do I assess for $p(\chi_1+\ldots+\chi_{10} = 7)$?' I could tell you the number, but I don't think that I will, at least not now. This number represents a personal, subjective assessment of mine, and *that is all*. There may well be other Totreps around, who believe just as strongly in the seven axioms, but who come up with different numbers, just as there are Totreps around who like apples more than I do, and oranges less. [Narrator's note: See the final comment at the end of this chapter.] Instead of telling you my assessment, I'd prefer to tell you how I arrived at that assessment, because I think that this will help you come up with an assessment of your own.

"First, with regard to that bozo Dwight, let me say that I happen to assess

$$p(\chi_1 = 1) = p(\chi_2 = 1) = \ldots = p(\chi_{10} = 1) = .55.$$

That is, the probability of heads on any one flip is .55, but I *don't* agree with his formula (11.1), that

$$p(\chi_1 + \ldots + \chi_{10} = 7) = \frac{10!}{7!3!}(.55)^7(.45)^3.$$

Dwight said that he got his formula because the trials were independent. Well, I know what independence means. Two events a and b are *independent with respect to the probability measure p* if

$$p(a \cap b) = p(a)p(b).$$

Assuming that these are non-null events, an equivalent, somewhat more transparent way of saying this is that either $p(a|b) = p(a)$ or $p(b|a) = p(b)$ – if one of these three equations holds, they all do. Take $p(a|b) = p(a)$ – this means that if someone gives me the information that the true state of the world is in the event b, I don't change my assessment of how likely a is. That is, *I* don't think that there is any information in the statement that 'b prevails' concerning the likelihood of a. I hate to be pedantic, but let me stress that independence is a subjective property – I might not assess two events as independent that another Totrep would – it all depends on the probability measure p, and thus, indirectly, on the individual's subjective preferences. Now are successive tack tosses independent? *I* don't assess them as being so. If I did, I would say that

$$p(\chi_{1001} = 1) = p(\chi_{1001} = 1 | 1 \text{ head in first 1000 tosses})$$

$$= p(\chi_{1001} = 1 | 999 \text{ heads in first 1000 tosses}).$$

But I certainly don't believe this – the first probability is .55 as I told you before, the second is pretty damn close to zero, and the third is close to one. There's a lot of information in the first 1000 tosses about the 1001st, and I certainly wouldn't ignore that info or say it is of no use in assessing the probability of heads on the 1001st toss. Maybe Dwight means 'independence' in some other sense than the one above, or maybe he means to say that the tosses are independent with respect to some 'ideal' probability measure q, but I'm sure not interested in 'ideal' probability measures, and I assume you're not either, if you want to use this to help make a choice among lotteries.

"Dwight also mentioned the strong law of large numbers – saying that it showed that

$$\lim_{n\to\infty} (\chi_1 + \ldots + \chi_n)/n = p(\chi_1 = 1).$$

That is, the limiting empirically observed frequency of heads will equal the probability of heads on any single trial. He might believe this is true, but I sure don't – I'd be very surprised to find the empirically observed frequency of heads settling down at .55 exactly. If you look up the strong law in a math book, you'll see why I think that Dwight is wrong about this. The strong law when specialized to this context says something like: If $\{\chi_n\}$ is a sequence of zero-one random variables that are independent and identically distributed with respect to a probability measure q, then

$$q(\{s \in S : \lim_{n\to\infty} (\chi_1(s) + \ldots + \chi_n(s))/n = q(\chi_1 = 1)\}) = 1.$$

(There is a technical requirement needed to prove this – q must be σ-additive on a certain sub-σ-algebra of A – but let me ignore this technicality.) In words, any Totrep who assesses these tack flips as independent and indentically distributed would assess probability one to the event that the long run frequency of heads will approach that Totrep's assessment of the probability of heads on any single toss. That is a remarkable consequence of independence, but since I don't assess the tack tosses as independent, and I don't think you do either, it is also remarkably useless.

"I have one more comment to make about Dwight, but let me turn now to what Ralph had to say. Rather surprisingly (to me at least), Ralph has gotten the mechanics right, although he doesn't seem to know why they are right. My question for him is the same as Dwight's – what is this prior distribution a distribution for? Ralph said something like, 'It's the distribution of the probability of heads on any one toss,' but that's silly - the probability of heads on any toss is .55 – there is nothing random about that.

"I don't think that Ralph can answer this question, but I sure can. We've already discussed why I don't assess successive tack flips as independent. But I do think that the sequence of tack flips has a property that is nearly as powerful as independence, called *exchange-ability* or *symmetric dependence*. For example, I think that

$$p(\chi_1 = 1, \chi_2 = 0, \chi_3 = 1, \chi_4 = 1) = p(\chi_3 = 1, \chi_4 = 0, \chi_2 = 1, \chi_1 = 1).$$

Notice that what I've done here is to keep the same 'outcomes' (heads, tails, heads, heads) but I've permuted the indices of the random variables. More generally if $\{k_1, k_2, \ldots, k_n\}$ is any permutation of $\{1, 2, \ldots, n\}$ for any n, then my assessment for the joint distribution of the random vectors $(\chi_1, \chi_2, \ldots, \chi_n)$ and $(\chi_{k_1}, \chi_{k_2}, \ldots, \chi_{k_n})$ are the same. This is a hard property to wrap your head around at first, but I think that if you think about it, you'll come to view it as quite intuitive in this context, and you'll want *your* subjective probability distribution to have this property.

"Now for the punchline: There is a very famous theorem, known as de Finetti's theorem, which can be specialized to this context as follows:

If $\{\chi_1, \chi_2, \ldots\}$ is an exchangeable sequence of zero-one random variables (that is, with respect to a probability measure p), then
(a) $p(\{s \in S : \lim_{n \to \infty}(\chi_1(s) + \ldots + \chi_n(s))/n \text{ exists}\}) = 1$, and
(b) letting $\alpha(s)$ be the limit of $(\chi_1(s) + \ldots + \chi_n(s))/n$ for those s for which this limit exists,

$$p(\chi_1 + \ldots, \chi_n = m) = E[\frac{n!}{m!(n-m)!}\alpha(s)^m(1 - \alpha(s))^{n-m}; p].$$

This is, despite appearances, quite transparent. Part (a) says that if I assess the sequence as being exchangeable, then I assess probability one that there will be a limiting empirical frequency for the frequency of heads. Of course, I'm not sure a priori what that limiting empirical frequency will be – it is a random variable $\alpha(s)$. Since it is random, it has a cumulative distribution function (it takes on values in the interval $[0, 1]$, remember). Let me define

$$F(\gamma) = p(\{s \in S : \alpha(s) \le \gamma\}) \text{ for } \gamma \in [0, 1].$$

That is, $F(\gamma)$ is the probability that I assess that the limiting empirical frequency will be γ or less. Then part (b) says that to compute things like $p(\chi_1 + \ldots + \chi_{10} = 7)$, I do just what Ralph told me to do (using the distribution function F instead of the density function f)

$$p(\chi_1 + \ldots + \chi_{10} = 7) = \int_0^1 \frac{10!}{7!3!} \gamma^7 (1-\gamma)^3 dF(\gamma).$$

If F has a continuous density, then it is exactly Ralph's formula (11.2). (There is one technicality I ought to mention – to prove this result, I require that p is σ-additive on the same sub-σ-algebra as is required for the strong law. But don't worry too much about that – if I took the time to explain the whole thing to you, you wouldn't find the assumption too hard to swallow.)

"Now to answer the question that I posed for Ralph. His prior distribution is my assessment for the distribution of the limiting empirical frequency of heads, where I assess that such a limit will be observed *because* I assess successive tosses to be exchangeable. That 'because' is quite important – what legitimizes Ralph's formula and the procedure is the qualitative property of exchangeability. In fact, the theorem has a converse – if I didn't view the sequence as exchangeable, then I can't use Ralph's formula – the theorem is an 'if and only if' result.

"As a practical matter, then I'm going to do just what Ralph says to do, with one step added in front:

(1) I decide that I assess the sequence as being exchangeable.

(2) I subjectively assess the probability distribution for the limiting empirical frequency, or what Ralph calls his prior.

(3) I compute things like $p(\chi_1 + \ldots + \chi_{10} = 7)$ using the formula – note that

$$p(\chi_n = 1) = \int_0^1 \gamma dF(\gamma) = E[\alpha(s); p];$$

this is how I got the .55 I told you about earlier.

"I feel like I'm beginning to bore you [I nod], but I have a few more points to make. The first is: Why am I assessing the distribution for the limiting empirical frequency and then using the formula to compute other assessments, rather than trying to make a few direct assessments such as $p(\chi_1 + \ldots + \chi_{10} = 7)$? After all, they are both judgment calls on my part. The reason is simple – I find it *easier* to do the former than the latter – if I found the latter easier I would do that. The point of this theory – going from the qualitative judgment in step 1 to the formula – is that it allows me to make an assessment that I find relatively easy (an assessment for F) that can then be used to make assessments I find more difficult, such as the assessment of $p(\chi_1 + \ldots + \chi_{10} = 7)$. But 'easier' and 'more difficult' are subjective things – you should do whatever you find easiest.

"Second, remember Ralph saying that as he obtained more sample evidence, his prior distribution would collapse to a distribution degenerate at the observed frequency of heads? Well, the sort of thing he's describing is the computation of a simple conditional probability, such as

$$p(\{s \in S : \alpha(s) \leq \gamma\} \mid \{s \in S : \sum_{j=1}^{1000} \chi_j(s)/1000 = .567\}).$$

You can do this quite easily, noting that

$$p\{s \in S : \alpha(s) \leq \gamma \text{ and } \sum_{j=1}^{n} \chi_n(s) = m\}) =$$

$$\int_0^\gamma \frac{n!}{m!(n-m)!} \beta^m (1-\beta)^{n-m} dF(\beta).$$

If you do this computation for any reasonable prior F (roughly, ones that put positive mass in neighborhoods of .567), you'll see that his statement was correct.

"Third, part (b) in de Finetti's theorem can be restated: Conditional on the value of $\alpha(s)$ being γ, the random variables $\chi_1, \chi_2, \ldots$ are independent and identically distributed, with $p(\chi_n = 1|\alpha(s) = \gamma) = \gamma$. If you're worried about me conditioning on a null event, imagine that $\alpha(s)$ has a discrete distribution with mass at γ. Even if this isn't the case, the statement I've written makes mathematical sense, although it's a little hard to explain this precisely unless you know a lot more mathematics than I think you do. So maybe when Dwight said that the flips were independent, what he meant was that they are conditionally independent *given* the value of $\gamma(s)$. But I don't think he meant this, quite. In order to assign probabilities to the outcomes of a random event, Dwight requires that the event or experiment be repeatable – then the probability of an outcome is just the long run frequency of that outcome. And Dwight is never willing to make any numerical statement about a particular repeatable experiment until he has a goodly amount of frequency data. That's why he calls himself a frequentist. On the other hand, I am willing to quantify any subjective uncertainty in my mind with probabilities, whether this is the repeatable kind of uncertainty or not. My probability assessment for the limiting empirical frequency is a good example of this, although I can give a starker example. Consider the probability that New York is closer to the North Pole than is, say, Madrid. Dwight presumably would say – it's either zero or one, by which I assume he means that New York is either closer or it isn't. But the same thing is true if I pull a coin out of my pocket and flip it. Either it will come up heads or it will be tails. It will be one or the other, so (by Dwight's logic) shouldn't the probability be either zero or one? I only understand probability as quantification of personal uncertainty, as part of a representation of my preferences. I really have a lot of trouble in understanding how Dwight can differentiate between the coin flip and the New York/Madrid question."

[Narrator's note: A round of applause for the cast, please.]

DE FINETTI'S THEOREM

In the above discussion, Totrep described de Finetti's theorem in the simple case of Bernoulli (zero-one) random variables. Here is a more general version of the theorem:

The setup is a state space S with A the algebra of all subsets of S and p a probability measure on A. You may presume that this p arises from a preference relation $\succ$ among acts (based on S), although this interpretation is not necessary for what follows. If you liked the story of Totrep, Social Scientist, expressing "more likely than" judgments, that is also consistent with what follows.

Also given is a sequence of random variables – function $Z_n : S \rightarrow R$. (Technical aside: Let A^* be the σ-algebra of S generated by all sets of the form $\{s : Z_1(s) \leq z_1, \ldots, Z_n(s) \leq z_n\}$ for all finite n, where $z_1, \ldots, z_n \in R$. The theorem requires that p be σ-additive on A^*.)

Definition (11.3). The sequence $\{Z_n\}$ is said to be *exchangeable* if the joint distribution of $(Z_1, \ldots, Z_n)$ is the same as that of $(Z_{k_1}, \ldots, Z_{k_n})$, for all n and permutations $\{k_1, \ldots, k_n\}$ of $\{1, \ldots, n\}$. Put another way: Let $F_n(z_1, \ldots, z_n)$ be the joint cumulative distribution function of the random vector $(Z_1, \ldots, Z_n)$. That is,

$$F_n(z_1, \ldots, z_n) = p(Z_1 \leq z_1, \ldots, Z_n \leq z_n).$$

Then $\{Z_n\}$ is exchangeable if, for all n, F_n is a symmetric function of its n arguments.

Next, for $n = 1, 2, \ldots$ and $z \in R$, define $\zeta_n(z, \cdot) : S \to R$ and $\xi_n(z, \cdot) : S \to R$ by

$$\zeta_n(z, s) = \begin{cases} 1 & \text{if } Z_n(s) \leq z, \\ 0 & \text{if } Z_n(s) > z, \end{cases}$$

and

$$\xi_n(z, s) = \frac{1}{n} \sum_{i=1}^{n} \zeta_i(z, s).$$

In words, $\xi_n(z, s)$ is the fraction of the first n observations that fall at or below level z, if the state of the world is s. So if we graphed $\xi_n(z, s)$ as a function of z (for a particular s), we'd have the empirical frequency function for the first n observations.

Theorem (11.4). The sequence $\{Z_n\}$ is exchangeable if and only if:
(a) There exists a function $\xi : R \times S \to [0, 1]$ such that for each s, $\xi(\cdot, s)$ is a distribution function, and

$$p(\{s \in S : \lim_{n \to \infty} \xi_n(z, s) = \xi(z, s) \text{ for continuity points of } \xi(\cdot, s)\}) = 1.$$

(b) $F_n(z_1, \ldots, z_n) = E[\xi(z_1, s) \cdot \xi(z_2, s) \cdot \ldots \cdot \xi(z_n, s); p]$.

This looks much more complicated than it really is. It can be paraphrased: If (and only if) you assess that $\{Z_n\}$ is exchangeable, then when you form the empirical frequency functions $\xi_n(\cdot, s)$, with probability one they will converge to some (random) limit distribution function $\xi(\cdot, s)$. And (this is a rather rough paraphrase of part (b)) if you condition on this limit distribution function, the $\{Z_n\}$ sequence is a sequence of independent and identically distributed random variables with distribution function $\xi(\cdot, s)$. Very roughly put – exchangeability is the same as "independent and identically distributed with an a priori *unknown* distribution function", a distribution function that will emerge from the frequency distribution of an infinite sequence of observations.

The original reference for de Finetti's theorem is "La Prevision ...," *Ann. Inst. Henri Poincaré.* A translation into English can be found in the book of readings edited by Kyburg and Smokler (1964). Substantial generalizations can be found in Hewitt and Savage (1956)., A slightly weaker version of the theorem is proven by Loeve in his book in probability theory (page 365). Also, Feller gives a partial proof for the simple Bernoulli case in his *Introduction to Probabilty Theory*, Vol. II, p. 229. Feller also discusses an important technical caveat – it is necessary that the sequence $\{Z_n\}$ is infinite for the theorem to be true. Any/all of these references will show that this is a very deep theorem, and one that requires much mathematical sophistication to prove. It turns out that, for the Bernoulli case, there is an incredibly "slick" proof using the convergence theorem for backward martingales – this proof can be found in Chapter 9 of Chung (1971).

DE FINETTI'S THEOREM AS THE
FUNDAMENTAL THEOREM OF (MOST) STATISTICS

Much (perhaps most) of statistics comes down to "sampling from a population with unknown distribution function," where typically a large numbers assumption is used to justify the view that the samples are i.i.d. with the unknown distribution. Taking a subjectivist view of probability, de Finetti's theorem can be seen as providing the qualitative justification for such a point of view – if you (the statistician) assess ex ante that the samples are exchangeable (and coming from a large population), then and only then is it legitimate to view the samples as "independent and identically distributed with unknown distribution function." What separates classical statistics from Bayesian statistics is that Bayesian statistics considers the distribution of the unknown distribution function – this is the Bayesian prior distribution.

In classical statistics, this distribution is generally swept under the rug – sometimes it is implicitly assumed to be completely diffuse, as in MLE point estimation – other times it is ignored entirely; only conditional probability statements are made, as in confidence interval construction. This is not *entirely* unreasonable – if we're looking for statements based on a certain set of data that *all* Totreps can agree upon, and if all Totreps assess that exchangeability is appropriate in a certain context, then the sorts of conditional probability statements that fill texts on classical statistics are statements that would be unanimously held. (I believe that most controversies in statistics concerning misspecification of models, etc., can be reduced to arguments about whether a certain exchangeability assumption is indeed valid. However I am not much of an empiricist, and you should take this opinion with a grain or two of salt.) It would, after all, be hard to get unanimous subjective assessments on the prior, and it wouldn't do (would it?) to fill scholarly journals with probabilistic statements that are mixtures of the author's subjective prior and data that have been collected. In any case, if one makes this sort of interpretation of classical statistics, then de Finetti's theorem and the qualitative property of exchangeability become fundamental to the subject; it is, once we agree on the right specification, what all Totreps agree upon. (But see the final section of this chapter.)

BAYESIAN INFERENCE AND DE FINETTI'S THEOREM AS NORMATIVE DECISION TOOLS

The normative usefulness of de Finetti's theorem is so apparent that even MBA students buy it without blinking. Situations where exchangeability is a natural assumption abound – quality control and marketing surveys are obvious examples. A typical story is that you aren't sure about the reliability of a piece of equipment, or what proportion of your clientele will purchase a certain good – and the data that you have are naturally assessed as being independent conditional on an unknown parameter – that is, exchangeable plus, where the plus is a parametric specification of the unknown distribution. Then the representation in de Finetti's theorem, together with your prior assessment on the parameter value and the data, give you sufficient joint probabilities with which to calculate the appropriate conditional probability distribution of the parameter, conditional on the data.

Since Bayes' formula is used in constructing these conditionals, the rubric Bayesian inference is often employed to describe this process. All this is somewhere between obvious (I hope) and boring (I fear), so let us look at a more interesting application.

Suppose that you were building a nuclear power plant, the safety of which is dependent on a certain device working. You assess probability 10^{-3} that this device will fail in a one year period. These odds aren't safe enough given the consequences of failure by the device, but you can install these devices in parallel so that all must fail if there's to be trouble. Moreover, parallel installation is such that the failure of one doesn't effect the others in any way that would cause the others to fail. So if you put, say, four of these devices in parallel, you get that the probability that all four fail within a year is

$$p(\#1 \text{ fails}) \cdot p(\#2 \text{ fails}) \cdot p(\#3 \text{ fails}) \cdot p(\#4 \text{ fails}) = (10^{-3})^4 = 10^{-12}.$$

Right? No, this is wrong.

It is wrong on two related counts. First, while the failure of one of the devices may not directly cause the others to fail, the reason that the first one failed may also be a reason that the others fail. For example, if there is a fire at the plant which causes the first system to burn, the same fire may well consume one or more of the other systems. If such causes of failure as this exist, then we can't assume that failure of the four systems is independent, as we did in the calculation.

But suppose that there are no "joint causes" such as fire. Even then the analysis just done may be wrong. When we assess probability .001 that one of these systems will fail, we are making an assessment. But we should admit the possibility that we are miscalibrated. Put another way, if you are told that the first three of the four systems failed within a year, that might well cause you do doubt the initial .001 assessment, and it might lead you to revise upwards the conditional probability that the fourth system did/will fail. Now there is a sense in which this is just the same sort of thing as fire as a joint cause of failure – one suspects, if the first three systems do fail in a year, that there has been some design flaw or some overlooked factor in the plant that the system can't cope with. And, of course, this design flaw or this overlooked factor will then have an effect on the fourth system. But however we put it, the problem remains – failure of the four systems are not events that we are likely to assess as being independent, especially given the sparse data we are apt to have on how such devices perform in the field, and the calculation above does not give the joint probability that all four fail.

So how should we proceed in this sort of problem? While independence isn't a very reasonable assumption, exchangeability may well be. If the systems are identical, one would expect the probability distribution for the joint distribution of their failure to be symmetric, and it would be symmetric no matter how many systems there were. Then just as in a marketing survey or a quality control problem, which is what this is, in a sense, we can analyze the problem by assessing a prior on the "limiting proportion of systems that fail within the year" (which should have expectation .001). And then, if this distribution is given by $F : [0,1] \to [0,1]$, calculate the chance of all four failing as $\int_0^1 \gamma^4 F(d\gamma)$.

For more on this sort of application of de Finetti's theorem, see problem 2 and Harrison (1981).

UNANIMOUS PRIORS

In two places above, we referred to the fact that different Totreps might have different prior probability distributions over a given set of states of nature, even if both obey the Savage axioms. From the perspective of the axioms alone, it seems no more reasonable to suppose that there is some single correct prior than it is to assume that there is some single "correct" set of tastes over consequences. Nonetheless, it is widely held by economic theorists that there is a difference between probability assessments and tastes, and that two Totreps, given access to the same information and training, *ought* to come to the same conclusions as to the likelihoods of states. In other words, priors will be unanimously held by Totreps, although differences of opinion over the likelihood of certain states can arise between two Totreps if they have had access to different pieces of information. This point of view is often referred to as the Harsanyi Doctrine, after John Harsanyi, one of its strongest proponents. This book concerns single person choice theory and so the Harsanyi Doctrine and its many wonderful consequences are not really fit subjects for us. However I didn't want casually to lead you too far astray in terms of received doctrine (however strange I find that particular doctrine).

PROBLEMS

(1) Consider the Savage setup described by Totrep in this chapter. Suppose I tell you that:

(a) I view successive tack tosses as being exchangeable,

(b) I assess $p(\chi_1 = 1) = .3$,

(c) I assess $p(\chi_1 + \chi_2 + \chi_3 = 2) = .195$, and

(d) I assess probability one that the bias of the tack is one of .1 or .3 or .5 – that is $p(\alpha(s) = .1) + p(\alpha(s) = .3) + p(\alpha(s) = .5) = 1$.

Then what do I assess for $p(\chi_1 + \ldots + \chi_{10} = 3)$?

(2) In practical books on Decision Analysis, you will sometimes find something called a "calibration function." The idea is that, when a decision maker is making probability assessments, he or she might express poorly the assessments made. More specifically, we imagine that we look at a long stream of assessments made by this individual, all of which are (for simplicity) of the either-or outcome type. Very specifically, we imagine that we ask the individual a long series of questions of the following type:

"Which factor was the cause of more deaths in the US in 1976? (a) Heart attacks. (b) Accidents in the home."

The individual is told to say which outcome he or she thinks is more likely, and what he or she judges to be the chances of the more likely outcome, rounded, for simplicity, to the nearest .1. We group together all of those in which the individual says there is a chance of .7 of one outcome, and (suppose) we find that the predicted-to-be-more-likely outcome is in fact correct in 80 percent of these cases. Looking at the group where the decision maker assesses probability .8, (suppose) we find that he or she is right 90 percent of the time. And so on. The individual we are describing is then said to be underconfident in his or her judgment, since the odds this person expresses understates the degree of confidence that he or she should have in what he or she knows. And so, the practical book goes on to say, if you are this decision maker, you should be bolder in your assessments. Or if you rely on assessments by this decision maker, you should "recalibrate" any assessment this decision maker makes.

(A variation on this is to ask the decision maker a question such as:

"How far is it from New York to Tokyo in statute miles? Instead of giving a point estimate, give a range such that there is, in your judgment, a 25 percent chance that the distance is less than your smaller number, and a 25 percent chance that the distance is greater than your larger number. In other worlds, give me the 'interquartile' range of your probability assessment for this subjectively random variable."

And then, if the individual's range actually contains the answer, say, 70 percent of the time, you know the individual is too conservative, etc.)

Is it possible that a given Totrep, whose assessments obey all the laws of probability theory in a Savage setting, would be consistently "miscalibrated", in the sense that every event to which Totrep assesses .7 chance actually has a .8 chance of being correct, etc.? (The answer is no – the real question is: Why not?) And since the answer is no, what could possibly be the theoretical basis for all this blather in practical books on Decision Analysis?

12

Normative Uses
of These Models
on Subproblems

The story that motivates this chapter is the following. You (or Totrep) have to make a decision involving uncertainty. You are wondering whether it is appropriate to make this decision using the expected utility model – should you assess probability and a utility function and then compute expected utility? In other words, do the Savage or von Neumann-Morgenstern axioms apply?

What complicates this question is that there are other things going on in your life – there are other decisions to be made, other sources of uncertainty, etc. To apply one of these models, you have to make a choice: You can "do it right," by applying the model to the global decision problem that you face, or you can apply the expected utility model "locally" to the immediate problem that you face, abstracting away from the other considerations, sources of uncertainty, etc. *I will assume* (big assumption) that you are willing to sign off on applying the axioms globally – in the larger context the axioms do make sense to you. The question is, do the axioms also make sense locally? If the answer to this question is not yes, then we may be in trouble in terms of the usefulness of these models – if every time I want to use these models to choose among some gambles I must reconsider all decisions that I might be called upon to make sometime during my lifetime, then perhaps I had better forget these models as a practical tool of analysis.

This is a very complex issue, in part because it is so vague. The way in which I'll proceed is to show a few of the problems you can encounter in trying to apply these models locally, in one simple and concrete setting. In order to get things moving, I'll be making a few simplifying assumptions:

(1) All probabilities are objective. Thus we will be asking whether the von Neumann-Morgenstern (hereafter, NM) axioms apply.

(2) In the global problem, you are willing to buy the NM axioms – you maximize expected utility. Moreover, you have tastes that don't change with time or anything else of that sort – in a dynamic choice problem you're willing to regard the problem as static choice of a *best strategy*, per our discussion at the end of Chapter 10. I'll never be explicit about this in this chapter, but if you're observant, you'll see that I'm implicitly invoking this assumption all over the place. We'll take up this matter explicitly in the next chapter.

(3) One of the commonest misuses of this methodology is to use it in circumstances where it is hard to build an adequate model – because of any sort of emotional involvement on the part of the decision maker, for example. *This is a critical issue* in deciding whether to apply the methodology, but I am unable to say anything formal about it. So I'll leave this issue alone – for purposes of this chapter, we'll have enough to do to consider those things that we can formalize.

THE BASIC PROBLEM

We'll look at three variations on the following general theme. Consider a Totrep who lives for two periods, $t = 1, 2$. Totrep consumes dollar bills in each of these periods – denote the amounts of his consumption by c_1 and c_2, respectively. Totrep has a friendly banker who is willing to borrow and/or lend to Totrep at a per period interest rate of r, which, for simplicity, I'll take to be zero. Bankruptcy is not permitted in this society, and Totrep cannot and will not take any action that might leave himself bankrupt.

Totrep comes endowed with initial wealth w.

Totrep will have two sources of income. The first is a combination of income from labor and return from all the investments that he has previously made. This income may be random and will be received at date $t = 2$. The amount of this income will typically be denoted by y. Totrep *may* have some discretion as to the probability distribution of this income.

Totrep's other source of income is an extra investment or speculation that he is able to undertake. Imagine that Totrep's stock broker has just called him wanting to know if Totrep is willing to engage in a hitherto unforeseen venture. The amount of this extra payoff will be denoted by x.

Issues concerning the time at which Totrep learns about the resolution of any uncertainty that pertains will be a large part of this story: We leave the specification of this to the particular cases we'll examine.

The question is: Under what circumstances can Totrep apply the NM model to make decisions concerning the second income source x? That is, imagine that Totrep's broker has offered him a choice of several extra speculations. When can Totrep abstract away from all his other problems (his other investments, his consumption decision) and use an NM model to choose among the extra speculations?

We shall assume that Totrep believes in the NM axioms applied to consumption pairs (c_1, c_2) – that is, he wishes to take actions overall that will lead him to maximize the expectation of a strictly increasing function $U(c_1, c_2)$. This, we shall see, *induces* preferences over the possible second source gambles, and the question being asked is. When do those induced preferences satisfy the NM axioms on their own?

VARIATION #1:
STATISTICAL DEPENDENCE BETWEEN x AND y

Consider the following simplification of the above story. Totrep has no discretion as to the distribution of y. Totrep learns *nothing* about y until after he chooses c_1. The payment x is made in period 1, and the amount of the payment is known before c_1 must be chosen.

Let p denote the probability distribution function of x, and $q(\cdot|x)$ denote the conditional probability distribution function of y given x. That is, we allow the two sources of income to be statistically dependent.

Then Totrep's expected utility will be

$$\sum_x p(x) \max_{c_1} [\sum_y U(c_1, w + x - c_1 + y) q(y|x)].$$

A lot needs to be said about this expression. Note first that the maximization is pulled outside the second summation – this is because

Totrep has to choose c_1 *before* learning what y will be. (What would it look like if c_1 were chosen after learning what y is?) Second, consumption in period 2 is the expression $w + x - c_1 + y$ – this is the sum of what is left over in savings, if $w + x$ exceeds c_1, or is owed to the banker, if $w+x$ falls short of c_1, added to the amount of income y. (If the interest rate r were nonzero, we'd write $(1+r)(w+x-c_1)+y$ for c_2.) We should add bankruptcy constraints to the maximization problem; c_1 must be chosen so that $w + x - c_1 + y$ is greater or equal than zero with probability one. I'll never write this constraint in, but it will always be implicit in what I say.

Does this define (or induce) preferences over simple probability distributions p? And if so, are these preferences NM? That is, do they satisfy the NM axioms? It seems as if these questions can be answered affirmatively: If I define a function F on the space of simple probability distributions p on R by

$$(12.1) \qquad F(p) = \sum_x p(x) \max_{c_1} [\sum_y U(c_1, w + x - c_1 + y) q(y|x)],$$

then surely Totrep prefers p to p' if and only if $F(p) > F(p')$. And it is apparent that $F(p)$ satisfies $F(ap+(1-a)p') = aF(p)+(1-a)F(p')$, so by the mixture space theorem, Totrep's preferences over probability distributions on x satisfy the NM axioms.

But I've slipped one over on you here, if you bought my argument, that is. Presumably, changing from p to p' may change the conditional distribution of y given x. Put another way, it can be that there are two gambles over x with the *same* marginal distribution p, but one is statistically independent of y while the second is perfectly correlated with y. If I choose the first, I get a different overall expected utility than if I choose the second. This manifests itself in expression (12.1) as follows: Changing from one gamble on x to another may change *not only* the marginal distribution p but also the conditional distributions $q(\cdot|x)$.

So it is nonsense to ask whether preferences over lotteries on x are NM. Just knowing the marginal distribution on x – the things that NM theory takes as the primitive objects of choice – is *not* enough to tell you how good or bad is the lottery. You need to know the joint distribution of x and y. There is no way to consider separately preference over gambles on x, ...

... unless you make some simplifying assumption concerning the statistical relation between x and y, such as that they are always independent. That is, suppose Totrep's broker calls with some possible gambles that are all independent of Totrep's income from various sources. Then letting q be the marginal distribution of y, (12.1) simplifies to

$$(12.2) \qquad F(p) = \sum_x p(x) \max_{c_1} [\sum_y U(c_1, w + x - c_1 + y)q(y)].$$

In this case the logic employed above is legitimate – Totrep prefers one gamble p on x to a second p' iff $F(p) > F(p')$, and since $F(ap + (1-a)p') = aF(p) + (1-a)F(p')$, these preferences are NM. Indeed, a NM utility function u on x is easily seen to be

$$(12.3) \qquad u(x) = \max_{c_1} [\sum_y U(c_1, w + x - c_1 + y)q(y)].$$

The general topic of which this is an example has the rubric "the utility function for wealth" in the finance/economics literature. The analysis extends to multiple periods – the general result is: Preferences for lotteries affecting current wealth are NM if the gambles resolve immediately (see below) and if the gambles are independent of other income sources and (when appropriate) future investment/income opportunities. A good textbook in financial market theory will tell you all about this.

This leaves open one very important question – what do you do (if anything) when there is statistical dependence between x and y? You'll need to know more than just the distribution of x – at worst you'll need to know the entire joint distribution of x and y. Some analysis is possible that doesn't go quite so far, by assuming that all distributions are jointly Normal, say, it will be enough to know the means, variances, and covariances of x and y. I won't go into this subject in any detail here, but if you're interested, any treatment of the Capital Asset Pricing Model in finance will get you started along the proper development of such a theory.

VARIATION #2: DISCRETION AS TO y

Suppose we change the story just told a little bit, by assuming that Totrep has some discretion as to the distribution of y. The

choices of x that are offered are independent of all the possible choices
of y (so the problems raised in the previous section are not at issue),
but now Totrep can, upon choosing a distribution of x, simultaneously "change" the distribution of y. Let us suppose that Totrep has
available a finite set $\{q_1, \ldots, q_i, \ldots, q_I\}$ of possible distributions of y
from which he can choose. Let us also suppose that the choice of i
must be made prior to the date at which the outcome of x is known.
Then the value to Totrep of a distribution p on x is given by the
function F defined as

$$(12.4) \quad F(p) = \max_i \{ \sum_x p(x) \max_{c_1} [\sum_y U(c_1, w + x - c_1 + y) q_i(y)] \}.$$

That is, Totrep prefers p to p' iff $F(p) > F(p')$. Do preferences so
defined on the p's always satisfy the NM axioms (or do they ever
do so)? Since it is easy to see that in general, $F(ap + (1 - a)p') \neq
aF(p) + (1 - a)F(p')$, it is not obvious that the answer is yes. In
fact the answer in general will be no. I leave it to you to find an
example. Note, however, that if the choice of i needn't be made until
after Totrep learns the outcome x, then the value of a p is given by
F defined by

$$(12.5) \quad F(p) = \sum_x p(x) [\max_i \max_{c_1} [\sum_y U(c_1, w + x - c_1 + y) q_i(y)]].$$

This does satisfy $F(ap + (1 - a)p') = aF(p) + (1 - a)F(p')$ (proof?),
so that in this case preferences for lotteries on x are NM. (What is
the appropriate utility function?)

A slight variation on the above is as follows. Suppose that the
outcome of y is learned prior to the decision about c_1, but the decision about p and q_i must be made simultaneously. What is the
appropriate function F that gives the value to Totrep of a probability distribution p on x in this case? It is

$$(12.6) \quad F(p) = \max_i \sum_x p(x) [\sum_y q_i(y) [\max_{c_1} U(c_1, w + x - c_1 + y)]].$$

Again examples can be produced to show that if we define induced
preferences on p's in the natural fashion: $p \succ p'$ iff $F(p) > F(p')$,
then $\succ$ will not in general satisfy the NM axioms. This corresponds

to the following story: Totrep is simultaneously considering a number of different investments, all of which are statistically independent of each other. In the above setting, he is considering two – one with payoff x and the other with payoff y. He would like to "decouple" these decisions and consider each one separately – what we have above says that he cannot do this and hope to use an NM analysis on them separately. If he wants to use an NM analysis, he must look at the whole package.

There is one case where he can safely consider them separately using NM analyses and then pick the best out of each group. A necessary and sufficient condition for this to be legit is that the induced utility function for wealth, defined by (12.3), has constant absolute risk aversion. I leave it to you to prove this statement.

VARIATION #3:
TEMPORAL RESOLUTION OF UNCERTAINTY

In the last section, whether preferences were NM or not depended on whether the choice of q_i can be before or after the uncertainty concerning x resolved. That was one example of the general problem of temporal resolution of uncertainty. Here is another.

So far we've looked at cases where the outcome x was known *before* c_1 had to be chosen. Now we'll relax that assumption. To keep matters simple, assume that y is the constant zero – x represents all of Totrep's income in addition to his endowment w – and x is received in period two instead of in one.

Now consider the following: Suppose x gives Totrep either \$20,000 or \$10,000, each with probability 1/2. Think of x as being determined by a coin flip. We want Totrep to compare this with, say, \$13K for sure. If Totrep had NM preferences over gambles in x, he'd be able to get out his utility function u (presumably different from the one defined in (12.3), because we've changed the setup) and he'd compare $u(13K)$ with $(u(20K) + u(10K))/2$. Will this work?

Would this work for you? If you are a student, think of the prizes as representing *all* the income you'll receive from next September 1 for the year following, out of which you'll need to pay your all expenses except for tuition. You will be barred from taking a job, and if you have a working spouse, he/she will be forced to stop working. You can, however, carry over savings from this year and this coming summer. Would you prefer the gamble or the sure thing? If you aren't a student, pretend that you are.

As you ponder this question, keep in mind the following added complication (although it was really there all the time). I haven't told you yet whether I'll flip the coin today or next September 1, and I haven't told you when you will learn the outcome of the coin flip. Suppose you had a choice between the following four "gambles": (a) the sure $13K; (b) the risky gamble, with the coin flipped next 1 September at which point you learn the outcome; (c) the risky gamble, with the coin flipped today and you told the outcome next September 1; (d) the risky gamble, with the coin flipped today and you told the outcome today. I'm not sure how you'll compare (a) with (b), (c), and (d), but I'm fairly sure that you'll tell me that (d) is better than (b) and (c), which in turn are just as good as each other. This is because the information concerning how much you will be given might be valuable in planning this year's expenses – if you know you're going to get $20K, you can blow your savings account on an immediate trip to Hawaii – if it will be $10K, you'll try to save more. Since it is the information that is of value to you in planning your interim expenditures, (b) and (c) are the same thing. And since (d) gives you this information sooner, it is better than the other two.

However the gambles in (b), (c) and (d) have the same marginal distribution viewed as probability distributions on x. So if you had NM preferences over gambles on x, you'd rate all three as the same. Manifestly, you don't have NM preferences over gambles in x; you aren't even indifferent between two versions of the "same" gamble as represented by a probability distribution.

How can we see this in Totrep's problem? If he chooses the $13K for sure, he gets utility

(12.7) $$\max_{c_1} U(c_1, w - c_1 + 13K).$$

If he chooses the gamble and the coin is flipped after c_1 must be chosen, which is the case in gambles (b) and (c), then he gets

(12.8) $$\max_{c_1}[\frac{U(c_1, w - c_1 + 20K) + U(c_1, w - c_1 + 10K)}{2}].$$

And if he takes the gamble, the coin is flipped today, and he learns the outcome before c_1 must be chosen, which is (d), he gets

$$(12.9) \quad \frac{\max_{c_1} U(c_1, w - c_1 + 20K) + \max_{c_1'} U(c_1', w - c_1' + 10K)]}{2}.$$

It is easy to see that the quantity in (12.9) is at least as large as the quantity in (12.8) (do it), and except for very strange functions for U (given the interpretation), (12.9) strictly exceeds (12.8).

Just knowing the marginal distribution p of x is *not* enough to tell how much Totrep likes the gamble in x. We also need to know when Totrep will learn the outcome – before or after c_1 must be chosen. And the pattern of *resolution of uncertainty* needn't be one of the two simple ones discussed above, where either everything resolves before c_1 is chosen, or everything resolves afterwards. It is possible to have partial resolutions of uncertainty prior to the c_1 decision – for example, imagine that the \$20K/\$10K lottery is to be determined by the roll of a die – if the die comes out with one, two or three spots up, then the payoff will be \$20K, but \$10K will result from four, five or six spots up. Suppose the die is going to be rolled before the c_1 decision will be made, but all Totrep is told is whether the number of spots up was an even or an odd number – after Totrep chooses c_1 the exact number of spots is revealed to him. In this case, what replaces (12.8) and (12.9)? Totrep will (generally) like this partial resolution more than having to wait for any resolution and less than getting complete resolution immediately.

To describe Totrep's induced preferences on lotteries in x in this story, I need to know not only the marginal distribution of x (that is, p) but also the pattern of the resolution of uncertainty vis a vis the date when c_1 must be chosen. So Totrep's preferences for gambles on x could not possibly be NM – the objects of choice in that theory, marginal distributions, aren't rich enough to capture all that is essential to Totrep's preferences ...

... unless we make a simplifying assumption, such as all uncertainty resolves prior to the choice of c_1, or all uncertainty resolves after. If we restrict attention to either of these cases, then the marginal distribution p of x tell us everything else we need to know, and we can ask whether Totrep's preferences are NM.

Case 1. If all uncertainty resolves prior to the choice of c_1, then Totrep's preferences over gambles p are given by the function F defined by

$$F(p) = \sum_x p(x)[\max_{c_1} U(c_1, w - c + x)].$$

That is, p is better than p' for Totrep iff $F(p) > F(p')$. It is easy to see that in this case $F(ap + (1 - a)p') = aF(p) + (1 - a)F(p')$, and so preferences are NM with utility function u given by

$$u(x) = \max_{c_1} U(c_1, w - c + x).$$

Case 2. If all uncertainty resolves after the choice of c_1, then Totrep's preferences over gambles p are given by the function F defined by

$$F(p) = \max_{c_1}[\sum_x p(x)U(c_1, w - c + x)].$$

It is not hard to produce examples where $F(ap + (1-a)p') \neq aF(p) + (1 - a)F(p')$, but this is *not* enough to conclude that Totrep's preferences over p's are not NM – we need an example where no monotone transformation G of F satisfies $G(ap + (1 - a)p') = aG(p) + (1 - a)G(p')$. (Why is this necessary and sufficient?)

It is not hard to produce examples where this is so. Suppose, for example that $U(c_1, c_2) = \ln(c_1) + \ln(c_2)$. Let $w = 0$. Consider the gambles p and p', where p gives prizes 1 and 2, each with probability 1/2, and p' gives .6 and 6.702, each with probability 1/2. You can show that $F(p) = -.8004$, with corresponding $c_1 = .6096$. And $F(p') = -.8004$, with corresponding $c_1 = .3957$. Thus Totrep is indifferent between p and p'. If his preferences obeyed the NM axioms, he would have to be indifferent between each of these and their convex combination $(p + p')/2$. (Why?) But it's easy to see that Totrep strictly prefers both p and p' to $(p + p')/2$. (Why?) Totrep cannot have NM preferences.

In general, induced preferences depend on the pattern of resolution of uncertainty when in the larger model/context there are decisions to be made that are not included in the model of the subproblem. Only when all uncertainty resolves *before* any decisions must be made are you guaranteed that the induced preferences will be NM.

Any number of questions can be taken up at this point. For example:

(a) Fixing the date of resolution of uncertainty at some date *after* a decision must be made, are there circumstances where induced preferences obey the NM axioms?

(b) Can anything be said about preferences of "lotteries" where the date of resolution of uncertainty can vary? To do this, a necessary first step is to find some way to encode the pattern of resolution of uncertainty mathematically. If the answer to the first question is yes, does the NM expected utility structure have any role to play in representing such preferences?

(c) If an NM model is not exactly appropriate, how bad an approximation do you get by using one anyway? (This question could be asked of any of the problems discussed in this chapter.)

The papers that originally discussed temporal resolution of uncertainty are Dreze and Modigliani (1972), Mossin (1969), and Spence and Zeckhauser (1972). You will get a shot at some of the answers in the problems, but in case you get stuck, Kreps and Porteus (1978,1979) should be consulted.

SUMMARY

This chapter has surveyed some of the major problems encountered in applying the models of choice under uncertainty that we've previously developed to applications where, for reasons of tractability, not all of Totrep's important decisions are considered. When there is correlation between the gambles over which Totrep is optimizing and other uncertainty left out of the application, when other decisions are being made simultaneously to those in the application, or when the uncertainty of the gambles being optimized over resolves at dates in the future (after important decisions left out must be taken), then use of the standard models is *very* suspect and often quite wrong. We have seen these conclusions for the von Neumann-Morgenstern model. Similar conclusions can be obtained in settings appropriate for the Savage model. Since this includes just about every important economic/social decision making context that you are likely to encounter, there is obviously a need for care in application.

PROBLEMS

(1) Show that preferences defined on (simple) probability distributions according to the index $F(p)$ defined in (12.4) will not satisfy the NM axioms in general. Show that those given by the index $F(p)$ in (12.5) will satisfy the axioms, and give the appropriate utility function.

(2) For preferences defined by the index $F(p)$ defined by (12.6), show that a necessary and sufficient condition for those preferences to satisfy the NM axioms is that the induced utility function on wealth given by (12.3) has constant absolute risk aversion. For which $U(c_1, c_2)$ will this be true?

(3) Show that the quantity in (12.9) is always at least as large as the quantity in (12.8). For what functions $U(c_1, c_2)$ will (12.8) always be equal to (12.9)?

(4) Provide the details of the arguments and calculations for the example with log utility on page 174.

(5) In this problem, we look at a very simple version of the difficulty arising with temporal resolution of uncertainty. Consider an individual with the following choice problem. He must select an action a from a finite set of feasible actions $A = \{a_1, \ldots, a_N\}$. He must also select a lottery/probability distribution on a finite set of outcomes $Z = \{z_1, \ldots, z_N\}$. What makes this a problem concerning temporal resolution of uncertainty is that the individual must choose the action at the same time that the probability distribution is chosen, before the uncertainty in that probability distribution resolves. Let P denote the set of all probability distributions on Z. We suppose that there is a function $V : Z \times A \to R$ such that the individual's preferences on $P \times A$ are given by

$$(12.9) \quad (p, a) \succ (p', a') \text{ iff } \sum_{n=1}^{N} p(z_n) V(z_n, a) > \sum_{n=1}^{N} p'(z_n) V(z_n, a').$$

Assume that for $n = 1, \ldots, N$, $V(z_n, a_n) > V(z_n, a_m)$ for all $m \neq n$.

Define a new binary relation $\succ$ on P by

$$p \succ p' \text{ iff } \max_{a \in A} \sum_{n=1}^{N} p(z_n) V(z_n, a) > \max_{a \in A} \sum_{n=1}^{N} p'(z_n) V(z_n, a).$$

It is natural to interpret $\succ$ as the individual's induced preference for lotteries, assuming that whatever lottery he chooses, he simultaneously takes the best action for that lottery. We are interested in whether $\succ$ satisfies the von-Neumann-Morgenstern axioms – that is, whether there exists a function $u : Z \rightarrow R$ such that

(12.10) $$p \succ p' \text{ iff } \sum_{n=1}^{N} p(z_n) u(z_n) > \sum_{n=1}^{N} p'(z_n) u(z_n).$$

(a) Show that in general, no such function U will exist. [Hint: Suppose $V(z_1, a_1) = V(z_2, a_2)$ and think about the lottery which gives z_1 with probability 1/2 and z_2 with probability 1/2.]

(b) Show that a sufficient condition for there to exist such a function u is that

(12.11) $$V(z, a) = f(a) + g(a)h(z),$$

where $g(a) > 0$ for every a.

The last part of the problem is to show that (12.11) is not just sufficient – it is also necessary. Do this in the following three steps. On any step, you may assume the previous ones even if you haven't proven them.

(c) Let δ_m denote the probability distribution with probability one attached to z_m. Then show that for any $p \in P$ and δ_m, there exists $\alpha > 0$ such that for all $\beta < \alpha$

$$\max_{a \in A} \sum_{n=1}^{N} [\beta p(z_n) + (1 - \beta) \delta_m(z_n)] V(z_n, a)$$

$$= \sum_{n=1}^{N} [\beta p(z_n) + (1 - \beta) \delta_m(z_n)] V(z_n, a_m).$$

That is, a_m is optimal for all distributions p which are "close" to δ_m. [Hint: Use the assumption given immediately after (12.9). It isn't necessary to assume that u exists as in (12.10) for this step.]

(d) Show that if u exists as in (12.10), then for $m = 1, \ldots, N$

$$p \overset{\cdot}{\succ} p' \text{ iff } \sum_{n=1}^{N} p(z_n)V(z_n, a_m) > \sum_{n=1}^{N} p'(z_n)V(z_n, a_m).$$

[Hint: The words "substitution axiom" should appear prominently in your solution.]

(e) Show that if u exists as in (12.10), then V has the form (12.11). [Hint: The words "uniqueness result" should appear prominently in your solution.]

(If this hasn't exhausted you, see if you can relate this back to the problem of our Totrep choosing consumption in a two period problem, where first period consumption has to be chosen before uncertainty pertaining to second period income resolves.)

(6) Suppose that Totrep faces some uncertainty about a prize he will receive from a finite set Z. This uncertainty resolves in (possibly) two stages – at date $t = 1$ there may be partial resolution of uncertainty, and at date $t = 2$, any remaining uncertainty will resolve. Formally, we let P be the space of all probability distributions on Z, and we let Π be the space of all simple probability distributions on P. Elements $\pi \in \Pi$ are called "two stage temporal lotteries", where the idea is that for $\pi \in \Pi$, Totrep learns at date $t = 1$ the outcome of π, which is a "one stage temporal lottery" $p \in P$, which then resolves at $t = 2$, giving a prize in Z. Note that, as elements of Π, a 50-50 gamble with prizes, say, z and z', which resolves entirely at $t = 1$ is a different animal from a gamble with the same prizes and the same probabilities that resolves at time $t = 2$. Specifically, the first is a mixture of two degenerate elements of P, while the second is a degenerate distribution in Π which gives (with probability one) a nondegenerate element of P. Moreover, each of these is distinct from: Roll a die, with prize z is the die has one, two or three spots up, and z' for four, five or six. Tell Totrep whether the die came up with an even or an odd number of spots at date $t = 1$, and tell Totrep the actual outcome at date $t = 2$.

Assume that Totrep has preferences over Π given by $\succ$.

As you will recognize, Π is a mixture space in the usual fashion, so it makes mathematical sense to assume the three mixture space axioms for $\succ$.

Now consider $\succ$ restricted to those elements of Π that are degenerate lotteries (giving prizes in P with certainty). Specifically, define a binary relation $\succ^2$ on P by

$$p \succ^2 p' \text{ iff } \delta_p \succ \delta_{p'},$$

where δ_p is the degenerate lottery (in Π) that gives $p \in P$ with certainty. Since $\succ^2$ is a binary relation on P, and P is manifestly a mixture space, it makes mathematical sense to assume that $\succ^2$ satisfies the three mixture space axioms on P.

Finish the following representation theorem: For a binary relation $\succ$ on Π, define $\succ^2$ on P as above. Then $\succ$ satisfies the three mixture space axioms on Π and $\succ^2$ satisfies the three mixture space axioms on P if and only if....

13

Dynamic Choice Theory and the Choice of Opportunity Sets

Near the end of Chapter 10, we introduced the standard manner of handling dynamic choice problems, namely to reduce them to a static choice of strategy. In this chapter, I will propose an alternative. It is easiest to begin with a specific and concrete choice problem; philosophical musings about the general problem of dynamic choice will come after you have seen the specifics.

BASIC SETUP

As a budding Totrep, you are faced with a complex decision today at lunchtime. You must decide what to have for lunch, and at the same time you must decide where to make reservations for tonight's dinner. There are several restaurants at which you might dine tonight – you know them all well, and you are certain of the menu of meals that they serve and the prices of the meals. For the sake of concreteness, let us suppose that there are four restaurants at which you might dine, with the following menus:

Menu #1: {steak, pasta},
Menu #2: {chicken, fish},
Menu #3: {chicken},
Menu #4: {fish, pasta}.

This means: At restaurant #2 chicken and fish are served, etc. To simplify matters, we assume that similarly titled meals at different restaurants are the same – same quality, same price, etc.

For lunch, you can have either veal or tuna-fish.

You are on a strict expense account budget that makes it impossible to have both veal for lunch and steak for supper, but any other combination is possible.

Then in terms of the objects of immediate choice, you have at the moment eight possible choices. (I'll abbreviate all meals by their first letters).

$$(v, \{p\}), (v, \{c, f\}), (v, \{c\}), (v, \{f, p\}),$$

$$(t, \{s, p\}), (t, \{c, f\}), (t, \{c\}), (t, \{f, p\}).$$

Note that I've represented each of the eight objects as a pair – lunch, the opportunity set for dinner. Note how veal and menu #1 results in $(v, \{p\})$ and not $(v, \{s, p\})$ – if you have veal, steak is out of your opportunity set.

How do we handle this choice problem? The methodology of Chapter 2 suggests that we look at a binary relation $\succ$ representing your preferences among the eight possible meal-menu pairs, and we assume that you choose a $\succ$-best pair. That's not much help. If there was some uncertainty floating around – say, you aren't sure about the menu at one or more of the restaurants – then all the things we've discussed since Chapter 4 might apply. My point is: as a choice problem of the sort we've been discussing, this complex situation fits nicely, *assuming* that these meal-menu pairs are the basic items of choice. But presumably that isn't how you would look at this problem. You might think ahead to what you'll want to (or will) choose at the restaurant in each case, and use that to figure out how good is each menu. That is, you might use the structure in this problem and the fact that this is one choice in an ongoing sequence of choices, resulting in a history of meals, in order to decide what to do now. Put descriptively, if I'm trying to describe your behavior today, I might do well to consider what these sorts of considerations will imply about your choices today. If I assume just a modicum of rationality on your part, I can assume that you will select according to some preference relation on meal-menu pairs. But I may be able to narrow down the possible preference relations that you might employ if I consider this as part of an ongoing dynamic choice problem.

The formal problem that we'll consider generalizes just a bit the situation above. There will be a finite set X of consumption bundles for today, and another finite set Y will represent the possible consumption bundles for tomorrow (or tonight). Typical elements of X will be denoted by x, x', etc. and of Y by y, y', etc. The collection of "opportunity sets of tomorrow's consumption," the set of all nonempty subsets of Y, will be denoted by A, with typical elements a, a', etc. *Today*, Totrep is choosing among pairs from $X \times A$, or pairs of the form: a consumption bundle for today, an opportunity set from which consumption tomorrow will be chosen.

Totrep will be presumed to have preferences over the space $X \times A$, given by a preference relation $\succ$. We are interested in what can be said about this preference relation – what restrictions on it are natural for a rational Totrep.

We shall be interested in the relation $\succ$ only (except insofar as other relations are helpful in characterizing it). A set of questions related to the ones that we shall ask would concern not only Totrep's preferences/choice behavior today (on $X \times A$) but also his preferences tomorrow (on Y). But for the time being we shall *not* be concerned explicitly with second period preferences/choice behavior. Thus the subject for now is more properly termed "preference for opportunity sets from dynamic choice considerations" instead of dynamic choice theory.

THE STANDARD MODEL

From a normative perspective, the natural solution to the restaurant problem calls for a little bit of introspection. You could conceivably wind up with one of the following eight combinations of meals:

$$(v, s), (v, p), (v, c), (t, s), (t, p), (t, c), (t, f).$$

(I haven't deleted (v, s) from this list, because I don't want feasibility constraints to impinge at this stage.) So you should first decide how you feel about these eight possible meal-meal pairs. Let me suppose that your underlying preferences for these eight are given by a preference relation $\overset{\cdot}{\succ}$ defined as

$$(v, s) \overset{\cdot}{\succ} (v, c) \overset{\cdot}{\succ} (t, s) \overset{\cdot}{\sim} (v, f) \overset{\cdot}{\succ} (t, c) \overset{\cdot}{\sim} (t, p) \overset{\cdot}{\succ} (v, p) \overset{\cdot}{\succ} (t, f).$$

Then in comparing, say $(v, \{c, f\})$ vs. $(t, \{s, p\})$, it seems natural to say that the first meal-menu pair is better, as the best meal-meal combination (in terms of $\overset{\cdot}{\succ}$) "in" the first meal-menu pair is (v,c), which is $\overset{\cdot}{\succ}$-better than the $\overset{\cdot}{\succ}$-best meal-meal pair (namely (t,s)) in the second meal-menu pair. Following this logic, the relation $\overset{\cdot}{\succ}$ above induces the following relation on the eight available pairs of meals and menus:

$$(v,\{c,f\}) \sim (v,\{c\}) \succ (t,\{s,p\}) \sim (v,\{f,p\}) \succ$$

$$(t,\{c,f\}) \sim (t,\{c\}) \sim (t,\{f,p\}) \succ (v,\{p\}).$$

This introspective-normative approach is derived from the following logic. All the decision maker cares about is the final result – the pair of meals (x,y) that is consumed. So the decision maker should decide how he feels about these simplest/most basic items. Having decided on basic preferences over pairs of meals, the decision maker should set out *now* to do whatever is necessary to obtain the best pair among those available. In the example, this would be to choose either $(v,\{c,f\})$ or $(v,\{c\})$ over the other six meal-menu pairs (to be followed with the choice of chicken later).

This is sometimes called the *strategic* or *dynamic programming* approach. "Strategic" refers to the implicit principle that today's choice ought to be one step in the implementation of the best overall strategy for dynamic choice. Of course, this is what lies behind the discussion at the end of Chapter 10 concerning the selection of a best strategy. As we observed then, this is the approach championed by most of the "classics" – see for example Savage (1972, p.15ff.)

In the general context of X, Y, A, etc. this would be formalized as follows:

Take as primitive a preference relation as $\overset{\cdot}{\succ}$ on $X \times Y$, and *define* a binary relation $\succ$ on $X \times A$ from $\overset{\cdot}{\succ}$ by

(13.1) $(x,a) \succ (x',a')$ if for all $y' \in a'$ there exists $y \in a$ such that $(x,y) \overset{\cdot}{\succ} (x',y')$.

Proposition (13.2). For an arbitrary preference relation $\overset{\cdot}{\succ}$ on $X \times Y$, $\succ$ defined on $X \times A$ by (13.1) is a preference relation.

A complementary descriptive approach to the normative approach above would be to say that a binary relation $\succ$ on $X \times A$ is *strategically rational* if there exists some preference relation $\overset{\cdot}{\succ}$ on $X \times Y$ such that (13.1) holds with the "if" replaced by an "iff".

That is, we observe (through choices and/or questionnaire data) the binary relation $\succ$, and we seek to explain/model $\succ$ by the thought process implicit in (13.1). If we can do this – if we can produce a $\dot{\succ}$ that rationalizes $\succ$ in this sense, then we say that $\succ$ is strategically rational.

Of course, not every binary relation $\succ$ on $X \times A$ is strategically rational. Proposition (13.2) makes obvious one necessary condition: $\succ$ will have to be a preference relation. But this is not sufficient. Consider, for example, an individual who says (in part) that

$$(t, \{s\}) \succ (t, \{s, p\}).$$

This will be impossible to rationalize as in (13.1). (Why?) Or suppose we found an individual who said that

$$(t, \{c, f\}) \succ (t, \{s\}) \succ (t, \{c\}) \succ (t, \{f\}).$$

This will also be impossible to explain as in (13.1) (Why?)

Proposition (13.3). A binary relation $\succ$ on $X \times A$ is strategically rational if and only if it is a preference relation and it satisfies

(13.4) $(x, a) \succeq (x, a')$ implies $(x, a) \sim (x, a \cup a')$.

I leave the proofs of this proposition and the one previous as exercises.

The term strategically rational is certainly value-laden – it sounds as if any behavior $\succ$ not satisfying this property would have to be crazy. But do you think that this is so? Can you imagine any circumstances where you would want to express preferences as in, say, the two examples above? Let me give each one a try in turn.

CHANGING TASTES AND SOPHISTICATED CHOICE

The Totrep who expressed the preferences $(t, \{s\}) \succ (t, \{s, p\})$ explains: "I'm on a diet and am terribly weak-willed. If I make reservations at the restaurant $\{s, p\}$, I know what will happen – I'll see pasta on the menu and choose it, thereby breaking my diet. Better to avoid the temptation, hence my strict preference for $(t, \{s\})$ over $(t, \{s, p\})$."

This Totrep continues: "I know that when I get to the restaurant of my choice, my behavior will be governed by a preference relation $\succ^x$ over Y, where the meal x that I had for lunch may impact on my preferences. So when I look right now at a pair (x, a), I know that I'm really looking at the result (x, y) where y is the $\succ^x$-best item in a. (What if $\succ^x$ rates two meals in a as being equally good? That's a good question. Since this is just meant to be an introduction to this subject, let me assume that this *never* happens – each $\succeq^x$ is antisymmetric.) I'll write $(x, c_x(a))$ for the pair (x, y) such that y is $\succ^x$-best in a.

"Right now I have preferences over pairs (x, y) given by a preference relation $\succ$ on $X \times Y$. So, being a sophisticated fellow, if I've got a choice between (x, a) and (x', a'), I think ahead to the eventual outcomes $(x, c_x(a))$ and $(x', c_{x'}(a'))$ that will ensue and compare those two. I say

(13.5) $(x, a) \succ (x', a')$ iff $(x, c_x(a)) \succ (x', c_{x'}(a'))$.

"Note that if right now I think $(t, s) \succ (t, p)$, yet I know that $p \succ^t s$, then it makes sense (follows (13.5)) for me to prefer strictly $(t, \{s\})$ to $(t, \{s, p\})$, which I do."

In the literature, this is called the changing tastes with sophisticated choice model. The main characteristics of choice according to this model are (a) an individual may act to constrain his/her future opportunities, in order not to have the opportunity to make a bad choice later on, so that (b) an individual may take an immediate action that appears suboptimal from the point of view of the dynamic programming/strategic approach in order to control his/her later preferences. The truly classic reference in the literature to this sort of consideration is found in the *Odyssey*, where Odysseus lashes himself to the mast (constrains his later options) in order to hear the Sirens' song.

From a theoretical point of view, an interesting question is: Which binary relations $\succ$ on $A \times X$ can be modelled in the above fashion? The answer to this question is neither pleasant nor intuitive – if you are up to a challenge, give it a shot. (I don't believe that the answer is published anywhere.)

This model of changing tastes appears first in the economics literature, as far as I know, in Strotz (1955). Since then there has been some of development of the theoretical model, and some work on applications, to things like forced savings programs and Christmas Clubs, the optimal amount of an addictive drug to take, and so on. There has also been some dispute as to whether any change from the standard model (13.1) is really necessary – see Stigler and Becker (1977) (only the title is in Latin). Of course, preferences defined on $X \times A$ using (13.5) will in general not be describable using the standard model, since preferences using the standard model will never strictly prefer a smaller opportunity set to one larger. Hence this dispute must be about whether the model is necessary for specific applications.

PREFERENCE FOR FLEXIBILITY

Our second Totrep expresses the following preferences (among others)

$$(t, \{c, f\}) \succ (t, \{s\}) \succ (t, \{c\}) \succ (t, \{f\}).$$

Note that (13.2) is violated so that no rationalization by (13.1) is possible. This particular Totrep explains:

"Always supposing that I have tuna for lunch, I can't be sure what I'll want to have when dinner-time rolls around. I can think of three possibilities: (i) Steak most preferred, chicken second, fish third; (ii) chicken first, then steak and then fish; (iii) fish first, then steak, and then chicken. So if I take the menu $\{f\}$, I'll get my first choice one third of the time and my third choice two thirds of the time. The menu $\{c\}$ will get me one first place, one second and one third. The menu $\{s\}$ will get me one first and two seconds. And the menu $\{c, f\}$ will get me two firsts and a second. I think that the three 'future preference profiles' above are equally likely, hence I express the preferences given above."

This explanation by Totrep suggests the following representation: There is a (for simplicity) finite set of "states of Totrep's preferences" S, which will determine how Totrep ranks meal-pairs. Formally, there is a function

$$u : X \times Y \times S \to R$$

where $u(x, y, s)$ is the "utility" attached to the pair of meals (x, y) in the state s. Totrep will learn the true state s tonight/tomorrow

– so if he consumes x for lunch and has menu a available, in state s he'll net the utility

$$\max_{y \in a} u(x, y, s).$$

Totrep thinks that the probability of state s occuring is $p(s)$ and he is an "expected utility maximizer" – so an index of the meal-menu pair (x, a) is

$$\sum_{s \in S} p(s)[\max_{y \in a} u(x, y, s)].$$

We remarked in Chapter 4 (and again in Chapter 7) that when utility is state dependent, probabilities over states are meaningless – these probabilities can be absorbed into the function u. Thus we make the following definition:

A binary relation $\succ$ on $X \times A$ can be *rationalized by an uncertainty-about-future-tastes model* if there exist a finite set S and a function $u : X \times Y \times S \to R$ such that

(13.6) $(x, a) \succ (x', a')$ iff $\sum_x \max_{y \in a} u(x, y, s) > \sum_s \max_{y' \in a'} u(x', y', s).$

In this definition, notice that the states s have no particular physical meaning. In particular, S, like u, is derived from preferences.

What binary relations $\succ$ on $X \times A$ fit this definition? One obvious necessary condition is that $\succ$ is a preference relation. (Why is this obviously necessary?) A second necessary condition is that

(13.7)   if $a \supseteq a'$, then for all $x, (x, a) \succeq (x, a')$.

That is, a bigger menu (in terms of set inclusion) is as good as a smaller one. (Contrast this with the sorts of preferences discussed in the preceding section on changing tastes.) Condition (13.7) can be termed *preference for flexibility* – Totrep seeks (at least weakly) to keep options open.

A third necessary condition is that, for all a'',

(13.8) if $a \supseteq a'$ and $(x, a) \sim (x, a')$, then $(x, a \cup a'') \sim (x, a' \cup a'')$.

The idea here is that if $a \supseteq a'$ and $(x, a) \sim (x, a')$, then the added flexibility that results from having a instead of a' is worthless. So if both a and a' are enlarged together (by tacking a'' onto each), the added flexibility of $a \cup a''$ over $a' \cup a''$ is also worthless.

Proposition (13.9). A binary relation $\succ$ on $X \times A$ can be rationalized as in (13.6) if and only if $\succ$ is a preference relation and satisfies (13.7) and (13.8).

That is, the three necessary conditions are also sufficient. This is a fairly nice result (but in just a moment you will see why I'm prejudiced in its favor). Properties (13.7) and (13.8) are fairly intuitive, and the proposition says that any preference relation satisfying them can be modelled in a way that bears the interpretation of uncertainty about future tastes.

The property "preference for flexibility" (13.7) was proposed as a reasonable replacement for (13.4) in Koopmans (1964). In this article, Koopmans suggests the uncertainty-about-future-tastes representation, but he did not make any formal connections between the two. The representation has been used in a number of economic contexts, notably in Goldman (1974), where liquidity demand for money is derived from uncertainty about future tastes. The proposition above is proved, and this general subject is further discussed and developed in Kreps (1979).

DISCUSSION

It is patent that dynamic choice is of crucial importance in many important economic (and other) decisions. Consider the selection of any capital asset or savings instrument, or decisions concerning education and jobs; any decision where the individual is making a choice that has an "opportunity set" component to it. The standard models of these choices, at least in the economics literature, have used the general methodology outlined at the end of Chapter 10 – the individual has a lifetime utility function (or overall preferences), solves a complicated dynamic programming problem to find out what the value of any asset/education/etc. will be, and chooses accordingly. In other words, dynamic choice is treated as nothing more than the choice of an optimal strategy.

As a descriptive model, this doesn't seem adequate. It is hard to find anyone who would maintain that individuals, in these sorts of choice situations, don't sometimes act to constrain their own later options, or sometimes act to preserve later options for no apparent reason, or do many other things that the standard model misses. But it is equally hard, if not harder, to find any formal, mathematical development of dynamic choice that encompasses such considerations. The reason for this is simple: Formal choice theory has not dealt well at all with models of dynamic choice beyond the standard "dynamic choice equals static choice of a strategy." I hope that the preceding discussion, incomplete and rudimentary as it is, indicates that this needn't be so and that, in particular, a way to proceed is to study formally the static choice of opportunity sets, and then (something we haven't done) to knit together sensibly those static choices into a truly dynamic framework.

PROBLEMS

(1) Prove Propositions (13.2) and (13.3).

(2) Prove that the representation (13.6) implies properties (13.7) and (13.8). If you are up to a challenge, prove that if $\succ$ is a preference relation satisfying (13.7) and (13.8) (and X and Y are finite sets!), then a representation of the form (13.6) holds.

(3) If you are really up to a challenge, consider the obvious multiperiod analogue of (13.6). Take, say, a three meal formulation, where X is a finite set of possible breakfasts, Y is a finite set of possible lunches, and Z is a finite set of possible dinners. Let A be the set of all nonempty subsets of Z, and let B be the set of all nonempty subsets of $Y \times A$. Totrep's choice in the morning is some $(x, b) \in X \times B$. The representation sought is that there exist finite sets S and T and a function $U : X \times Y \times Z \times S \times T$ such that the index of a pair (x, b) is given by

$$\sum_{s \in S} \max_{(y,a) \in b} \sum_{t \in T} \max_{z \in a} U(x, y, z, t, s).$$

Can you find "nice" properties of a binary relation $\succ$ on $X \times B$ that are necessary and sufficient for this sort of representation?

14

The Experimental Evidence

The models of choice that we have developed are meant to serve both as normative guides for decision making and as descriptive models of how individuals choose. Whether they are really suitable normatively is a matter for the individual decision maker to decide; knowing some of the limitations in theory (from Chapter 12), you are in a relatively good position to decide whether, in a particular situation, you want your choice behavior to conform to one of these models. In this final chapter, I want to touch briefly on evidence concerning the use of these models for descriptive purposes.

In descriptive applications, these models are used to describe the behavior of individuals within a larger context of a market or some other organization. The analyst asks what will be the overall outcomes within the market/organization if individuals act according to one of these models. This manner of application presupposes that these models do a good job of describing individual behavior. So it is natural to test that hypothesis experimentally and/or emprically. I want to introduce some of the more damning experimental evidence, damning in the sense that the models tend to be disconfirmed in certain systematic ways.

This is an enormous subject, and I am not going to do more than give the briefest of introductions to it. Machina (1987, forthcoming) are the places to go if you find your curiosity aroused by this.

To begin, I should say how the experimental evidence is collected. The typical methodology is to ask individuals from a subject population how they would choose in a number of binary choice settings. That is, one asks the subjects a long list of questions like: Would you rather have (a) $1000 for sure or (b) a .9 probability chance of getting $2000 and a .1 chance of getting $0? Now the subjects are not really getting their preferred gambles; this is all pretend. And, indeed, this is often a point of criticism of these studies; critics will say that the subjects, since it is pretend, don't take the exercise seriously. A variation on this criticism is that the subjects typically used, college students, are not very important economically. Even if college students don't conform to the classic models, this criticism goes, important economic decision makers do, and that is what is important to the application of these models in economics. (In the case of some experiments of this sort, the experimenter is very well supported financially, and then the subject may get, say, one of the choices made, randomly selected. There are reasons why this procedure isn't quite kosher, however; see Karni and Saffra (1987).)

This is not the place to get into such criticisms of (these) experimental methods in economics. The reader must decide how troubling is the evidence I'm about to cite, a decision that I hope will be made only after consuming more than the very quick skim of the evidence that follows.

THE ALLAIS PARADOX

The first and most famous violation of the standard models of choice under uncertainty is due to Allais (1953). Allais' basic experimental result has be replicated many, many times, in many forms, and I will report here on the particular experimental results of Kahneman and Tversky (1979). Among the questions asked of subject were the following two. (I am modifying the questions of Kahneman and Tversky by changing the monetary units for purposes of presentation; their article should be consulted for the exact details of their results.) First, choose between the two gambles A and B with objective uncertainty depicted in figure 14.1. Then choose between the two gambles C and D depicted in figure 14.2. If you have never seen this stuff before, it might be instructive to ask yourself: How would you yourself choose in each of these two situations?

In the first choice situation, Kahneman and Tversky observe that 82% choose the gamble B. While in the second situation, 83% choose C. This means that *at least* 65% of their subjects choose B in the first case and C in the second. But this pair of choices is inconsistent with the von Neumann-Morgenstern model of expected utility. If u is the individual's von Neumann-Morgenstern utility function, a preference for B over A means that $u(2400) > .33u(2500) + .66u(2400) + .01u(0)$, or $.34u(2400) > .33u(2500) + .01u(0)$. Similarly, a choice of

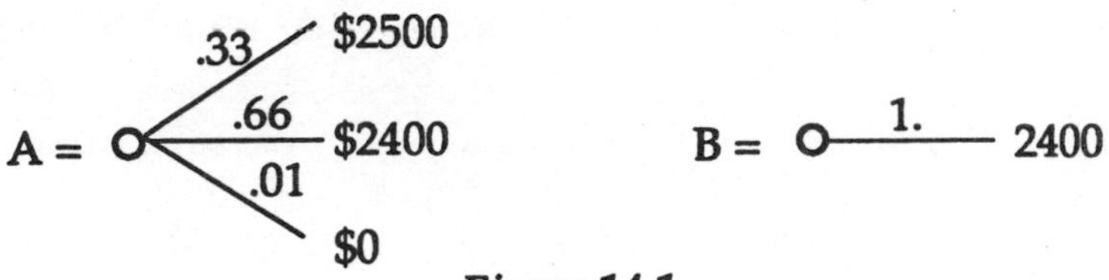

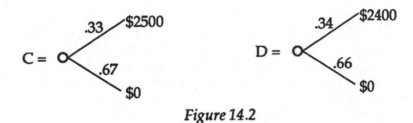

Figure 14.1

Figure 14.2

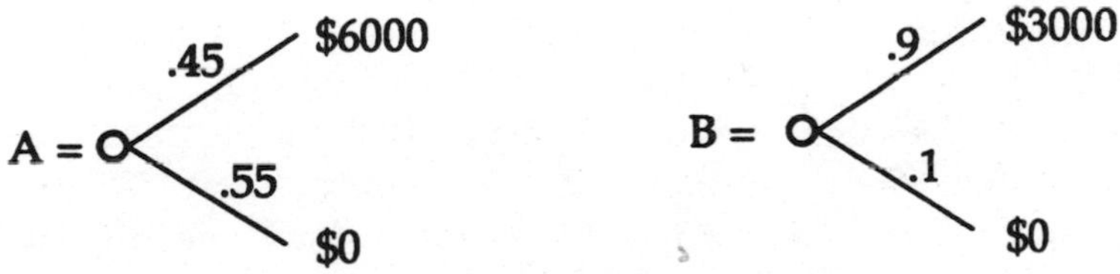

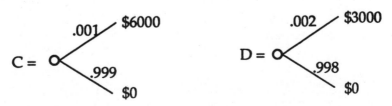

Figure 14.3

Figure 14.4

C over D means that $.33u(2500) + .67u(0) > .34u(2400) + .66u(0)$, or $.33u(2500) + .01u(0) > .34u(2400)$. These two inequalities can hardly be consistent.

You can view this result as a violation of the substitution axiom. According to the substitution axiom, a preference for B over A implies a preference for $2400 for sure over $2500 with probability 33/34 and $0 with probability 1/34. (Why?) Indeed, I would imagine that most people would express precisely this preference. But then the substitution axiom applied to this would say that $.34\delta_{2400} + .66\delta_0 \succ .34(33/34\delta_{2500} + 1/34\delta_0) + .66\delta_0$, which is precisely the reverse of what was seen in the C vs. D comparison.

In the case of this particular pair of choices, Kahneman and Tversky explain what is happening as a "certainty effect" wherein individuals tend to put more weight on what is certain when comparing with events that are viewed as being very likely, but not completely certain. In other words, B is better than A because in B there is no chance of not getting a prize (of getting $0); the one-in-a hundred chance in A is too great a risk to take. But when you compare C with D, there is a substantial chance of getting $0 in either case, and the slightly worse odds in C are more than compensated for by the greater prize that may be won.

Kahneman and Tversky go on to demonstrate a number of other violations of the substitution axiom. For example, they ask subjects to choose between A and B in figure 12.3 and between C and D in figure 12.4. They find that 86% take B over A, and 73% take C over D. So at least 59% of the subjects must simultaneously prefer B to A and C to D, which of course is inconsistent with the substitution axiom. (Why?) They explain this as a "possibility" effect – people tend to treat all small but still positive chances of a prize as being similar. That is, in figure 12.3, you are giving up a substantial amount of probability to double the size of the prize you might win. While in figure 12.4, you'll only win if you are lucky in either case, so why not win a prize twice as large?

What does one do with preferences of these sorts? A lot of the recent literature has gone into devising variations and adaptations of the expected utility model which will accomodate such choices. (Indeed, Kahneman and Tversky themselves propose one variation, although it varies from the classic model on a number of other dimensions as well.) Machina (1987, forthcoming) should be consulted for a survey.

THE ELLSBERG PARADOX

In the previous sets of choices, probabilities were given exogenously; it was the von Neumann-Morgenstern model of choice under uncertainty that was at issue. Problems of a different sort arise experimentally when there is subjective uncertainty. The seminal paper in this vein is Ellsberg (1961).

One variation on the Ellsberg paradox runs as follows. I have an urn with 300 balls in it. Some of the balls are red, some blue, and some yellow. All the balls are the same size and weight, and they are not distinguished in any was except in color. I am willing to tell you that precisely 100 of the balls are red. I am unwilling to say how many are blue and how many yellow, except that, of course, the total number of blue and yellow is 200. I will reach into this urn without looking and draw out one of the balls at random. I want to know your preferences between gambles based on the outcome of this random event. In all these gambles, you will either win $1000 or you will win nothing.

First, would you prefer (A) to get $1000 if the ball drawn out is red and zero if it is blue or yellow, or (B) to get $1000 if the ball drawn out is blue and zero if red or yellow?

Second, would you prefer (C) to get $1000 if the ball drawn out is blue or yellow and zero if it is red, or (D) to get $1000 if the ball drawn out is red or yellow and zero if it is blue?

Many respondents (perhaps you) prefer A to B and C to D. The explanation for such a pair of preferences is that in A, you know the odds are 1/3 of winning the prize. In B, you are unsure of the odds. In C, you know the odds are 2/3 of winning, while in D, you are unsure of the odds. Now in B and D, the odds "average" 1/3 and 2/3, respectively. But the odds are ambiguous. So it feels better to take the gambles with the known odds, given that those with the ambiguous odds are not substantially better "on average." You might even try to say (if you have these preferences) that "risk aversion" explains your choices, where you are averse to the risk of not knowing the odds precisely.

Of course, such a pair of preferences is inconsistent with the Anscombe-Aumann and Savage models. Those models hold that you should assess probabilities for the subjectively uncertain events, probabilities that add up to one, and then choose whichever gamble gives the highest subjective expected utility. In this case, it seems most natural to assess probability 1/3 to the event that the ball drawn is red, and to assess that the events "a blue ball is drawn" and "a yellow ball is drawn" are equally likely. (The Comte d'Alembert from Chapter 11 would certainly agree to this.) This, in turn, implies (if you conform to the models) that each event has probability 1/3, and you are indifferent between A and B and betweeen C and D. But whatever probabilities you assess for the three events, if you strictly prefer A to B, then you must strictly prefer D to C, since the winning event in C is the complement of the winning event in A, and the winning event in D is the complement of the winning event in B.

Still, many individuals do prefer A to B and C to D, on just the sort of grounds given above – they averse to gambling when the odds are ambiguous. There has been rather less work done on trying to modify the standard models to accomodate this, but two recent and very intriguing approaches to this are Segal (1987) and Schmeidler (1988).

FRAMING EFFECTS

To illustrate this class of problems with the classic models, I take an example from Tversky and Kahneman (1981). Answer the following question; then take a two minute break, and answer the one following that:

> Imagine that the U.S. is preparing for the outbreak of an unusual Asian disease, which is expected to kill 600 people. Two alternative programs to combat the disease have been proposed. Assume that the exact scientific esitmate of the consequences of the program are as follows:
>
> If program A is adopted, 200 people will be saved.
>
> If program B is adopted, there is 2/3 probability that no one will be saved, and 1/3 probability that 600 people will be saved.

Take the two-minute break now.

Imagine that the U.S. is preparing for the outbreak of an

unusual Asian disease, which is expected to kill 600 people. Two alternative programs to combat the disease have been proposed. Assume that the exact scientific esitmate of the consequences of the program are as follows:

If program C is adopted, 400 people will die with certainty.

If program D is adopted, there is 2/3 probability that 600 people will die, and 1/3 probability that no one will die.

When Tversky and Kahneman posed these questions to a group of subjects, 72% of the subjects chose A over B, and 78% chose D over C. Hence at least 50% chose A over B and D over C. But if you look, you'll see that A is identical to C and B is identical to D.

It is entirely possible that the subjects of this experiment didn't take the time to think this through. After all, there is no way that you can convince the subjects to such an experiment that their choices are really going to matter. But if we take these results (and others like them) at face value, we see a phenomenon of enormous consequence to the models discussed in this book: The way in which a decision problem is framed or posed can effect the choices made by decision makers. Tversky and Kahneman would say that the problem in this case is that individuals tend to think of decisions in terms of deviations from the status quo, where the framing of the question can establish the status quo. So that in the first question, by talking about how many people will be saved, we've framed the question so that the unlucky 600 are dead, and we are bringing them back to life – in that case, better to save some people for sure. In the second question, the frame is such that they are still with us, and your decision sends some to their death. Hence D is preferred; do you really want to send 400 people to their death with no hope of cure?

There are a number of different demonstrations of how framing matters to decision makers; some further examples are given in Kahneman and Tversky (1979), for example, and Machina (1987, forthcoming) gives many further references.

One can take the position that framing, per se, doesn't pose an enormous problem for descriptive applications of choice theory, insofar as, in building the model, one incorporates into the model the frame that faces the decision maker. But the models that are typical of the literature are not very good at paying attention to framing issues, so the evidence that framing matters is, at least, troublesome to most applications of the theory.

SUMMARY

This has been the briefest of introductions to some of the categories of experimental evidence concerning the descriptive validity
of the models developed in this book. In fact, we have left out entire other categories of problems, such as problems with transitivity or
with the notion that choice is stable through time or doesn't depend on
"unchosen, hence irrelevant alternatives." There is experimental (and
empirical) evidence that individuals are very poor intuitive statisti-
cians – they see patterns in data that aren't there, and they sometimes
overprocess the data that they do have. And faced with complex decision problems, people use heuristic procedures which sometimes bias
their choices in ways that the standard models don't capture. (We discussed one facet of this in Chapter 13, concerning choice in dynamic
choice settings.)

These data provide a continuing challenge to the theorist, a challenge to develop and adapt the standard models so that they are more
descriptive of what we see. It will be interesting to see what will be
in a course on choice theory in ten or twenty years time.

PROBLEMS

(1) Show directly that the preferences expressed in the Ellsberg paradox violate of Savage's Axiom (9.3). Can you produce one (or more)
axioms in the Anscombe-Aumann setting which are violated by the
Ellsberg paradox preferences?

(2) Kahneman and Tversky (1979) gives the following example of a
violation of the von Neumann-Morgenstern expected utility model.
Ninety-five subjects were asked:

"Suppose you consider the possibility of insuring some property against
damage, e.g., fire or theft. After examining the risks and the premium, you find that you have no clear preference between the options
of purchasing insurance or leaving the property uninsured.

"It is then called to your attention that the insurance company offers a new program called *probabilistic insurance*. In this program you pay half of the regular premium. In case of damage, there is a 50 percent chance that you pay the other half of the premium and the insurance company covers all the losses; and there is a 50 percent chance that you get back your insurance payment and suffer all the losses...

"Recall that the premium is such that you find this insurance is barely worth its cost.

"Under these circumstances, would you purchase probabilistic insurance?"

And 80 percent of the subjects said that they wouldn't. Ignore the time value of money. (Because the insurance company gets the premium now, or half now and half later, the interest that the premium might earn can be consequential. I want you to ignore such affects. To do this, you could assume that if the insurance company does insure you, the second half of the premium must be increased to account for the interest the company has foregone. While if they do not, when they return the first half premium, they must return it with the interest it has earned. But it is easiest simply to ignore these complications altogether.) The question is: Does this provide a violation of the von Neumann-Morgenstern model, if we assume (as is typical) that all expected utility maximizers are risk neutral or risk averse? Is someone who definitely turns down probabilistic insurance in preference to full insurance or none, between which he is indifferent, exhibiting behavior that is inconsistent with the model, with risk neutrality or aversion a maintained hypothesis? Show first that the answer is yes. Then reconsider some of the discussion of Chapter 12, and show that the answer is no.

References

Allais, M. (1953), "Le comportement de l'homme rationnel devant de risque: Critique des postulats et axiomes de l'ecole Americaine," *Econometrica*, Vol. 21, 503-546.

Anscombe, F. J. and R. J. Aumann (1963), "A definition of subjective probability," *Annals of Mathematical Statistics*, Vol. 34, 199-205.

Chung, K. L. (1974), *A Course in Probability Theory*, 2nd edition, Academic Press, New York.

de Finetti, B. (1937), "La prevision: ses lois logiques, ses sources subjectives," *Annales de l'Institute Henri Poincaré*, Vol. 7, 1-68. Translated to English by H. E. Kyburg and reprinted in Kyburg and Smokler (1964).

Dreze, J. and F. Modigliani (1972), "Consumption decisions under uncertainty," *Journal of Economic Theory*, Vol. 5, 165-177.

Ellsberg, D. (1961), "Risk, ambiguity, and the Savage axioms," *Quarterly Journal of Economics*, Vol. 75, 643-669.

Feller, W. (1971), *An Introduction to Probability Theory and Its Applications, Volume 2*, 2nd edition, John Wiley and Sons, New York.

Fishburn, P. (1970), *Utility Theory for Decision Making*, John Wiley and Sons, New York. Reprinted by Krieger Press, Huntington, New York, 1979.

Goldman, S. M. (1974), "Flexibility and the demand for money," *Journal of Economic Theory*, Vol. 9, 203-222.

Herstein, I. N. and J. Milnor (1953), "An axiomatic approach to measurable utility," *Econometrica*, Vol. 21, 291-297.

Hewitt, E. and L. J. Savage (1956), "Symmetric measures on Cartesian products," *Transactions of the American Mathematics Society*, Vol. 80, 470-501.

Kahneman, D. and A. Tversky (1979), "Prospect theory: An analysis of decision under risk," *Econometrica*, Vol. 47, 263-91.

Karni, E. and Z. Saffra (1987), " 'Preference reversal' and the observability of preferences by experimental methods," *Econometrica*, Vol. 55, 675-686.

Koopmans, T. C. (1964), "On the flexibility of future preferences," in *Human Judgments and Optimality*, M. W. Shelly and G. L. Bryan (eds.), John Wiley and Sons, New York.

Kraft, C. H., J. W. Pratt and A. Seidenberg (1959), "Intuitive probability on finite sets," *Annals of Mathematical Statistics*, Vol. 30, 408-419.

Krantz, D. H., R. D. Luce, P. Suppes and A. Tversky (1971), *Foundations of Measurement*, Vol. 1, Academic Press, New York.

Kreps, D. M. (1979), "A representation theorem for 'preference for flexibility'," *Econometrica*, Vol. 47, 565-577.

Kreps, D. M. and E. L. Porteus (1978), "Temporal resolution of uncertainty and dynamic choice theory," *Econometrica*, Vol. 46, 185-200.

Kreps, D. M. and E. L. Porteus (1979), "Temporal von Neumann-Morgenstern and induced preferences," *Journal of Economic Theory*, Vol. 20, 81-109.

Kyburg, H. E., and H. E. Smokler, eds. (1964), *Studies in Subjective Probability*, John Wiley and Sons, New York.

Loeve, M. (1963), *Probability Theory*, 3rd edition, Van Nostrand, Princeton.

Machina, M. (1987), "Choice under uncertainty: Problems solved and unsolved," *Economic Perspectives*, Vol. 1, 121-154.

Machina, M. (forthcoming), *The Economic Theory of Individual Choice Under Uncertainty: Theory, Evidence and New Directions*, Cambridge University Press, Cambridge.

Mossin, J. (1969), "A note on uncertainty and preference in a temporal context," *American Economic Review*, Vol. 59, 172-173.

Pratt, J. W. (1964), "Risk aversion in the small and in the large," *Econometrica*, Vol. 32, 122-136.

Rothschild, M. and J. Stiglitz (1970), "Increasing risk. I: A definition," *Journal of Economic Theory*, Vol. 2, 225-243.

Rothschild, M. and J. Stiglitz (1971), "Increasing risk. II: Its economic consequences," *Journal of Economic Theory*, Vol. 3, 66-84.

Rothschild, M. and J. Stiglitz (1973), "Addendum to increasing risk," *Journal of Economic Theory*, Vol. 5, 300.

Savage, L. J. (1954), *The Foundations of Statistics*, John Wiley and Sons, New York. Revised and enlarged edition, Dover, New York, 1972.

Schmeidler, D. (1988), "Subjective probability and expected utility without additivity," mimeo, Tel Aviv University.

Segal, U. (1987), "The Ellsberg paradox and risk aversion: An anticipated utility approach," mimeo, forthcoming in the *International Economic Review*.

Spence, A. M. and R. Zeckhauser (1972), "The effect of the timing of consumption decisions and the resolution of lotteries on the choice of lotteries," *Econometrica*, Vol. 40, 401-403.

Stigler, G. J. and G. S. Becker (1977), "De gustibus non est disputandum," *American Economic Review*, Vol. 67, 76-79.

Strotz, R. (1955), "Myopia and Inconsistency in Dynamic Utility Maximization," *Review of Economic Studies*, Vol. 23, 165-180.

Tversky, A. and D. Kahneman (1981), "The framing of decisions and the psychology of choice," *Science*, Vol. 211, 453-458.

Index

Dickinson, M. H., Farley, C.T., Full, R. J., Koehl, M. A. R., Kram, R. and Lehman, S. (2000) How animals move: an integrative view. *Science* **288**, 100–106.

Dickinson, S. (1929) The efficiency of bicycle-pedalling, as affected by speed and load. *Journal of Physiology* **67**, 242–255.

Dimery, N. J., Alexander, R. McN. and Ker, R. F. (1986) Elastic extensions of leg tendons in the locomotion of horses (*Equus caballus*). *Journal of Zoology* **210**, 415–425.

Dixon, A. F. G., Croghan, P. C. and Gowing, R. P. (1990) The mechanism by which aphids adhere to smooth surfaces. *Journal of Experimental Biology* **152**, 243–253.

Domenici, P. and Blake, R. W. (1997) The kinematics and performance of fish fast-start swimming. *Journal of Experimental Biology* **200**, 1165–1178.

Donovan, D. A. and Carefoot, T. H. (1997) Locomotion in the abalone *Haliotis kamtschatkana*: pedal morphology and cost of transport. *Journal of Experimental Biology* **200**, 1145–1153.

Drucker, E. G. and Jensen, J. S. (1996) Pectoral fin locomotion in the striped surfperch, II: Scaling swimming kinematics and performance at a gait transition. *Journal of Experimental Biology* **199**, 2243–2252.

Drucker, E. G. and Lauder, G. V. (1999) Locomotor forces on a swimming fish: Three-dimensional vortex wake dynamics quantified using digital particle image velocimetry. *Journal of Experimental Biology* **202**, 2393–2412.

Drucker, E. G. and Lauder, G. V. (2000) A hydrodynamic analysis of fish swimming speed: Wake structure and locomotor force in slow and fast labriform swimmers. *Journal of Experimental Biology* **203**, 2379–2393.

Drucker, E. G. and Lauder, G. V. (2001) Wake dynamics and fluid forces of turning maneuvers in sunfish. *Journal of Experimental Biology* **204**, 431–442.

Dudley, R. (2000) *The Biomechanics of Insect Flight*. Princeton University Press, Princeton, N.J.

Dudley, R. and Ellington, C. P. (1990a) Mechanics of forward flight in bumblebees, I: Kinematics and morphology. *Journal of Experimental Biology* **148**, 19–52.

Dudley, R. and Ellington, C. P. (1990b) Mechanics of forward flight in bumblebees, II: Quasi-steady lift and power requirements. *Journal of Experimental Biology* **148**, 53–88.

Eaton, M. D., Evans, D. L., Hodgson, D. R. and Rose, R. J. (1995a) Maximum accumulated oxygen deficit in thoroughbred horses. *Journal of Applied Physiology* **78**, 1564–1568.

Eaton, M. D., Evans, D. L., Hodgson, D. R. and Rose, R. J. (1995b) Effect of treadmill inclination and speed on metabolic rate during exercise in thoroughbred horses. *Journal of Applied Physiology* **79**, 951–957.

Ebensperger, L. A. and Bozinovic, F. (2000) Energetics and burrowing behaviour in the semifossorial degu *Octodon degu* (Rodentia: Octodontidae). *Journal of Zoology* **252**, 179–186.

Economos, A. C. (1983) Elastic and/or geometric similarity in mammalian design? *Journal of Theoretical Biology* **103**, 167–172.

Edman, K. A. P. (1979) The velocity of unloaded shortening and its relation to sarcomere length and isometric force in vertebrate muscle fibres. *Journal of Physiology* **291**, 143–159.

Edman, K. A. P., Mulieri, L. A. and Scubon-Mulieri, B. (1976) Non-hyperbolic force–velocity relationship in single muscle fibres. *Acta Physiologica Scandinavica* **98**, 143–156.

Edman, K. A. P., Elzinga, G. and Noble, M. I. M. (1978) Enhancement of mechanical performance by stretch during tetanic contractions of vertebrate skeletal muscle fibres. *Journal of Physiology* **281**, 139–155.

Edwards, E. B. and Gleeson, T. T. (2001) Can energetic expenditure be minimized by performing activity intermittently? *Journal of Experimental Biology* **204**, 599–605.

Elder, H. Y. (1973) Direct peristaltic progression and the functional significance of the dermal connective tissue during burrowing in the polychaete *Polyphysia crassa* (Oersted). *Journal of Experimental Biology* **58**, 637–655.

Ellers, O. (1995) Form and motion of *Donax variabilis* in flow. *Biological Bulletin* **189**, 138–147.

Ellington, C.P. (1984) The aerodynamics of hovering insect flight, III: Kinematics. *Philosophical Transactions of the Royal Society B* **305**, 41–78.

Ellington, C. P., Machin, K. E. and Casey, T. M. (1990) Oxygen consumption of bumblebees in forward flight. *Nature* **347**, 472–473.

Ellington, C. P., van den Berg, C., Willmott, A. P. and Thomas, A. L. R. (1996) Leading-edge vortices in insect flight. *Nature* **384**, 628–630.

Elliott, J. P., Cowan I. McT. and Holling, C. S. (1977) Prey capture by the African lion. *Canadian Journal of Zoology* **55**, 1811–1828.

Emerson, S. B. (1985) Jumping and leaping. In M. Hildebrand, D. M. Bramble, K. F. Liem, and D. B. Wake (editors), *Functional Vertebrate Morphology*, pp. 58–79. Belknap Press, Cambridge, MA.

Emerson, S. B. and Diehl, D. (1980) Toe pad morphology and mechanisms of sticking in frogs. *Biological Journal of the Linnean Society* **13**, 199–216.

English, A. W. (1976) Limb movements and locomotor function in the California sea lion (*Zalophus californianus*). *Journal of Zoology* **178**, 341–364.

Ennos, A. R. (1989) The kinematics and aerodynamics of the free flight of some Diptera. *Journal of Experimental Biology* **142**, 49–85.

Evans, M. E. G. (1972) The jump of the click beetle (Coleoptera, Elateridae)—A preliminary study. *Journal of Zoology* **167**, 319–336.

Farley, C. T. and Ko, T. C. (1997) Mechanics of locomotion in lizards. *Journal of Experimental Biology* **200**, 2177–2188.

Fedak, M. A., Heglund, N. C. and Taylor, C. R. (1982) Energetics and mechanics of terrestrial locomotion, II: Kinetic energy changes of the limbs as a function of speed and body size in birds and mammals. *Journal of Experimental Biology* **97**, 23–40.

Ferry, L. A. and Lauder, G. V. (1996) Heterocercal tail function in Leopard sharks: a three-dimensional kinematic analysis of two models. *Journal of Experimental Biology* **199**, 2253–2268.

Fieler, C. L. and Jayne, B. C. (1998) Effects of speed on the hindlimb kinematics of the lizard *Dipsosaurus dorsalis*. *Journal of Experimental Biology* **201**, 609–622.

Fierstine, H. L. and Walters, V. (1968) Studies of locomotion and anatomy of scombroid fishes. *Memoirs of the Southern California Academy of Sciences* **6**, 1–31.

Fish, F. E. (1993) Power output and propulsive efficiency of swimming bottlenose dolphins (*Tursiops truncatus*). *Journal of Experimental Biology* **185**, 179–193.

Fish, F. E. (1996) Transitions from drag-based to lift-based propulsion in mammalian swimming. *American Zoologist* **36**, 628–641.

Fish, F. E. (1998) Comparative kinematics and hydrodynamics of odontocete cetaceans: morphological and ecological correlates with swimming performance. *Journal of Experimental Biology* **201**, 2867–2877.

Flammang, P., Michel, A., van Cauwenberge, A., Alexandre, H. and Jangoux, M. (1998) A study of the temporary adhesion of the podia in the sea star *Asterias rubens* (Echinodermata, Asteroidea) through their footprints. *Journal of Experimental Biology* **201**, 2383–2395.

Fleagle, J. G. (1974) The dynamics of a brachiating siamang (*Hylobates* [*Symphalangus*] *syndactylus*). *Nature* **248**, 259–260.

Francis, L. (1991) Sailing downwind: Aerodynamic performance of the *Velella* sail. *Journal of Experimental Biology* **158**, 117–132.

Full, R. J. (1987) Locomotion energetics of the ghost crab, I: Metabolic cost and endurance. *Journal of Experimental Biology* **130**, 137–153.

Full, R. J. and Tu, M. S. (1990) Mechanics of six-legged runners. *Journal of Experimental Biology* **148**, 129–146.

Full, R. J. and Tu, M. S. (1991) Mechanics of a rapid running insect: two-, four- and six-legged locomotion. *Journal of Experimental Biology* **156**, 215–231.

Full, R. J. and Tullis, A. (1990) Energetics of ascent: Insects on inclines. *Journal of Experimental Biology* **149**, 307–317.

Full, R. J., Blickhan, R. and Tu, M. S. (1991) Leg design in hexapedal runners. *Journal of Experimental Biology* **158**, 369–390.

Full, R. J., Zuccaerello, D. A. and Tullis, A. (1990) Effect of variation in form on the cost of terrestrial locomotion. *Journal of Experimental Biology* **150**, 233–246.

Full, R. J., Yamauchi, A. and Jindrich, D. L. (1995) Single leg force production: Cockroaches righting and running on photoelastic gelatin. *Journal of Experimental Biology* **198**, 2441–2452.

Gal, J. M. and Blake, R. W. (1988a) Biomechanics of frog swimming, I: Estimation of the propulsive force generated by *Hymenochirus boettgeri*. *Journal of Experimental Biology* **138**, 399–411.

Gal, J. M. and Blake, R. W. (1988b) Biomechanics of frog swimming, II: Mechanics of the limb beat cycle in *Hymenochirus boettgeri*. *Journal of Experimental Biology* **138**, 413–429.

Gambaryan, P. P. (1974) *How Mammals Run*. Wiley, New York.

Gans, C. (1968) Relative success of divergent pathways of amphisbaenian specialisation. *American Naturalist* **102**, 345–362.

Gans, C. (1984) Slide-pushing—A transitional locomotor method of elongate squamates. *Symposium of the Zoological Society of London* **52**, 13–26.

Gans, C. (1992) Electromyography. In A. A. Biewener (editor), *Biomechanics: Structures and Systems*, pp. 175–204. IRL Press, Oxford, UK.

Gans, C. and Gasc, J.-P. (1990) Tests on the locomotion of the elongate and limbless reptile *Ophisaurus apodus* (Sauria, Anguidae). *Journal of Zoology* **220**, 517–536.

Garland, T. (1983) The relation between maximal running speed and body mass in terrestrial mammals *Journal of Zoology* **199**, 157–170.

Gibo, D. L. and Pallett, M. J. (1979) Soaring flight of monarch butterflies, *Danaus plexippus* (Lepidoptera: Danaidae), during the late summer migration in southern Ontario. *Canadian Journal of Zoology* **57**, 1393–1401.

Glasheen, J. W. and McMahon, T. A. (1996a) A hydrodynamic model of locomotion in the basilisk lizard. *Nature* **380**, 340–342.

Glasheen, J. W. and McMahon, T. A. (1996b) Size-dependence of water-running ability in basilisk lizards (*Basiliscus basiliscus*). *Journal of Experimental Biology* **199**, 2611–2618.

Gorb, S., Gorb, E. and Kastner, V. (2001) Scale effects on the attachment pads and friction forces in syrphid flies (Diptera, Syrphidae). *Journal of Experimental Biology* **204**, 1421–1431.

Gordon, A. M., Huxley, A. F. and Julian, F. J. (1966) The variation of isometric tension with sarcomere length in vertebrate muscle fibres. *Journal of Physiology* **184**, 170–192.

Gordon, C. N. (1980) Leaping dolphins. *Nature* **287**, 759.

Gosline, J. M. and Shadwick, R. E. (1983) The role of elastic energy storage mechanisms in swimming: An analysis of mantle elasticity in escape jetting in the squid, *Loligo opalescens. Canadian Journal of Zoology* **61**, 1421–1431.

Gosline, J. M., Steeves, J. D., Harman, A. D. and DeMont, M. E. (1983) Patterns of circular and radial muscle activity in respiration and jetting of the squid *Loligo opalescens. Journal of Experimental Biology* **104**, 97–109.

Grand, T. I. (1977) Body weight: Its relation to tissue composition, segment distribution, and motor function. *American Journal of Physical Anthropology* **47**, 211–240.

Gray, J. (1933) Studies in animal locomotion, I: The movement of fish with special reference to the eel. *Journal of Experimental Biology* **10**(4), 88–104.

Gray, J. (1968) *Animal Locomotion*. Weidenfeld & Nicolson, London.

Gray, J. and Hancock, G. J. (1955) The locomotion of sea urchin spermatozoa. *Journal of Experimental Biology* **32**, 802–814.

Gray, J. and Lissmann, H. W. (1938) Locomotory reflexes in the earthworm. *Journal of Experimental Biology* **15**, 506–517.

Gray, J. and Lissmann, H. W. (1964) The locomotion of nematodes. *Journal of Experimental Biology* **41**, 135–154.

Greene, P. R. (1985) Running on flat turns: Experiments, theory, and applications. *Journal of Biomechanical Engineering* **107**, 96–103.

Griffiths, R. I. (1991) Shortening of muscle fibres during stretch of the active cat medial gastrocnemius muscle: The role of tendon compliance. *Journal of Physiology* **436**, 219–236.

Grodnitsky, D. L. (1999) *Form and Function of Insect Wings*. Johns Hopkins University Press, Baltimore.

Günther, M. M., Ishida, H., Kumakura, H. and Nakano, Y. (1989) The jump as a fast mode of locomotion in arborial and terrestrial biotopes. *Zeitschrift für Morphologie und Anthropologie* **78**, 341–372.

Hall-Craggs, E. B. C. (1965) An analysis of the jump of the lesser galago (*Galago senegalensis*). *Journal of Zoology* **147**, 20–29.

Hammond, L., Altringham, J. D. and Wardle, C. S. (1998) Myotomal slow muscle function of rainbow trout *Onchorhynchus mykiss* during steady swimming. *Journal of Experimental Biology* **201**, 1659–1671.

Hayes, G. and Alexander, R. McN. (1983) The hopping gaits of crows (Corvidae) and other bipeds. *Journal of Zoology* **200**, 205–213.

He, P. and Wardle, C. S. (1988) Endurance at intermediate swimming speeds of Atlantic mackerel, *Scomber scombrus* L., herring, *Clupea harengus* L., and saithe, *Pollachius virens* L. *Journal of Fish Biology* **33**, 255–266.

Hedenström, A. and Liechti, F. (2001) Field estimates of body drag coefficient on the basis of dives by passerine birds. *Journal of Experimental Biology* **204**, 1167–1175.

Heglund, N. C., Taylor, C. R. and McMahon, T. A. (1974) Scaling stride frequency and gait to animal size: Mice to horses. *Science* **186**, 1112–1113.

Heglund, N. C., Fedak, M. A., Taylor, C. R. and Cavagna, G. A. (1982) Energetics and mechanics of terrestrial locomotion, IV: Total mechanical energy changes as a function of speed and body size in birds and mammals. *Journal of Experimental Biology* **97**, 57–66.

Heglund, N. C., Willems, P. A., Penta, M. and Cavagna, G. A. (1995) Energy-saving gait mechanics with head-supported loads. *Nature* **375**, 52–54.

Herbert, R. C., Young, P. G., Smith, C. W., Wootton, R. J. and Evans, K. E. (2000) The hind wing of the desert locust (*Schistocerca gregaria* Forskål), III: A finite element analysis of a deployable structure. *Journal of Experimental Biology* **203**, 2945–2955.

Hertel, H. (1966) *Structure, Form and Movement*. Reinhold, New York.

Herzog, W. and Leonard, T. R. (1991) Validation of optimization models that estimate the forces exerted by synergistic muscles. *Journal of Biomechanics* **24** (suppl. 1), 31–39.

Hess, F. and Videler, J. J. (1984) Fast continuous swimming of saithe (*Pollachius virens*): A dynamic analysis of bending moments and muscle power. *Journal of Experimental Biology* **109**, 229–251.

Hildebrand, M. (1976) Analysis of tetrapod gaits: general considerations and symmetrical gaits. In R. M. Herman, S. Grillner, P. S. G. Stein, and D. G. Stuart (editors), *Neural Control of Locomotion*, pp.203–236. Plenum, New York.

Hildebrand, M. (1977) Analysis of asymmetrical gaits. *Journal of Mammalology* **58**, 131–156.

Hill, A. V. (1950) The dimensions of animals and their muscular dynamics. *Science Progress* **38**, 209–230.

Hove, J. R., O'Bryan, L. M., Gordon, M. S., Webb, P. W. and Weihs, D. (2001) Boxfishes (Teleostei: Ostraciidae) as a model system for fishes swimming with many fins: kinematics. *Journal of Experimental Biology* **204**, 1459–1471.

Howland, H. C. (1974) Optimal strategies for predator avoidance: The relative importance of speed and manoeuvrability. *Journal of Theoretical Biology* **47**, 333–350.

Hoyt, D. F. and Taylor, C. R. (1981) Gait and the energetics of locomotion in horses. *Nature* **292**, 239–240.

Hoyt, D. F., Wickler, S. J. and Cogger, E. A. (2000) Time of contact and step length: the effect of limb length, running speed, load carrying and incline. *Journal of Experimental Biology* **203**, 221–227.

Hui, C. A. (1987) The porpoising of penguins: An energy-conserving behavior for respiratory ventilation? *Canadian Journal of Zoology* **65**, 209–211.

Hui, C. A. (1988) Penguin swimming, I: Hydrodynamics. *Physiological Zoology* **61**, 333–343.

Hunter, R. D. and Elder, H. Y. (1989) Burrowing dynamics and energy cost of transport in the soft-bodied marine invertebrates *Polyphysia crassa* and *Priapulus caudatus*. *Journal of Zoology* **218**, 209–222.

Huxley, A. F. (1957) Muscle structure and theories of contraction. *Progress in Biophysics and Biophysical Chemistry* **7**, 255–318.

Irschick, D. J., Austin, C. C., Petren, K., Fisher, R. N., Losos, J. B. and Ellers, O. (1996) A comparative analysis of clinging ability among pad-bearing lizards. *Biological Journal of the Linnean Society* **59**, 21–35.

Irschick, D. J. and Jayne, B. C. (1999) Comparative three-dimensional kinematics of the hindlimb for high-speed bipedal and quadrupedal locomotion of lizards. *Journal of Experimental Biology* **202**, 1047–1065.

James, R. S. and Johnston, I. A. (1998) Scaling of muscle performance during escape responses in the fish *Myoxocephalus scorpius* L. *Journal of Experimental Biology* **201**, 913–923.

Jayes, A. S. and Alexander, R. McN. (1978) Mechanics of locomotion of dogs (*Canis familiaris*) and sheep (*Ovis aries*). *Journal of Zoology* **185**, 289–308.

Jayes, A. S. and Alexander, R. McN. (1980) The gaits of chelonians: Walking techniques for very low speeds. *Journal of Zoology* **191**, 353–378.

Jayne, B. C. and Davis, J. D. (1991) Kinematics and performance capacity for the cocertina locomotion of a snake (*Coluber constrictor*). *Journal of Experimental Biology* **156**, 539–556.

Jenkins, F. A. (1971) Limb posture and locomotion in the Virginia opossum (*Didelphis marsupialis*) and in other non-cursorial mammals. *Journal of Zoology* **165**, 303–315.

Jenkins, F. A. and McClearn, D. M. (1984) Mechanisms of hind foot reversal in climbing mammals. *Journal of Morphology* **182**, 197–219.

Jenkins, F. A., Dial, K. P. and Goslow, G. E. (1988) A cineradiographic analysis of bird flight: The wishbone in starlings is a spring. *Science* **241**, 1495–1498.

Johannson, L. C. and Norberg, U. M. L. (2001) Lift-based paddling in diving grebe. *Journal of Experimental Biology* **204**, 1687–1696.

Jones, C. D. R., Jarjou, M. S., Whitehead, R. G. and Jequier, E. (1987) Fatness and the energy cost of carrying loads in African women. *The Lancet* **1987**, 1331–1332.

Jones, F. R. H. (1952) The swimbladder and the vertical movement of teleostean fishes, II: The restriction to rapid and slow movements. *Journal of Experimental Biology* 29, 94–109.

Jones, F. R. H. and Marshall, N. B. (1953) The structure and functions of the teleostean swimbladder. *Biological Reviews* 28, 16–83.

Jones, F. R. H. and Scholes, P. (1985) Gas secretion ond resorption in the swimbladder of the cod *Gadus morhua*. *Journal of Comparative Physiology B* 155, 319–331.

Jones, H. D. (1973) The mechanism of locomotion of *Agriolimax reticulatus* (Mollusca: Gastropoda). *Journal of Zoology* 171, 489–498.

Jones, H. D. and Trueman, E. R. (1970) Locomotion of the limpet, *Patella vulgata* L. *Journal of Experimental Biology* 52, 201–216.

Josephson, R. K. (1985) Mechanical power output from striated muscle during cyclic contraction. *Journal of Experimental Biology* 114, 493–512.

Josephson, R. K. (1993) Contraction dynamics and power output of skeletal muscle. *Annual Reviews of Physiology* 55, 525–546.

Josephson, R. K. (1997a) Power output from a flight muscle of the bumblebee *Bombus terrestris*, II: Characterization of the parameters affecting power output. *Journal of Experimental Biology* 200, 1227–1239.

Josephson, R. K. (1997b) Power output from a flight muscle of the bumblebee *Bombus terrestris*, III: Power during simulated flight. *Journal of Experimental Biology* 200, 1241–1246.

Josephson, R. K. and Stevenson, R. D. (1991) The efficiency of a flight muscle from the locust *Schistocerca americana*. *Journal of Physiology* 442, 413–429.

Josephson, R. K., Malamud, J. G. and Stokes, D. R. (2000)Asynchronous muscle: a primer. *Journal of Experimental Biology* 203, 2713–2722.

Katz, S. L. and Gosline, J. M. (1993) Ontogenetic scaling of jump performance in the African desert locust (*Schistocerca gregaria*). *Journal of Experimental Biology* 177, 81–111.

Katz, S. L., Shadwick, R. E. and Rapoport, H. S. (1999) Muscle strain histories in swimming milkfish in steady and sprinting gaits. *Journal of Experimental Biology* 202, 529–541.

Kellermayer, M. S. Z., Smith, S. B., Granzier, H. L. and Bustamante, C. (1997) Folding–unfolding transitions in single titin molecules characterized with laser tweezers. *Science* 276, 1112–1116.

Ker, R.F. (1992) Tensile fibres: Strings and straps. In J. F. C. Vincent (editor), *Biomechanics: Materials*, pp. 75–97. IRL Press, Oxford, UK.

Ker, R.F., Bennett, M. B., Bibby, S. R., Kester, R. C. and Alexander, R. McN. (1987) The spring in the arch of the human foot. *Nature* 325, 147–149.

Ker, R.F., Bennett, M. B., Alexander, R. McN. and Kester, R. C. (1989) Foot strike and the properties of the human heel pad. *Proceedings of the Institution of Mechanical Engineers, Part H* 203, 191–196.

Kesel, A. B. (2000) Aerodynamic characteristics of dragonfly wing sections compared with technical aerofoils. *Journal of Experimental Biology* 203, 3125–3135.

Kitamura, K., Tokunaga, M., Iwane, A. H. and Yanagida, T. (1999) A single myosin head moves along an actin filament with regular steps of 5.3 nanometres. *Nature* 397, 129–134.

Knower, T., Shadwick, R. E., Katz, S. L., Graham, J. B. and Wardle, C. S. (1999) Red muscle activation patterns in yellowfin (*Thunnus albacares*) and skipjack (*Katsuwonus pelamis*) tunas during steady swimming. *Journal of Experimental Biology* **202**, 2127–2138.

Kohlhage, K. and Yager, J. (1994) An analysis of swimming in remipede crustaceans. *Philosophical Transactions of the Royal Society B* **346**, 213–221.

Komi, P. V. and Bosco, C. (1978) Utilization of stored elastic energy in leg extensor muscles by men and women. *Medicine and Science in Sports* **10**, 261–265.

Kram, R. (1996) Inexpensive load carrying by rhinoceros beetles. *Journal of Experimental Biology* **199**, 609–612.

Kram, R. and Taylor, R. C. (1990) Energetics of running: A new perspective. *Nature* **346**, 265–267

Kram, R., Domingo, A. and Ferris, D. P. (1997) Effect of reduced gravity on the preferred walk–run transition speed. *Journal of Experimental Biology* **200**, 821–826.

Kubow, T. M. and Full, R. J. (1999) The role of the mechanical system in control: a hypothesis of self-stabilization in hexapedal runners. *Philosophical Transactions of the Royal Society B* **354**, 849–861.

Kuo, A. D. (1999) Stabilization of lateral motion in passive dynamic walking. *International Journal of Robotics Research* **18**: 917–930.

Kvist, A., Lindström, Å., Green, M., Piersma, T. and Visser, G. H. (1998) Carrying large fuel loads during sustained bird flight is cheaper than expected. *Nature* **413**, 730–732.

LaBarbara, M. (1983) Why the wheels won't go. *American Naturalist* **121**, 395–408.

Lang, T. G. (1975) Speed, power and drag measurements of dolphins and porpoises. In T. Y.-T. Wu, C. J. Brokaw, and C. Brennan (editors), *Swimming and Flying in Nature*, **2**, 553–572. Plenum, New York.

Langman, V. A., Roberts, T. J., Black, J., Maloiy, G. M. O., Heglund, N. C., Weber, J.-M., Kram, R. and Taylor, C. R. (1995) Moving cheaply: Energetics of walking in the African elephant. *Journal of Experimental Biology* **198**, 629–632.

Lännergren, J. (1978) The force–velocity relation of isolated twitch and slow muscle fibres of *Xenopus laevis*. *Journal of Physiology* **283**, 501–521.

Lapennas, G. N. and Schmidt-Nielsen, K. (1977) Swimbladder permeability to oxygen. *Journal of Experimental Biology* **67**, 175–196.

Lasiewski, R. C. (1963) Oxygen consumption of torpid, resting, active and flying hummingbirds. *Physiological Zoology* **36**, 122–140.

Lauder, G. V. (1980) The suction feeding mechanism in sunfishes (*Lepomis*): An experimental analysis. *Journal of Experimental Biology* **88**, 49–72.

Lawrence, M. J. and Brown, R. W. (1974) *Mammals of Britain: Their Tracks Trails and Signs*. Blandford, London.

Le Cren, E. D. and Holdgate, M. W. (editors) (1962) *The Exploitation of Natural Animal Populations*. Oxford University Press, Oxford, UK.

Liechti, F., Hedenström, A. and Alerstam, T. (1994) Effects of sidewinds on optimal flight speeds of birds. *Journal of Theoretical Biology* **170**, 219–225.

Lighthill, M. J. (1960) Note on the swimming of slender fish. *Journal of Fluid Mechanics* **9**, 305–317.

Lighthill, M. J. (1970) Aquatic animal propulsion of high hydromechanical efficiency. *Journal of Fluid Mechanics* **44**, 265–301.

Lighthill, M. J. (1971) Large-amplitude elongated-body theory of fish locomotion. *Proceedings of the Royal Society B* **179**, 125–138.

Lighthill, M. J. (1973) On the Weis-Fogh mechanism of lift generation. *Journal of Fluid Mechanics* **60**, 1–17.

Lighthill, M. J. (1976) Flagellar hydrodynamics. *SIAM Review* **18**, 161–230.

Lindstedt, S. L., Hokanson, J. F., Wells, D. J., Swain, S. D., Hoppeler, H. and Navarro, V. (1991) Running energetics in the pronghorn antelope. *Nature* **353**, 748–750.

Lindström, Å. (1991) Maximum fat deposition rates in migrating birds. *Ornis Scandinavica* **22**, 12–19.

Lissmann, H. W. (1945a) The mechanism of locomotion in gastropod molluscs, I: Kinematics. *Journal of Experimental Biology* **21**, 58–69.

Lissmann, H. W. (1945b) The mechanism of locomotion in gastropod molluscs, II: Kinetics. *Journal of Experimental Biology* **22**, 37–50.

Lissmann, H. W. (1950) Rectilinear locomotion in a snake (*Boa occidentalis*). *Journal of Experimental Biology* **26**, 267–279.

Liu, H., Ellington, C. P., Kawachi, K., van den Berg, C. and Wilmott, A. (1998) A computational fluid dynamic study of hawkmoth hovering. *Journal of Experimental Biology* **201**, 461–477.

Loeb, G. E. and Gans, C. (1986) *Electromyography for Experimentalists*. University of Chicago Press, Chicago.

Long, J. H., McHenry, M. J. and Boetticher, N. C. (1994) Undulatory swimming: How traveling waves are produced and modulated in sunfish (*Lepomis gibbosus*). *Journal of Experimental Biology* **192**, 129–145.

Lou, F., Curtin, N. A. and Woledge, R. C. (1997) The energetic cost of activation of white muscle fibres from the dogfish *Scyliorhinus canicula*. *Journal of Experimental Biology* **200**, 495–501.

Lou, F., van der Laarse, W. J., Curtin, N. A. and Woledge, R. C. (2000) Heat production and oxygen consumption during metabolic recovery of white muscle fibres from the dogfish *Scyliorhinus canicula*. *Journal of Experimental Biology* **203**, 1201–1210.

Lovvorn, J. R., Croll, D. A. and Liggins, G. A. (1999) Mechanical versus physiological determinants of swimming speeds in diving Brünnich's guillemots. *Journal of Experimental Biology* **202**, 1741–1752.

Lutz, G. J. and Rome, L. C. (1994) Built for jumping: The design of the frog muscular system. *Science* **263**, 370–372.

MacGillivray, P. S., Anderson, E. J., Wright, G. M. and DeMont, M. E. (1999) Structure and mechanics of the squid mantle. *Journal of Experimental Biology* **202**, 683–695.

Machin, K. E. and Pringle, J. W. S. (1959) The physiology of insect fibrillar muscle, II: Mechanical properties of a beetle flight muscle. *Proceedings of the Royal Society B* **151**, 204–225.

Madin, L. P. (1990) Aspects of jet propulsion in salps. *Canadian Journal of Zoology* **68**, 765–777.

Maganaris, C. N. and Paul, J. P. (2000) Load–elongation characteristics of in vivo human tendon and aponeurosis. *Journal of Experimental Biology* **203**, 751–756.

Maganaris, C. N., Baltzopoulos, V. and Sargeant A. J. (1998) In vivo measurements of the triceps surae complex architecture in man: Implications for muscle function. *Journal of Physiology* **512.2**, 603–614.

Magnuson, J. J. (1970) Hydrostatic equilibrium of *Euthynnus affinis*, a pelagic teleost without a gas bladder. *Copeia* **1970**, 56–85.

Magnuson, J. J. (1973) Comparative study of adaptations for continuous swimming and hydrostatic equilibrium of scombroid and xiphoid fishes. *Fishery Bulletin* **71**, 337–356.

Magnuson, J. J. (1978) Locomotion by scombrid fishes: Hydromechanics, morphology and behaviour. In W. S. Hoar and D. J. Randall (editors), *Fish Physiology*, **7**, 239–313. Academic Press, New York.

Maitland, D. P. (1992) Locomotion by jumping in the Mediterranean fruit-fly larva *Ceratitis capitata*. *Nature* **355**, 159–161.

Maloiy, G. M. O., Heglund, N. C., Prager, L. M., Cavagna, G. A. and Taylor, C. R. (1986) Energetic cost of carrying loads: Have African women discovered an economic way? *Nature* **319**, 668–669.

Manton, S. M. (1973) The evolution of arthropodan locomotory mechanisms, Part 11: Habits, morphology and evolution of the Uniramia (Onychophora, Myriapoda, Hexapoda) and comparisons with the Arachnida, together with a functional review of uniramian musculature. *Journal of the Linnean Society (Zoology)* **53**, 257–375.

Margaria, R. (1976) *Biomechanics and Energetics of Muscular Exercise*. Clarendon, Oxford, UK.

Marsh, R. L. (1988) Ontogenesis of contractile properties of skeletal muscle and sprint performance in the lizard *Dipsosaurus dorsalis*. *Journal of Experimental Biology* **137**, 119–139.

Marsh, R. L. (1994) Jumping ability of anuran amphibians. *Advances in Veterinary Science and Comparative Medicine: Comparative Vertebrate Exercise Physiology* **38B**, 51–111.

Marsh, R. L. and Olson, J. M. (1994) Power output of scallop adductor muscle during contractions replicating the in vivo mechanical cycle. *Journal of Experimental Biology* **193**, 139–156.

Marsh, R. L., Olson, J. M. and Gusik, S. K. (1992) Mechanical performance of scallop adductor muscle during swimming. *Nature* **357**, 411–413.

Martin, A. W. and Fuhrman, F. A. (1955) The relationship between summated tissue respiration and metabolic rate in the mouse and dog. *Physiological Zoology* **28**, 18–34.

Martinez, M. M. (2001) Running in the surf: Hydrodynamics of the shore crab *Grapsus tenuicrustatus*. *Journal of Experimental Biology* **204**, 3097–3112.

Maybury, W. J. and Rayner, J. M. V. (2001) The avian tail reduces body parasitic drag by controlling flow separation and vortex shedding. *Proceedings of the Royal Society B* **268**, 1405–1410.

Maybury, W. J., Rayner, J. M. V. and Couldrick, L. B. (2001) Lift generation by the avian tail. *Proceedings of the Royal Society B* **268**, 1443–1448.

McCay, M. G. (2001) Aerodynamic stability and maneuverability of the gliding frog *Polypedates dennysi*. *Journal of Experimental Biology* **204**, 2817–2826.

McCutchen, C. W. (1977) Froude propulsive efficiency of a small fish, measured by wake visualisation. In T. J. Pedley (editor), *Scale Effects in Animal Locomotion*, pp. 339–363. Academic Press, London.

McGahan, J. (1973) Flapping flight of the Andean condor in nature. *Journal of Experimental Biology* **58**, 239–253.

McGeer, T. (1990a) Passive dynamic walking. *International Journal of Robotics Research* **9**, 62–82.

McGeer, T. (1990b) Passive bipedal running. *Proceedings of the Royal Society B* **240**, 107–134.

McGeer, T. (1993) Dynamics and control of bipedal locomotion. *Journal of Theoretical Biology* **163**, 277–314.

McGhee, R. B. and Frank, A. A. (1968) On the stability properties of quadrupedal creeping gaits. *Mathematical Biosciences* **3**, 331–351.

McMahon, T. A. (1971) Rowing: A similarity analysis. *Science* **173**, 349–351.

McMahon, T. A. (1973) Size and shape in biology. *Science* **179**, 1201–1204.

McMahon, T. A. (1975) Allometry and biomechanics: limb bones in adult ungulates. *American Naturalist* **109**, 547–563.

McMahon, T.A. (1984) *Muscles, Reflexes, and Locomotion*. Princeton University Press, Princeton, NJ.

McMahon, T. A. (1985) The role of compliance in mammalian running gaits. *Journal of Experimental Biology* **115**, 263–282.

McMahon, T.A. and Bonner, J. T. (1983) *On Size and Life*. Scientific American Library, New York.

McMahon, T. A. and Cheng, G. C. (1990) The mechanics of running: How does stiffness couple with speed? *Journal of Biomechanics* **23**, suppl. 1, 65–78.

McMahon, T. A. and Greene, P. R. (1978) Fast running tracks. *Scientific American* **239** (6), 148–163.

McMahon, T. A. and Kronauer, R. E. (1976) Tree structures: Deducing the principle of mechanical design. *Journal of Theoretical Biology* **59**, 443–466.

Meldrum, D. J., Dagosto, M. and White, J. (1997) Hindlimb suspension and hind foot reversal in *Varecia variegata* and other arboreal mammals. *American Journal of Physical Anthropology* **103**, 85–102.

Mill, P. J. and Pickard, R. S. (1975) Jet propulsion in an anisopteran dragonfly larva. *Journal of Comparative Physiology A* **97**, 329–338.

Miller, D. I. (1975) Biomechanics of swimming. *Exercise and Sport Science Reviews* **3**, 219–248.

Miller, J. B. (1975) The length–tension relationship of the dorsal longitudinal muscle of a leech. *Journal of Experimental Biology* **62**, 43–53.

Milligan, B. J., Curtin, N. A. and Bone, Q. (1997) Contractile properties of obliquely striated muscle from the mantle of squid (*Alloteuthis subulata*) and cuttlefish (*Sepia officinalis*). *Journal of Experimental Biology* **200**, 2425–2436.

Minetti, A E. (1995) Optimum gradient of mountain paths. *Journal of Applied Physiology* **79**, 1698–1703.

Minetti, A. E. (1998) The biomechanics of skipping gaits: A third locomotor paradigm? *Proceedings of the Royal Society B* **265**, 1227–1235.

Minetti, A. E. and Alexander, R. McN. (1997) A theory of metabolic costs for bipedal gaits. *Journal of Theoretical Biology* **186**, 467–476.

Minetti, A. E., Ardigo, L. P. and Saibene, F. (1994) The transition between walking and running in humans: Metabolic and mechanical aspects at different gradients. *Acta Physiologica Scandinavica* **150**, 315–323.

Minetti, A. E., Pinkerton, J. and Zamparo, P. (2001) From bipedalism to bicyclism: Evolution in energetics and biomechanics of historic bicycles. *Philosophical Transactions of the Royal Society B* **268**, 1351–1360.

Mochon, S. and McMahon, T. A. (1980) Ballistic walking: An improved model. *Mathematical Biosciences* **52**, 241–260.

Molloy, J. E., Burns, J. E., Kendrick-Jones, J., Tregear, R. T. and White, D. C. S. (1995) Movement and force produced by a single myosin head. *Nature* **378**, 209–212.

Müller, U. K., van den Heuvel, B. L. E., Stamhuis, E. J. and Videler, J.J. (1997) Fish foot prints: Morphology and energetics of the wake behind a continuously swimming mullet (*Chelon labrosus* Risso). *Journal of Experimental Biology* **200**, 2893–2906.

Nachtigall, W. (1960) Über Kinematik, Dynamik und Energetik des Schwimmens einheimischer Dytisciden. *Zeitschrift für Vergleichende Physiologie* **43**, 48–118.

Nachtigall, W. (1965) Locomotion: Swimming (hydrodynamics) of aquatic insects. In M. Rockstein (editor), *The Physiology of Insecta*, **2**, 255–281. Academic Press, New York.

Nachtigall, W. and Bilo, D. (1980) Strömungsanpassung des Pinguins beim Schwimmen unter Wasser. *Journal of Comparative Physiology A* **137**, 17–26.

Nachtigall, W. and Kempf, B. (1971) Vergleichende Untersuchungen zur flugbiologischen Funktion des Daumenfittichs (*Alula spuria*) bei Vogeln. *Zeitschrift für vergleichende Physiologie* **71**, 326–341.

Nachtigall, W. and Wieser, J. (1966) Profilmessungen am Taubenflugel. *Zeitschrift für vergleichende Physiologie* **52**, 333–346.

Napier, J. R. and Walker, A. C. (1967) Vertical clinging and leaping—A newly recognised category of locomotor behaviour of Primates. *Folia Primatologia* **6**, 204–219.

Nevenzel, J. C., Rodegker, W., Mead, J. F. and Gordon, M. S. (1966) Lipids of the living coelacanth, *Latimeria chalumnae*. *Science* **152**, 1753–1755.

Nigg, B. M. (1986) *Biomechanics of Running Shoes*. Human Kinetics, Champaign, IL.

Nigg, B. M., Bahlsen, H. A., Luethi, S. M. and Stokes, S. (1987) The influence of running velocity and midsole hardness on external impact forces in heel–toe running. *Journal of Biomechanics* **20**, 951–959.

Norberg, U. M. (1975) Hovering flight in the pied flycatcher (*Ficedula hypoleuca*). In T. Y.-T. Wu, C. J. Brokaw, and C. Brennen (editors) *Swimming and Flying in Nature*, **2**, pp.869–881. Plenum, New York.

Norberg, U. M. and Rayner, J. M. V. (1987) Ecological morphology and flight in bats (Mammalia: Chiroptera): Wing adaptations, flight performance, foraging strategy and echolocation. *Philosophical Transactions of the Royal Society B* **316**, 335–427.

Norberg, U. M. L., Brooke, A. P. and Trewhella, W. J. (2000) Soaring and non-soaring bats of the family Pteropidae (flying foxes, *Pteropus* spp.): Wing morphology and flight performance. *Journal of Experimental Biology* **203**, 651–664.

Nudds, R. L. and Bryant, D. M. (2000) The energetic cost of short flights in birds. *Journal of Experimental Biology* **203**, 1561–1572.

O'Dor, R. K. and Webber, D. M. (1986) The constraints on cephalopods: Why squid aren't fish. *Canadian Journal of Zoology* **64**, 1591–1605.

Pandolf, K. B, Haisman, M. F. and Goldman, R. F. (1976) Metabolic energy expenditure and terrain coefficients for walking on snow. *Ergonomics* **19**, 683–690.

Parrott, G. C. (1970) Aerodynamics of gliding flight of a black vulture *Coragyps atratus. Journal of Experimental Biology* **53**, 363–374.

Parsons, P. E. and Taylor, C. R. (1977) Energetics of brachiation versus walking: A comparison of a suspended and an inverted pendulum mechanism. *Physiological Zoology* **50**, 182–189.

Pelster, B. and Scheid, P. (1992) Counter-current concentration and gas secretion in the fish swimbladder. *Physiological Zoology* **65**, 1–16.

Pendergast, D. R., Bushnell, D., Wilson, D. W. and Cerretelli, P. (1989) Energetics of underwater swimming with SCUBA. *European Journal of Applied Physiology* **59**, 342–350.

Pendergast, D. R., Tedesco, M., Nawrocki, D. M. and Fisher, N. M. (1996). Energetics of kayaking. *Medicine and Science in Sports and Exercise* **28**, 573–580.

Pennycuick, C. J. (1960) Gliding flight of the fulmar petrel. *Journal of Experimental Biology* **37**, 330–338.

Pennycuick, C. J. (1967) The strength of the pigeon's wing bones in relation to their function. *Journal of Experimental Biology* **46**, 219–233.

Pennycuick, C. J. (1968a) A wind-tunnel study of gliding flight in the pigeon *Columba livia. Journal of Experimental Biology* **49**, 509–526.

Pennycuick, C. J. (1968b) Power requirements for horizontal flight in the pigeon, *Columba livia. Journal of Experimental Biology* **49**, 527–555.

Pennycuick, C. J. (1971a) Gliding flight of the White-backed vulture *Gyps africanus. Journal of Experimental Biology* **55**, 13–38.

Pennycuick, C. J. (1971b) Control of gliding angle in Rüppell's griffon vulture *Gyps rüppellii. Journal of Experimental Biology* **55**, 39–46.

Pennycuick, C. J. (1971c) Gliding flight of the dog-faced bat *Rousettus aegyptiacus* observed in a wind tunnel. *Journal of Experimental Biology* **55**, 833–845.

Pennycuick, C. J. (1972) Soaring behaviour and performance of some East African birds, observed from a motor glider. *Ibis* **114**, 178–218.

Pennycuick, C. J. (1975) Mechanics of flight. In D. S. Farnell, J. R. King, and A. S. Parkes (editors), *Avian Biology,* **5**, 1–75. Academic Press, London.

Pennycuick, C. J. (1978) Fifteen testable predictions about bird flight. *Oikos* **30**, 165–176.

Pennycuick, C. J. (1982) The flight of petrels and albatrosses (Procellariiformes), observed in South Georgia and its vicinity. *Philosophical Transactions of the Royal Society* **300**, 75–106.

Pennycuick, C. J. (1983) Thermal soaring compared in three dissimilar tropical bird species, *Fregata magnificens, Pelecanus occidentalis* and *Coragyps atratus. Journal of Experimental Biology* **102**, 307–325.

Pennycuick, C. J. (1997) Actual and "optimal" flight speeds: Field data reassessed. *Journal of Experimental Biology* **200**, 2355–2361.

Pennycuick, C. J. (2001) Speeds and wingbeat frequencies of migrating birds compared with calculated benchmarks. *Journal of Experimental Biology* **204**, 3283–3294.

Pennycuick, C. J. and Lock, A. (1976) Elastic energy storage in primary feather shafts. *Journal of Experimental Biology* **64**, 677–689.

Pennycuick, C. J. and Scholey, K. D. (1984) Flight behaviour of Andean condors *Vultur gryphus* and turkey vultures *Cathartes aura* around the Paracas Peninsula, Peru. *Ibis* **126**, 253–256.

Pennycuick, C. J., Fuller, M. R. and McAllister, L. (1989) Climbing performance of Harris' hawks (*Parabuteo unicinctus*) with added load: implications for muscle mechanics and for radiotracking. *Journal of Experimental Biology* **142**, 17–29.

Pennycuick, C. J., Alerstam, T. and Hedenström, A. (1997) A new low-turbulence wind tunnel for bird flight experiments at Lund University, Sweden. *Journal of Experimental Biology* **200**, 1441–1449.

Peplowski, M. M. and Marsh, R. L. (1997) Work and power output in the hindlimb muscles of Cuban tree frogs *Osteopilus septentrionalis. Journal of Experimental Biology* **200**, 2861–2870.

Peters, R. H. (1983) *The Ecological Implications of Body Size.* Cambridge University Press, Cambridge, UK.

Piersma, T. (1998) Phenotypic flexibility during migration: Optimization of organ size contingent on the risks and rewards of fueling and flight. *Journal of Avian Biology* **29**, 511–520.

Prandtl, L. and Tietjens, O. G. (1957) *Applied Hydro- and Aerodynamics*, 2 ed. 2. Dover, New York.

Prange, H. D. and Schmidt-Nielsen, K. (1970) The metabolic cost of swimming in ducks. *Journal of Experimental Biology* **53**, 763–777.

Preuschoft, H. and Demes, B. (1984) Biomechanics of brachiation. In H. Preuschoft, D. J. Chivers, W. Y. Brockelman, and N. Creel (editors), *The Lesser Apes: Evolutionary and Behavioral Biology*, pp. 96–118. Edinburgh University Press, Edinburgh.

Pugh, L. G. C. E. (1971) The influence of wind resistance in running and walking and the mechanical efficiency of work against horizontal or vertical forces. *Journal of Physiology* **213**, 255–276.

Pugh, L. G. C. E. (1974) The relation of oxygen uptake and speed in competition cycling and comparative observations on the bicycle ergometer. *Journal of Physiology* **241**, 795–808.

Quilliam, T. A. (editor) (1966) The mole: its adaptation to an underground environment. *Journal of Zoology* **149**, 31–114.

Quillin, K. J. (1998) Ontogenetic scaling of hydrostatic skeletons: Geometric, static stress and dynamic stress scaling of the earthworm *Lumbricus terrestris. Journal of Experimental Biology* **201**, 1871–1883.

Quillin, K. J. (1999) Kinematic scaling of locomotion by hydrostatic animals: Ontogeny of peristaltic crawling by the earthworm *Lumbricus terrestris. Journal of Experimental Biology* **202**, 661–674.

Rayner, J. M. V. (1979) A new approach to animal flight mechanics. *Journal of Experimental Biology* **80**, 17–54.

Rayner, J.M.V. (1985a) Linear relations in biomechanics: The statistics of scaling functions. *Journal of Zoology A* **206**, 415–439.

Rayner, J.M.V. (1985b) Bounding and undulating flight in birds. *Journal of Theoretical Biology* **117**, 47–77.

Rayner, J.M.V. (1986) Vertebrate flapping flight mechanics and aerodynamics, and the evolution of flight in bats. In W. Nachtigall (editor), *Biona Report*, 5: *Bat Flight*, 27–74. Fischer, Heidelberg.

Rayner, J. M. V. (1987) Form and function in avian flight. *Current Ornithology* **5**, 1–66.

Rayner, J.M.V. (1993) On aerodynamics and the energetics of vertebrate flapping flight. *Contemporary Mathematics* **141**, 351–400.

Rayner, J. M. V. (1994) Aerodynamic corrections for the flight of birds and bats in wind tunnels. *Journal of Zoology* **234**, 537–563.

Rayner, J.M.V. (1995) Flight mechanics and constraints on flight performance. *Israel Journal of Zoology* **41**, 321–342.

Rayner, J. M. V. (1999) Estimating power curves of flying vertebrates. *Journal of Experimental Biology* **202**, 3449–3461.

Rayner, J. M. V. and Thomas, A. R. L. (1991) On the vortex wake of an animal flying in a confined volume. *Philosophical Transactions of the Royal Society B* **334**, 107–117.

Rayner, J. M. V., Jones, G. and Thomas, A. (1986) Vortex flow visualizations reveal change of upstroke function with flight speed in microchiropteran bats. *Nature* **321**, 162–164.

Reilly, T., Secher, N., Snell, P. and Williams, C. (1990) *Physiology of Sports*. Spon, London.

Richmond, F. J. R. (1998) Elements of style in neuromuscular architecture. *American Zoologist* **38**, 729–742.

Ritter, D. (1992) Lateral bending during lizard locomotion. *Journal of Experimental Biology* **173**, 1–10.

Ritter, D. (1995) Epaxial muscle function during locomotion in a lizard (*Varanus salvator*) and the proposal of a key innovation in the vertebrate axial musculoskeletal system. *Journal of Experimental Biology* **198**, 2477–2490.

Roberts, T. J., Marsh, R. L., Weyand, P. G. and Taylor, C. R. (1997) Muscular force in running turkeys: The economy of minimizing work. *Science* **275**, 1113–1115.

Roberts, T. J., Chen, M. S. and Taylor, C. R. (1998a) Energetics of bipedal running, II: Limb design and running mechanics. *Journal of Experimental Biology* **201**, 2753–2762.

Roberts, T. J., Kram, R., Weyand, P. G. and Taylor, C. R. (1998b) Energetics of bipedal running, I: Metabolic cost of generating force. *Journal of Experimental Biology* **201**, 2745–2751.

Röll, B. (1995) Epidermal fine structure of the toe tips of *Sphaerodactylus cinereus* (Reptilia, Gekkonidae). *Journal of Zoology* **235**, 289–300.

Rome, L. C. and Sosnicki, A. A. (1991) Myofilament overlap in swimming carp, II: Sarcomere length changes during swimming. *American Journal of Physiology* **260**, C289–C296.

Rome, L. C., Loughna, P. T. and Goldspink, G. (1984) Muscle fiber activity in carp as a function of swimming speed and muscle temperature. *American Journal of Physiology* **247**, R272–R279.

Rome, L. C., Funke, R. P., Alexander, R. McN., Lutz, G., Aldridge, H. Scott, F. and Freadman, M. (1988) Why animals have different muscle fibre types. *Nature* **335**, 824–827.

Rome, L. C., Syme, D. A., Hollingworth, S., Lindstedt, S. L. and Baylor, S. M. (1990a) The whistle and the rattle: The design of sound producing muscles. *Proceedings of the National Academy of Science* **93**, 8095–8100.

Rome, L. C., Sosnicki, A. A. and Goble, D. O. (1990b) Maximum velocity of shortening of three fibre types from horse soleus muscle: implications for scaling with body size. *Journal of Physiology* **431** 173–185.

Roos, P. J. (1964) Lateral bending in newt locomotion. *Koninklijke Nederlands Akademie van Wetenschappen. Proceedings C* **67**, 223–232.

Rosén, M. and Hedenström, A. (2001) Gliding flight in a jackdaw: A wind tunnel study. *Journal of Experimental Biology* **204**, 1153–1166.

Rosenberger, L. J. (2001) Pectoral fin locomotion in batoid fishes: Undulation *versus* oscillation. *Journal of Experimental Biology* **204**, 379–394.

Rosenberger, L. J. and Westneat, M. W. (1999) Functional morphology of undulatory pectoral fin locomotion in the stingray *Taeiura lymma* (Chondichthyes: Dasyatidae). *Journal of Experimental Biology* **202**, 3523–3539.

Rubin, C. T. and Lanyon, L. E. (1982) Limb mechanics as a function of speed and gait: A study of functional strains in the radius and tibia of horse and dog. *Journal of Experimental Biology* **101**, 187–211.

Ruegg, J. C. (1968) Contractile mechanisms of smooth muscle. *Symposia of the Society for Experimental Biology* **22**, 45–66.

Russell, A. P. (1975) A contribution to the functional morphology of the foot of the tokay, *Gekko gecko* (Reptilia, Gekkonidae). *Journal of Zoology* **176**, 437–476.

Savaglio, S. and Carbone, V. (2000) Scaling in athletic world records. *Nature* **404**, 244.

Schaeffer, P. J., Conley, K. E. and Linstedt, S. L. (1996) Structural correlates of speed and endurance in skeletal muscle: the rattlesnake tail shaker muscle. *Journal of Experimental Biology* **199**, 351–358.

Schmidt-Nielsen, K. (1984) *Scaling: Why Is Animal Size So Important?* Cambridge University Press, Cambridge, UK.

Schmitz, F. W. (1960) *Aerodynamik des Flügmodells*, ed. 4. Lange, Duisberg.

Scholey, K. (1986) The climbing and gliding locomotion of the giant red flying squirrel *Petaurista petaurista* (Sciuridae). In W. Nachtigall (editor), *Biona Report*, **5**: *Bat Flight*, 187–204. Fischer, Heidelberg.

Schrank, A. J., Webb, P. W. and Mayberry, S. (1999) How do body and paired-fin positions affect the ability of three teleost fishes to maneuver around bends? *Canadian Journal of Zoology* **77**, 203–210.

Secor, S. M., Jayne, B. C. and Bennett, A. F. (1992) Locomotor performance and energetic cost of sidewinding by the snake *Crotalus cerastes*. *Journal of Experimental Biology* **163**, 1–14.

Sepulveda, C. and Dickson, K. A. (2000) Maximum sustainable speeds and cost of swimming in juvenile kawakawa tuna (*Euthynnus affinis*) and chub mackerel (*Scomber japonicus*). *Journal of Experimental Biology* **203**, 3089–3101.

Seymour, M. K. (1969) Locomotion and coelomic pressure in *Lumbricus terrestris* L. *Journal of Experimental Biology* **51**, 47–58.

Seymour, M. K. (1971) Burrowing behaviour in the European lugworm *Arenicola marina* (Polychaeta: Arenicolidae). *Journal of Zoology* **164**, 93–132.

Shadwick, R. E., Katz, S. L., Korsmeyer, K. E., Knower, T. and Covell, J. W. (1999) Muscle dynamics in skipjack tuna: Timing of red muscle shortening in relation to activation and body curvature during steady swimming. *Journal of Experimental Biology* **202**, 2139–2150.

Sharp, N. C. C. (1997) Timed running speed of a cheetah (*Acinonyx jubatus*). *Journal of Zoology* **241**, 493–494.

Spedding, G. R. (1987a) The wake of a kestrel (*Falco tinnunculus*) in gliding flight. *Journal of Experimental Biology* **127**, 45–57.

Spedding, G. R. (1987b) The wake of a kestrel (*Falco tinnunculus*) in flapping flight. *Journal of Experimental Biology* **127**, 59–78.

Spedding, G. R. and Maxworthy, T. (1986) The generation of circulation and lift in a rigid two-dimensional fling. *Journal of Fluid Mechanics* **165**, 247–272.

Spedding, G. R., Rayner, J. M. V. and Pennycuick, C. J. (1984) Momentum and energy in the wake of a pigeon (*Columba livia*) in slow flight. *Journal of Experimental Biology* **111**, 81–102.

Spierts, I. L. Y. and van Leeuwen, J. L. (1999) Kinematics and muscle dynamics of C- and S-starts of carp (*Cyprinus carpio* L.). *Journal of Experimental Biology* **202**, 393–406.

Stelle, L. L., Blake, R. W. and Trites, A. W. (2000) Hydrodynamic drag in Steller sea lions (*Eumetopias jubatus*). *Journal of Experimental Biology* **203**, 1915–1923.

Stork, N. E. (1980) Experimental analysis of adhesion of *Chrysolina polita* (Chrysomelidae: Coleoptera) on a variety of surfaces. *Journal of Experimental Biology* **88**, 91–107.

Suarez, R. K. (1996) Upper limits to metabolic rates. *Annual Reviews of Physiology* **58**, 583–605.

Sugimoto, T. (1998) A theoretical analysis of sea-anchor soaring. *Journal of Theoretical Biology* **192**, 393–402.

Suter, R. B. and Wildman, H. (1999) Locomotion on the water surface: Hydrodynamic constraints on rowing velocity require a gait change. *Journal of Experimental Biology* **202**, 2771–2785.

Suter, R. B., Rosenberg, O., Loeb, S., Wildman, H. and Long, J. H. (1997) Locomotion on the water surface: Propulsive mechanisms of the fisher spider *Dolomedes triton*. *Journal of Experimental Biology* **200**, 2523–2538.

Tabor, D. (1991) *Gases, Liquids and Solids*, ed. 3. Cambridge University Press, Cambridge, UK.

Taylor, C. R., Caldwell, S. L. and Rowntree, V. J. (1972) Running up and down hills: some consequences of size. *Science* **178**, 1096–1097.

Taylor, C. R., Maloiy, G. M. O., Weibel, E. R., Langman, V. A., Kamau, J. M. Z., Seeherman, H. J. and Heglund, N. C. (1981) Design of the mammalian respiratory system, III: Scaling maximum aerobic capacity to body mass: Wild and domestic mammals. *Respiration Physiology* **44**, 25–37.

Taylor, C. R., Heglund, N. C. and Maloiy, G. M. O. (1982) Energetics and mechanics of terrestrial locomotion, I: Metabolic energy consumption as a function of speed and body size in birds and mammals. *Journal of Experimental Biology* **97**, 1–21.

Taylor, G. (1952) Analysis of the swimming of long narrow animals. *Proceedings of the Royal Society A* **214**, 158–183.

Taylor, G. M. (2000) Maximum force production: Why are crabs so strong? *Proceedings of the Royal Society B* **267**, 1475–1480.

Thomas, A. L. R. (1996) Why do birds have tails? The tail as a drag reducing flap, and trim control. *Journal of Theoretical Biology* **183**, 247–253.

Thompson, D. and Fedak, M. A. (1993) Cardiac responses of grey seals during diving at sea. *Journal of Experimental Biology* **174**, 139–164.

Thorpe, S. K. S., Li, Y., Crompton, R. H. and Alexander, R. McN. (1998) Stresses in human leg muscles in running and jumping determined by force plate analysis and from published magnetic resonance images. *Journal of Experimental Biology* **201**, 63–70.

Thorstensson, A. and Roberthson, H. (1987) Adaptations to changing speed in human locomotion: Speed of transition between walking and running. *Acta Physiologica Scandinavica* **131**, 211–214.

Thulborn, T. (1990) *Dinosaur Tracks.* Chapman & Hall, London.

Ting, L. H., Blickhan, R. and Full, R. J. (1994) Dynamic and static stability in hexapedal runners. *Journal of Experimental Biology* **197**, 251–269.

Tobalske, B. W. (1995) Neuromuscular control and kinematics of intermittent flight in European starlings (*Sturnus vulgaris*). *Journal of Experimental Biology* **198**, 1259–1273.

Tobalske, B. W. and Dial, K. P. (1994) Neuromuscular control and kinematics of intermittent flight in budgerigars. *Journal of Experimental Biology* **187** 1–18.

Tobalske, B. W. and Dial, K. P. (1996) Flight kinematics of black-billed magpies and pigeons over a wide range of speeds. *Journal of Experimental Biology* **199**, 263–280.

Tobalske, B. W., Peacock, W. L. and Dial, K. P. (1999) Kinematics of flap-bounding flight in the zebra finch over a wide range of speeds. *Journal of Experimental Biology* **202**, 1725–1739.

Triantafyllou, G., Triantafyllou, M. and Grosenbaugh, M. (1993) Optimal thrust development in oscillating foils with application to fish propulsion. *Journal of Fluids Structure* **7**, 205–224.

Trueman, E. R. (1967) The dynamics of burrowing in *Ensis* (Bivalvia). *Proceedings of the Royal Society B* **166**, 459–476.

Trueman, E. R. and Jones, H. D. (1977) Crawling and burrowing. In R. McN. Alexander and G. Goldspink (editors), *Mechanics and Energetics of Animal Locomotion*, pp. 204–221. Chapman & Hall, London.

Tucker, V. A. (1970) Energetic cost of locomotion in animals. *Comparative Biochemistry and Physiology* **34**, 841–846.

Tucker, V. A. (1972) Metabolism during flight in the laughing gull, *Larus atricilla*. *American Journal of Physiology* **222**, 237–245.

Tucker, V. A. (1992) Pitching equilibrium, wing span and tail span in a gliding Harris' hawk, *Parabuteo unicinctus*. *Journal of Experimental Biology* **165**, 21–41.

Tucker, V. A. (1995) Drag reduction by wing tip slots in a gliding Harris' hawk, *Parabuteo unicinctus*. *Journal of Experimental Biology* **198**, 775–781.

Tucker, V. A. (2000) Gliding flight: drag and torque of a hawk and falcon with straight and turned heads, and a lower value for the parasite drag coefficient. *Journal of Experimental Biology* **203**, 3733–3744.

Tucker, V. A. and Heine, C. (1990) Aerodynamics of gliding flight in a Harris' hawk, *Parabuteo unicinctus*. *Journal of Experimental Biology* **149**, 469–489.

Tucker, V. A. and Parrott, G. C. (1970) Aerodynamics of gliding flight in a falcon and other birds. *Journal of Experimental Biology* **52**, 345–367.

Tucker, V. A., Cade, T. J. and Tucker, A. E. (1998) Diving speeds and angles of a gyrfalcon (*Falco rusticolus*). *Journal of Experimental Biology* **201**, 2061–2070.

Van den Berg, C. and Rayner, J. M. V. (1995) The moment of inertia of bird wings and the inertial power requirement for flapping flight. *Journal of Experimental Biology* **198**, 1655–1664.

Van der Stelt, A. (1968) *Spiermechanica en myotoombouw bij vissen*. Thesis, University of Amsterdam.

Vandewalle, H., Peres, G., Heller, J., Panel, J. and Monod, H. (1987) Force–velocity relationship and maximal power on a bicycle ergometer: correlation with the height of a vertical jump. *European Journal of Applied Physiology* **56**, 650–656.

Van Lawick-Goodall, H. and van Lawick-Goodall, J. (1970) *Innocent Killers*. Collins, London.

Van Leeuwen, J. L. (1999) A mechanical analysis of myomere shape in fish. *Journal of Experimental Biology* **202**, 3405–3414.

Van Leeuwen, J. L. and Kier, W. M. (1997) Functional design of tentacles in squid: linking sarcomere ultrastructure to gross morphological dynamics. *Philosophical Transactions of the Royal Society B* **352**, 551–571.

Van Leeuwen, J. L. and Spoor, C. W. (1992) Modelling mechanically stable muscle architectures. *Philosophical Transactions of the Royal Society B* **336**, 275–292.

Van Leeuwen, J. L. and Spoor, C. W. (1993) Modelling the force equilibrium in unipennate muscles with in-line tendons. *Philosophical Transactions of the Royal Society B* **342**, 321–333.

Van Leeuwen, J. L., Jayes, A. S. and Alexander, R. McN. (1981) Estimates of mechanical stresses in tortoise leg muscles during walking. *Journal of Zoology* **195**, 53–69.

Van Vleet, E. S., Candileri, S., McNellie, J., Reinhardt, S. B., Conkright, M. E. and Zwissler, A. (1984) Neutral lipid components of eleven species of Caribbean sharks. *Comparative Biochemistry and Physiology B*, **79**, 549–554.

Videler, J. J. (1993) *Fish Swimming*. Chapman & Hall, London.

Videler, J. and Groenewold, A. (1991) Field-measurements of hanging flight aerodynamics in the kestrel *Falco tinnunculus*. *Journal of Experimental Biology* **155**, 519–530.

Videler, J. and Kamermans, P. (1985) Difference between upstroke and downstroke in swimming dolphins. *Journal of Experimental Biology* **119**, 265–274.

Videler, J. J., Müller, U. K. and Stamhuis, E. J. (1999) Aquatic vertebrate locomotion: Wakes from body waves. *Journal of Experimental Biology* **202**, 3423–3430.

Vogel, S. (1967). Flight in *Drosophila*, III: Aerodynamic characteristics of fly wings and wing models. *Journal of Experimental Biology* **46**, 431–443.

Vogel, S. (1981) *Life in Moving Fluids: The Physical Biology of Flow*. Willard Grant Press, Boston.

Wainwright, S. A., Biggs, W. D., Currey, J. D. and Gosline, J. M. (1976) *Mechanical Design in Organisms*. Wiley, New York.

Wakeling, J. M. and Ellington, C. P. (1997) Dragonfly flight, I: Gliding flight and steady-state aerodynamic forces. *Journal of Experimental Biology* **200**, 543–556.

Wakeling, J. M. and Johnston, I. A. (1999) White muscle strain in the common carp and red to white muscle gearing ratios in fish. *Journal of Experimental Biology* **202**, 521–528.

Walker, G., Yule, A. B. and Ratcliffe, J. (1985) The adhesive organ of the blowfly, *Calliphora vomitoria*: A functional approach (Diptera: Calliphoridae). *Journal of Zoology A* **205**, 297–307.

Walker, J. A. (2000) Does a rigid body limit maneuverability? *Journal of Experimental Biology* **203**, 3391–3396.

Walker, J. A. and Westneat, M. W. (1997) Labriform propulsion in fishes: Kinematics of flapping flight in the bird wrasse *Gomphosus varius* (Labridae). *Journal of Experimental Biology* **200**, 1549–1569.

Walker, J. A. and Westneat, M. W. (2000) Mechanical performance of aquatic rowing and flying. *Proceedings of the Royal Society B* **267**, 1875–1881.

Wallace, H. R. (1958) Movement of eelworms, I: The influence of pore size and moisture content of the soil on the migration of larvae of the beet eelworm, *Heterodera schachtii* Schmidt. *Annals of Applied Biology* **46**, 74–85.

Wallace, H. R. (1959) The movement of eelworms in water films. *Annals of Applied Biology* **47**, 366–370.

Walters, V. and Fierstine, H. L. (1964) Measurements of swimming speeds of yellowfin tuna and wahoo. *Nature* **202**, 208–209.

Walton, M., Jayne, B. C. and Bennett, A. F. (1990) The energetic cost of limbless locomotion. *Science* **249**, 524–527.

Ward, S., Rayner, J. M. V., Möller, U., Jackson, D. M., Nachtigall, W. and Speakman, J. R. (1999) Heat transfer from starlings *Sturnus vulgaris* during flight. *Journal of Experimental Biology* **202**, 1589–1602.

Wardle, C. S., Videler, J. J. and Altringham, J. J. (1995) Tuning in to fish body waves: Body form, swimming mode and muscle function. *Journal of Experimental Biology* **198**, 1629–1636.

Warren, R. D. and Crompton, R. H. (1997) Locomotor ecology of *Lepilemur edwardsi* and *Avahi occidentalis*. *American Journal of Physical Anthropology* **104**, 471–486.

Warren, R. D. and Crompton, R. H. (1998) Diet, body size and the energy costs of locomotion in saltatory primates. *Folia Primatologia* **69** (suppl. 1), 86–100.

Watabe, S. and Hartshorne, D. J. (1990) Paramyosin and the catch mechanism. *Comparative Biochemistry and Physiology B* **96**, 639–646.

Weast, R. C. (editor) (1987) *CRC Handbook of Chemistry and Physics*, ed. 68. CRC Press, Boca Raton, FL.

Webb, P. W. (1971) The swimming energetics of trout, II: Oxygen consumption and swimming efficiency. *Journal of Experimental Biology* **55**, 521–540.

Webb, P. W. (1975) Hydrodynamics and energetics of fish propulsion. *Bulletin of the Fisheries Research Board of Canada* **190**, 1–158.

Webb, P. W. (1989) Station holding by three species of benthic fish. *Journal of Experimental Biology* **145**, 305–320.

Webb, P. W. (1992) Is the high cost of body/caudal fin undulatory swimming due to increased friction drag or inertial recoil? *Journal of Experimental Biology* **162**, 157–166.

Webb, P. W. (1993) The effect of solid and porous channel walls on steady swimming of steelhead trout *Onchorhynchus mykiss*. *Journal of Experimental Biology* **178**, 97–108.

Webb, P. W. (1994) The biology of fish swimming. In L. Maddock, Q. Bone, and J. M. V. Rayner (editors) *Mechanics and Physiology of Animal Swimming*. Cambridge University Press, Cambridge, UK.

Webber, D. M. and O'Dor, R. K. (1986) Monitoring the metabolic rate and activity of free-swimming squid with telemetered jet pressure. *Journal of Experimental Biology* **126**, 205–224.

Weihs, D. (1973) Mechanically efficient swimming techniques for fish with negative buoyancy. *Journal of Marine Research* **31**, 194–209.

Weimerskirch, H., Guionnet, T., Martin, J., Shaffer, S. A. and Costa, D. P. (2000) Fast and fuel efficient? Optimal use of wind by flying albatrosses. *Proceedings of the Royal Society B* **267**, 1869–1874.

Weimerskirch, H., Martin, J., Clerquin, Y., Alexandre, P. and Jiraskova, S. (2001) Energy saving in flight formation. *Nature* **413**, 697–698.

Weis-Fogh, T. (1960) A rubber-like protein in insect cuticle. *Journal of Experimental Biology* **37**, 889–906.

Weis-Fogh, T. (1972) Energetics of hovering flight in hummingbirds and *Drosophila*. *Journal of Experimental Biology* **56**, 79–104.

Weis-Fogh, T. (1973) Quick estimates of flight fitness in hovering animals, including novel mechanisms for lift production. *Journal of Experimental Biology* **59**, 169–230.

Wells, J. B. (1965) Comparison of mechanical properties between slow and fast mammalian muscles. *Journal of Physiology* **178**, 252–269

West, G. B., Brown, J. H. and Enquist, B. J. (1997) A general model for the origin of allometric scaling laws in biology. *Science* **276**, 122–126.

White, R. G. and Yousef, M. K. (1978) Energy expenditure in reindeer walking on roads and on tundra. *Canadian Journal of Zoology* **56**, 215–223.

White, T. D. and Anderson, R. A. (1994) Locomotor patterns and costs as related to body size and form in teiid lizards. *Journal of Zoology* **233**, 107–128.

Wickler, S. J., Hoyt, D. F., Cogger, E. A. and Hirschbein, M. H. (2000) Preferred speed and cost of transport: The effect of incline. *Journal of Experimental Biology* **203**, 2195–2200.

Wilga, C. D. and Lauder, G. V. (2000) Three-dimensional kinematics and wake structure of the pectoral fins during locomotion in leopard sharks *Triakis semifasciata*. *Journal of Experimental Biology* **203**, 2261–2278.

Williams, T. M. (1999) The evolution of cost efficient swimming in marine mammals: Limits to energetic optimization. *Philosophical Transactions of the Royal Society B* **354**, 193–201.

Willmott, A. P. and Ellington, C. P. (1997a) Measuring the angle of attack of beating insect wings: Robust three-dimensional reconstruction from two-dimensional images. *Journal of Experimental Biology* **200**, 2693–2704.

Willmott, A. P. and Ellington, C. P. (1997b) The mechanics of flight in the hawkmoth *Manduca sexta*, I: kinematics of hovering and forward flight. *Journal of Experimental Biology* **200**, 2705–2722.

Willmott, A. P. and Ellington, C. P. (1997c) The mechanics of flight in the hawkmoth *Manduca sexta*, II: Aerodynamic consequences of kinematic and morphological variation. *Journal of Experimental Biology* **200**, 2723–2745.

Willmott, A. P., Ellington, C. P. and Thomas, A. L. R. (1997) Flow visualisation and unsteady aerodynamics in the flight of the hawkmoth, *Manduca sexta*. *Philosophical Transactions of the Royal Society B* **352**, 303–316.

Wilson, J. A. (1975) Sweeping flight and soaring by albatrosses. *Nature* **257**, 307–308.

Wilson, R. S., Franklin, C. E. and James, R. S. (2000) Allometric scaling relationships of jumping performance in the striped marsh frog *Limnodynastes peronii*. *Journal of Experimental Biology* **203**, 1937–1946.

Winter, D. A. (1990) *Biomechanics and Motor Control of Human Movement*, ed. 2. Wiley, New York.

Winter, Y., Voigt, C. and von Helversen, O. (1997) Gas exchange during hovering flight in a nectar-feeding bat *Glossophaga soricina*. *Journal of Experimental Biology* **201**, 237–244.

Wirtz, P. and Ries, G. (1992) The pace of life reanalysed: Why does walking speed of pedestrians correlate with city size? *Behaviour* **123**, 77–83.

Withers, P. C. (1979) Aerodynamics and hydrodynamics of the "hovering" flight of Wilson's storm petrel. *Journal of Experimental Biology* **80**, 83–91.

Wittenberg, J. B., Schwend, M. J. and Wittenberg, B. A. (1964) The secretion of oxygen into the swim-bladder of fish, III: The role of carbon dioxide. *Journal of General Physiology* **48**, 337–355.

Woledge, R. C., Curtin, N. A. and Homsher, E. (1985) *Energetic aspects of muscle contraction* Academic Press, London.

Wolfgang, M. J., Anderson, J. M., Grosenbaugh, M. A., Yue, D. K. P. and Triantafyllou, M. S. (1999) Near-body flow dynamics in swimming fish. *Journal of Experimental Biology* **202**, 2303–2327.

Wood, J. (1970) A study of the instantaneous air velocities in a plane behind the wings of certain Diptera flying in a wind tunnel. *Journal of Experimental Biology* **52**, 17–25.

Wootton, R. J. (1995) Geometry and mechanics of insect hindwing fans: a modelling approach. *Proceedings of the Royal Society B* **262**, 181–187.

Wootton, R. J. (1999) Invertebrate paraxial locomotory appendages: design, deformation and control. *Journal of Experimental Biology* **202**, 3333–3345.

Yamaguchi, G. T., Sawa, A. G. U., Moran, D. W., Fessler, M. J. and Winters, J. M. (1990) A survey of human musculotendon actuator parameters. In J. M. Winters and S. L.-Y. Woo (editors), *Multiple Muscle Systems: Biomechanics and Movement Organization*. Springer, New York.

Yates, G. T. (1983) Hydromechanics of body and caudal fin propulsion. In P. W. Webb and D. Weihs (editors), *Fish Biomechanics*, pp. 177–213. Praeger, New York.

Yoda, K., Sato, K., Niizuma, Y., Kurita, M., Bost, C.-A., Le Mayo, Y. and Naito, Y. (1999) Precise monitoring of porpoising behaviour of Adélie penguins determined using acceleration data loggers. *Journal of Experimental Biology* **202**, 3121–3126.

Young, I. S., Alexander, R. McN., Woakes, A. J., Butler, P. J. and Anderson, L. (1992) The synchronisation of ventilation and locomotion in horses (*Equus caballus*). *Journal of Experimental Biology* **166**, 19–31.

Zamparo, P., Perini, R., Orizio, C., Sacher, M. and Ferretti, G. (1992) The energy cost of walking or running on sand. *European Journal of Applied Physiology* **65**, 183–187.

Zarrugh, M. Y., Todd, F. N. and Ralston, H. J. (1974) Optimization of energy expenditure during level walking. *European Journal of Applied Physiology* **33**, 293–306.

Index